It's Your Eternity

LAST BREATH – THEN WHAT?

CRAIG BELTRAND

ACKNOWLEDGMENTS:

Cover and Interior Design Services by Melinda Martin – Martin Publishing Services

PUBLISHING INFORMATION:

NLT *– Scripture is taken from the New Living Translation, copyright © 1996, 2004, 2007 by Tyndale House Foundation. All rights reserved.*

KJV *– Scripture is taken from the King James Version. Copyright © 1999 by New York: American Bible Society.*

NKJV*– Scripture is taken from the New King James Version*®. *Copyright © 1982 by Thomas Nelson. All rights reserved.*

NIV *– Scripture quotations marked (NIV) are taken from the Holy Bible, New International Version*®, *and NIV*®. *Copyright © 1973, 1978, 1984, 2011 by Biblica, Inc.* ™ *Used by permission of Zondervan. All rights reserved worldwide. The "NIV" and "New International Version" are trademarks registered in the United States Patent and Trademark Office by Biblica, Inc.* ™

ISBN: Paperback 978-1-7327625-7-2

Hardback 978-1-7327625-8-9

eBook   978-1-7327625-9-6

PUBLISHED BY: Southwestern Legacy Press, LLC

P.O. Box 1231

Gallatin, TN 37066

LIBRARY OF CONGRESS CATALOGING NUMBER (LCCN) 2020920767

LIBRARY CATALOGING:

Beltrand, Craig (Craig Beltrand) – Author

It's Your Eternity: Last Breath – Then What?

326 pages 23cm × 15cm (9in. × 6 in.)

DESCRIPTION:

"It's Your Eternity: Last Breath – Then What?"

Is an insightfully written narrative of Craig Beltrand's spiritual journey starting in 1979 as a carefree young United States Air Force officer whose main goal in life was to "eat, drink and be merry" while cruising the Montana back roads on motorcycles with his buddies. After a horrific accident, which he survives with only a minor scratch, he begins to ask "What if" questions about his "Eternity." Through intense study and examination of the Old Testament and New Testament biblical Scriptures and end times prophecy Craig becomes a committed believer in Jesus Christ. In **" It's Your Eternity: Last Breath–Then What?"** he invites you to join him on this journey.

CONTENTS

BIDDEN OR UNBIDDEN

During my assignment at Malmstrom Air Force Base, my buddies and I were always ready to share a few beers, jump on our motorcycles, and ride under the big skies of Montana. We were having a good time at a friend's party on base one day when one of the guys suggested we go for a ride. His suggestion produced an enthusiastic response since most of us welcomed the chance to take to the highway. My Triumph 750cc "Bonneville" was gassed up and ready to go, and so was I. Grabbing my helmet off the king and queen seat, I strapped it on for appearance's sake. Once we were off the base, it went right back onto the seat behind me, where it stayed anytime I was off base. I was wearing shorts, a tee-shirt, and flip-flops enjoying the sunshine on my head and feeling the air rushing across my body. As a twenty-five year old, United States Air Force officer, I was glad to break away from the rules and do what I wanted. We rode through small towns consisting of only one gas station, one grocery store, and usually two bars. The roar of my bike and the exhilaration of speed coupled with unrestricted freedom brought a sense of euphoria while we rode surrounded by wide-open spaces. After a time, that highway rush gave way to a thirst for more beers, and we pulled into our favorite roadside bar. We spent time in light-hearted conversations and lively teasing as we drank our beers and relished our partying. Eventually, it was time to go, so we went outside and got on our bikes. Uncharacteristically, I strapped on my helmet.

We headed back down the two-lane country road with a greater sense of cockiness fueled by the teasing and the beers. Already speeding, I decided to show off and began to pass a friend. I moved into the oncoming traffic lane and picked up speed. My buddy looked over at me and then glanced at his speedometer, which was registering ninety-five miles per hour! A vague sense of concern crept in as I suddenly felt my bike vibrate, but I pressed on. Then a significant wobble occurred, which became so severe the front wheel turned ninety degrees to the bike's path of forward motion. The right front fork hit the steering stop, broke through and smashed into the gas tank. I lost all control of my bike and became airborne, entering into what seemed to me to be a slow-motion trajectory. A rapid-moving episode of my life became frame-by-frame still shots in my mind. I saw myself moving up and over the front of the handlebars, and then cartwheeling into a mid-air summersault. With everything in motion, suddenly, I sensed something catching me and instantly knew I was going to be alright. Complete peace settled in. Searching for the source of a scraping sound, I looked behind me and saw part of my motorcycle. Looking backward caused the back of my helmet to scrape the pavement. As I made my full flip, my left foot smashed into the ground with such force, it tore open my skin and exposed my Achilles tendon. My spiraling flight came to an abrupt conclusion as I landed on my rear end and slid down the road with my shorts providing the only protection from the rough asphalt. It takes a while to stop when you are going ninety-five miles per hour, and the only brake you have is your bum. Finally stopping, I immediately jumped up, staring face-to-grill with a semi-trailer truck. It had skidded to a stop no more than twenty steps away from me. Quickly, I ran off the road to let him pass, shaking my fist and cursing as he slowly went by. I was utterly unclear about the source of my anger since I also was happy to be alive and amazed I was not gravely injured. I noticed the people in a nearby truck had watched the entire episode. I started waving my arms and shouting, "I'm alive! I'm alive!"

CHAPTER ONE

INTRODUCTION

S o, what's in your eternity? Standing with your feet firmly planted amid your daily life, you must ask yourself that question if you are to achieve any inner peace about your future. It is of paramount importance to explore the answer, and with serious contemplation resolve for yourself, in the depth of your soul, what you believe to be your answer to that question. Your eternal life depends on what you decide.

Who am I to dare ask you that question? I'm just an average guy who grew up with little substance in a smallish town. An ordinary man who has an acute awareness, as I drive around in my high-mileage Ford F-150 truck, that it will exist longer on Earth than I will. My search to find answers to unexplainable experiences led me to seek a response to the persistent, "What if?" question that was ever-present in the back of my mind. I once believed there is nothing after death. We are mortal beings. The only explanation for the life I once had was that every person's short bio was "born, lived, and died." That was it!

But, "What if?" kept surfacing and brought another compelling question. What if I were wrong? What if I were missing something significant? It took years of unexplainable events for me even to consider another possibility. I had no focus or thoughts about anything beyond the life I was living. I was young. I had the entire world before me. My mindset was, "Who cares about the stuff that won't happen for thirty or forty years?" After countless "otherworldly" occurrences, it became apparent to me there must be a supernatural existence of some sort. Could angels or perhaps demons really exist? Asking that question set me on a quest to investigate. My question to you, "What's in your eternity?" is my invitation to begin your investigation. Come, let us reason together, let us contemplate, and let us consider. Mankind's eternal brilliance shines during the time spent in these contemplative moments.

A base starting place is to acknowledge that physical bodies are mortal. Recognizing everyone's body dies, we must decide what will become of the soul and spirit. The importance of eternity comes from its Latin root word, "aeternalis." It means without beginning or end. Give yourself time to pause and reflect. What you decide will have a lasting impact on your life. Eternity is a very long time.

An eternity of some sort is coming soon enough, and when it does, it is forever. It is impossible to know when death will come, and when it does, it is too late to change our eternity. My intent is not to be harsh, but rather to invite you to consider the "What if." I know countless people think there is nothing after death. The ideas presented in this book are intended to provide a wake-up call to get you thinking critically about eternity before death happens. What if your theories and beliefs are wrong? You cannot verify your best guess as 100% correct unless you do some honest homework to prove or disprove it. There is a serious finality to this process. Regardless of what is on the other side, weigh your cost in the balance. It could be finding the One True God on one side of the scale, and nothing on the other side. There could be the One True God on one side and some other god on the other side. Only one outcome can be right; there is no middle ground on which to hedge your bets.

This cannot be a group or committee decision. Every person must searchingly look into their own eyes, in a mirror, and find an answer to bring peace within their core being. Let me encourage you to learn to think for yourself instead of following the "herd" or assuming some other highly intelligent person must know better than you. Learn to seek out and understand "all" sides to the story. If you get only one thing from my life experiences, it must be this: "It is Your Eternity; yours alone." It is worth your time to investigate, particularly since you cannot point the finger at anyone else when death comes. Your free will is powerful. Will you walk away from your past and create something new, or cling to your comfortable status quo? Why not at least investigate?

Before we investigate the realm of what happens after death, let's consider what happens during our lives. Throughout your life, have you perhaps had trouble explaining experiences that just couldn't be explained away by what we would classify as "natural" or "normal?" Are some of your experiences beyond what seems to be possible? Most people will answer "yes" to that question. People usually admit to experiencing out-of-the-ordinary things they can't explain. Others claim psychics, who knew nothing about them, told them something true about themselves. The information came through supernatural channels. Perhaps it was an event, like a motorcycle accident, when something unusual or surreal happened and there was no way to explain how it happened. What is the source of those events? Is the source working for good or evil?

While living life for today with a "who cares about tomorrow mindset," the one thing I knew for sure was I would die somewhere along the way. If you are like I was years ago, scratching your head, and wondering about things like horoscopes and psychic readings, you are probably wondering how that could be profitable. Based on all the advertising done to promote the psychic industry, apparently, psychic stuff pays well. People like me were not spending good money to hear nothing, and so they were getting supernatural information. Sorry for the bluntness, but try to understand that the source of that information is from the evil realm. The satanic realm has been watching you and me since birth. They observed all the details of our lives and communicated that to psychics or mediums and through other methods. This realm is an accomplished influencer because they have studied man since his creation in the Garden of Eden.

One day my wife and I had a visitor who, like us, was in their early sixties. While at our dinner table, this person mentioned their family was being unnerved by a few recent unexplainable events. Lights in the house were unexplainably turning on and off. On other occasions, while driving their new luxury sedan straight down a road on their way to work, the car horn would honk on its own. A friend of theirs organized a free psychic consultation giving the psychic no information about what was happening. During the encounter, the psychic described the different happenings down to the most exact details. The psychic also provided that individual with more information about their life that could be known only through supernatural means. While having this discussion with our visitor, my wife and I knew the direction this would take because of our experiences with supernatural beings. We explained that when it comes to externally observable events, there is not anything the devil and his source of demonic angels do not know. Actually, both good and dark forces are aware of all past and present human activities. Those strange events were an attempt to draw them into the dark world. We must be careful since dark sources are watching for opportunities to enter into our life.

Both the Jewish Bible, known as the Tanakh and the Christian

Bible, relate real accounts of mediums and psychic activity like our friend had experienced. The Tanakh and Old Testament tell of King Saul asking a psychic, or medium, to call up the prophet Samuel from the dead.[1] In the New Testament, a slave girl was being used to make money for her masters using her psychic abilities.[2] These were real activities and very lucrative undertakings. If they weren't, there would be no psychic readings, tarot cards, talking boards, and palm readings today. The Tanakh and the Christian Bible contain numerous historical accounts of similar incidences. This struggle between the same two supernatural forces, good and evil, started in the Garden of Eden with the real account of Adam and Eve.

These same two forces seek to influence the souls of people today. Weigh both sides of the argument carefully and choose wisely. What seems good today, through the wisdom of man, may mean nothing compared to the omniscient knowledge of the One True God. By default, not choosing a side means upon death, the enemy is victorious in having kept us distracted from weighing our eternity in the balance. Because of what Adam and Eve did, there is a physical death to our body, but not our soul and spirit, which are eternal. The soul is our inner person who defines us and drives our choices, words, and actions. Our spirit is the wireless communication feature enabling us to stay in intimate contact with God's Holy Spirit.

I'm human and far from perfect. Thankfully, The One True God is a God of profound grace. God knows all about our shortcomings. We do not differ from Adam and Eve. Without Grace, we would all be buried under a pile of legalistic laws and principles from which there is no escape. The beauty of Grace is the "free" and "unmerited" favor of

---

1 1 Sam. 28:7-21
2 Acts 16:16–23

God that sets us free from the consequences of all our mistakes. God chose Jesus as the bridge over our sin gap, allowing us access back to Him. Choosing to cross that bridge through Jesus does not mean we should turn around and take things for granted.

Grace is free. Yes, it is free, and I cannot say that enough! Jesus became the pardon and paid the price for our freedom. He came to set us free from all things. Grace cannot be earned, nor can it be unearned.[3] Once we choose Grace, it is up to us to use our free will to grow in our walk with God. Even better, it is not a requirement to mature in our walk because of God's free gift of Grace. Life is better when we do, but it is not a requirement. Don't take my word for it. Ask the One True God for proof. I did that years ago, and His answer has made all the difference to me. He wants you to ask Him so He can give you His answer.

Like every other human born, except Jesus, King David of Israel struggled with sinning, yet God loved his repentant heart. He committed adultery, lied, and then had the woman's husband murdered. But he had a heart that put God first when his sin was revealed to him, and he immediately repented.[4] Maybe you are not as thick-headed as me; however, even the best of us have issues, but if we have grief in our hearts over our sin and repent to God, then as the Bible states, sin will burn as wood, hay, or stubble at our judgment day.[5] Jesus paid the price for that to occur.

I take the Bible very literally, not symbolically, unless the Bible explicitly states otherwise. In my late twenties, I was firmly introduced to God after asking for proof of His existence. In the first of four su-

---

3 Eph. 2:8–10
4 Acts 13:22
5 1 Cor. 3:12–15

pernatural visions, not dreams, I was physically burned in The Lake of Fire. These supernatural experiences, vividly depicting teachings written about in the Bible thousands of years ago, convinced me the Bible is true. Having the words of an ancient book come to life convinced me I could believe it as it is written. I still had my free will to walk away from God, but from that point on, I knew the truth. I know Jesus is real because I personally and physically met Him. I know Satan is real because I also personally and physically met him. They are as real to me as anyone else I have ever met in my life.

Not everyone has the firsthand experience that I had. However, having open discussions with others showed me I was not alone. Jesus has been appearing to other people as He sees fit. The Bible tells us Jesus came to Earth to visit Apostle John at Patmos, as seen in the book of Revelation, and Apostle Paul in the barracks as written in Acts. Other documented meetings include His encounters with Noah, Abraham, Daniel, and various other people throughout history. God has never changed and cannot change; therefore, my experiences of meeting Him align with Scripture as written. Only two options exist for the source of what I have received; either they are from Jesus or Satan. Test them for yourself against Scripture.

I have two college degrees, one in electrical engineering and the other in business. I also have worked for over thirty years in the U.S. defense industry with multiple Top Secret clearances. I did not set out to write a book addressing eternity, but as I sought the One True God, I felt my journey wasn't for me alone. So here I am, asking you to test everything against Scripture to discern the Truth.

Mysterious experiences in my late 20's and early 30's initially challenged my engineering background. Once I understood that the Bible was real and filled with true account after true account, not just a bunch of cute stories, things started making sense. My experiences led me to know the importance of critical thinking. Was I getting all the facts when making decisions? Were there fake partial facts twisted together and pawned off as truth? We have to persevere in getting both sides of the story to learn the truth. It is vital to prevent our emotions and fear from getting in the way. The earlier account of the person with flashing lights and randomly honking car horn illustrates how their fear drove them to a psychic. This individual needed to "critically" think about the events that transpired. There are two sides to every story. It takes time and focus to dig for other possibilities and examine them for truth, but shouldn't your eternity be worth the effort? Shouldn't you do more than blindly accept what is said in the media or from friends? Take a step forward by asking the One True God for direction, wisdom, knowledge, and understanding to see both sides for what they are. You are the only one responsible for your eternity. If there is a God, He will know the very second you consider asking Him.

I always say to ask the One True God, because there are false gods happy to answer. Ask for the Top God of all supernatural powers, the God of gods. He is telepathic and instantly knows your thoughts. He is capable of blocking out the false gods and answers. Please note I did not say pray to Jesus, or the God of Abraham-Isaac-Jacob, or Joseph Smith's god, Baal or Hindu gods, etc. Just pray to the One True God, and He will answer. He did for me and has done it repeatedly for others over the history of mankind.

Eventually, my need to know more exceeded my resistance. Once I asked, the One True God answered. He is never asleep and will keep out the fake gods from answering you if you will call on Him. You want the Lord of lords to hear what is in your heart and give you a true answer. I asked for the One True God to respond. When I asked, I did not know who it was. In my heart, I wanted to know the truth. It turned out to be the God of the Bible who responded, and at first, I did not like the answer.

I struggled over it for about eighteen months. Finally, realizing my eternity was not something to dismiss, I began to work hard to understand the other side of the story. My due diligence and study convinced me to go all-in for Jesus. I am not quickly sold on things since I tend to be thick-headed and stubborn. Deciding for Him should have been a quick and simple decision, but that wasn't the case for me and may not be for you.

We all have free will to choose as we please. I had the option to turn against what I ultimately came to know as Truth. I have met others who have done that very thing, even after having an encounter with Jesus. I've had pleasant conversations with some of these seemingly nice people. When I mention the One True God, I can see a change in their eyes, which then subtly affects their countenance. Their supernatural demonic influencer knows I recognized he is there. When this happens, the person generally manifests anger and uses harsh words. I see something in their eyes that is not them. Their countenance changes quickly. It is like I am no longer talking with the same person. The interesting thing is that we were having a normal conversation, and I just brought God into the conversation to see what their reaction would be. There was no reason to get upset. Generally, people do not get angry, and it remains a calm conversation. However, when someone knows the truth and has decided against it, the enemy goes into overdrive to protect his territory. Dark forces know God can flip a person anytime until death. The bottom line is we all have free will, and some knowingly choose against God's plan for mankind. These events seemed rare in my early days, but have become more common today. Maybe my awareness has improved, and I am more likely to see the forces at work behind the person. Some of you who are on Jesus' team have probably wondered why someone, who seems so nice, can instantly flip and become hostile or even vile. When that happens, you have hit a nerve that alerts the enemy to bring a full-on charge to protect his turf and scare you off. Use Jesus' name to bind the enemy. Then do or say what God is telling you. God may say it is time to walk away, so listen and walk away. Remember, some people plant seedlings, and others water them, but only God causes the growth.[6] If God is saying walk away, then do it and leave the rest up to Him. Add them to your prayer list, because it is not over until God says it is over.

My meeting Jesus and demonic beings like Satan may seem hard to believe, yet it actually happened. I asked the One True God to reveal Himself, and supernatural things happened. You, too, should ask. It is simple enough. It may seem a bit unsettling at first, but God always hears and answers in His time. Today, numerous people seek "spirit guides" of all sorts, and Satan has adequate numbers in his army happy to fill the needs. Once at our local church, my wife and I were working with a young person who had spirit guides. He had a relationship with Jesus but did not want to give up his spirit guide friends. When asked why, he said the guides gave him power over women, which he did not otherwise have. He is not the only young person we have run into that confesses to meeting with friendly guides who help them. Most times, Satan's army plays both sides of the "good cop-bad cop" routine to keep them trapped. The good cop spirit guide protects them from the bad cop spirit guide. Many of them cannot sleep without a night light.

---

6 1 Cor. 3:6–7

Most dislike looking in mirrors. We can pretend there is no such thing as the supernatural world, or we can look for answers. The Scriptures in Ephesians 6:11–13 state, *We do not battle against flesh and blood, but rather against principalities, against powers, against spirits of darkness.* The Bible teaches that both good and bad angels exist. As mentioned earlier, either I was shown things by those representing good or those representing evil. Your job is to discern the Truth of the matter, with the One True God's help.

For Further Study

To invite you to understand what is in your eternity, The One True God is saying to you:

> *"Call to Me, and I will answer you, and show you*
> *great and mighty things, which you do not know."*

> —Jeremiah 33:3

- Romans 8:1–2; Galatians 5:1; John 8:32 & John 36; 2 Corinthians 3:17

- Revelation 1:10–19; Acts 23:11; Genesis 6:13–22; Genesis 17:5–22; Genesis 22:1–2, 22:11–18; Daniel 8:15–16; Daniel 9:20–22

CHAPTER TWO

MOTORCYCLE CRASH

I t is testimony time whenever someone asks me how, in my late twenties, I came to accept Jesus as my Lord and Savior. It's time to bear witness to my experience, make a public open and true declaration of what happened to bring me to the point of faith in Him, and to tell what proof I have of who He is. My testimony bears witness to an unusual encounter. So unique, in fact, I often am very self-conscious about telling this story. But considering God is telepathic, perfect, and infinite in capability; and that making the stars, heavens, and Earth is simple for Him, I realize while it is an out-of-the-ordinary human one, it is quite easily within His realm of activities. If I am concerned with how other people will receive my true account, I hesitate. Yet, it is a true account with a significant impact on those who will consider it, so I'm willing to risk the strange looks I get, the quiet disbelief some individuals register, and the extra distance often given to me by church people. It isn't about me proving my credibility; it is about His power and desire to come into an ordinary man's life, flip his apple cart, and change the course of that man's destiny. I am eternally grateful for the strong medicine He gave for thick-headed me; it was the only way to penetrate my way of thinking. He is an apple cart flipping God, who can be forceful, but allows us free will to ultimately choose our direction.

As I read the Bible, I discovered another thick-headed person who prompted God to use extreme ways to help him find the One

True God. Daniel 4 records the story. Nebuchadnezzar II was a super-powerful king who reigned longer than any other king during the Babylonian empire. He was so powerful he deliberately destroyed Solomon's Temple, the first temple the Israelites had built in Jerusalem. He was one of the "hard nuts to crack," just as I had been, but neither of us was too tough for God to crack. God brought him to his knees, and when He did, Nebuchadnezzar turned a completely different way and began to confess to all in his kingdom that the God of Israel was the One True God. Daniel 4:1–2 says that Nebuchadnezzar wrote to "all" the peoples, nations, and tongues of his vast empire, declaring the signs and wonders of the "Most High God" of Israel.

Extreme measures were used to bring Nebuchadnezzar to that place. One moment he was standing on the top of his royal palace looking over his great city while proclaiming the vastness of his power and glory. God spoke. He told the king he would be removed from the kingdom. The next moment, Nebuchadnezzar found himself forced away from the kingdom and driven into madness. For seven years, the exiled king lived like an animal; outdoors, exposed to the elements, and eating grass. When the seven years were completed, God restored his reasoning, and Nebuchadnezzar was changed forever.

Nebuchadnezzar could have shrugged his shoulders and walked away like nothing ever happened to him, but the fear of the One True God and his "Eternity" meant more to him. So, before his death, Nebuchadnezzar wrote the truth about the One True God and sent it throughout his vast kingdom. He revealed to "all" peoples, nations, and tongues who the One True God was. God has been continuously calling out to all of us throughout time. No one will have an excuse because God is innately all-knowing. The proclamation of Nebuchadnezzar ends with a strong message to all who will receive it;

God puts down any who walk in pride. He is able and willing to do that on this side of eternity, resulting in a better outcome than doing it on the other side, which involves the Lake of Fire in the second death. God does not destroy the soul and spirit of His created beings, whether they are fallen, demonic angels or men. The second death is permanent separation from God at the Lake of Fire.

My second death comment may raise some eyebrows, but the Bible says we can die twice. The first is the physical death of the body as we know it. In the second death, everyone who has experienced the first physical death has their body restored to a new but different alive state. Then they are banished with that new existence to spend all of their eternity in the Lake of Fire unless they choose to believe in Jesus and the One True God before their physical death. This somber ending is worth further thought and consideration. The God of the Bible says we will all have an eternity. It is not a case of you die, and there is nothing more after that.

My acceptance of Jesus and what He did for me was not an overnight experience. I knew there was a God right away, and I knew that it was the God talked about in the Bible. Still, it was not a simple decision for me to make. My reasons for stiff-arming God for about eighteen months were probably not much different from other people's reasons. Many think they know better than the infinite mind of God and knowingly take that to their grave. If this is the path you are on, please reconsider your eternity and ask Jesus to mend the breaches caused by man.

God continuously calling out to me, led me to ask Him to identify Himself. Only in retrospect, however, could I see the diversity and relentlessness of His efforts across the years of my life. When I was a child attending Sunday school classes, I heard the stories from the

Bible. But they seemed no different than comics found in the paper or magazines like Superman, Thor, Iron Man, etc. At that time, in my mind, there didn't seem to be anything more significant or more real than Santa Claus. When I found out that was a fraud, then nothing else was real either. It all became just a bunch of stories for little kids. I know that sounds a bit harsh, but I was just a kid, and that is what I thought. I grew up wondering what other lies my parents told me.

From my early days, I was drawn to the concrete, knowable things of life. Math and science seemed to be real. Putting heat under a beaker of water causes the water to become hot. I could know that because I could measure the change with a thermometer. Put something dissolvable like salt in water and the salt disappears. That was real and measurable by tasting the now salty water and observing the change in its boiling point with that thermometer. Those were real things. Other real things included playing sports or getting from point "A" to point "B" faster on my bike. I had no time for stuff I could not directly experience or prove, and that included Bible stories or other spiritual experiences about which I heard.

Spiritual teachings continued to come into my life. By the time I was in my mid-twenties, I knew a little bit about God and some other gods. There was the occasional run-in with a psychic reader, some daily horoscope predictions, Hare Krishna's at an airport, or a wedding at a church. I was living life on the edge, and it seemed improbable I would make it to thirty years of age. With frequent disconcerting supernatural happenings, I reached a place where I had to know if there was a supernatural force behind everything, the observable as well as the inexplicable. An insatiable need to know with certainty took hold of me and grew. Maybe it took me longer than most to get to that point, but I had become desperate to know. That eternity question dug in and would not let go of me. I had to know before I passed away if there was more, and if there was more, what was it all about? Rather than one single event, I experienced many events that fueled that desire. My most extraordinary experience came when an ordinary activity became a surreal adventure.

During my assignment at Malmstrom Air Force Base, my buddies and I were always ready to share a few beers, jump on our motorcycles, and ride under the big skies of Montana. We were having a good time at a friend's party on base one day when one of the guys suggested we go for a ride. His suggestion produced an enthusiastic response since most of us welcomed the chance to take to the highway. My Triumph 750cc "Bonneville" was gassed up and ready to go, and so was I. Grabbing my helmet off the king and queen seat, I strapped it on for appearance's sake. Once we were off the base, it went right back onto the seat behind me, where it stayed anytime I was off base. I was wearing shorts, a tee-shirt, and flip-flops enjoying the sunshine on my head and feeling the air rushing across my body. As a twenty-five year old, United States Air Force officer, I was glad to break away from the rules and do what I wanted. We rode through small towns consisting of only one gas station, one grocery store, and usually two bars. The roar of my bike and the exhilaration of speed coupled with unrestrict-ed freedom brought a sense of euphoria while we rode surrounded by wide-open spaces. After a time, that highway rush gave way to a thirst for more beers, and we pulled into our favorite roadside bar. We spent time in light-hearted conversations and lively teasing as we drank our beers and relished our partying. Eventually, it was time to go, so we went outside and got on our bikes. Uncharacteristically, I strapped on my helmet.

We headed back down the two-lane country road with a greater sense of cockiness fueled by the teasing and the beers. Already speeding, I decided to show off and began to pass a friend. I moved into the oncoming traffic lane and picked up speed. My buddy looked over at me and then glanced at his speedometer, which was registering ninety-five miles per hour! A vague sense of concern crept in as I suddenly felt my bike vibrate, but I pressed on. Then a significant wobble occurred, which became so severe the front wheel turned ninety degrees to the bike's path of forward motion. The right front fork hit the steering stop, broke through and smashed into the gas tank. I lost all control of my bike and became airborne, entering into what seemed to me to be a slow-motion trajectory. A rapid-moving episode of my life became frame-by-frame still shots in my mind. I saw myself moving up and over the front of the handlebars, and then cartwheeling into a mid-air summersault. With everything in motion, suddenly, I sensed something catching me and instantly knew I was going to be alright. Complete peace settled in. Searching for the source of a scraping sound, I looked behind me and saw part of my motorcycle. Looking backward caused the back of my helmet to scrape the pavement. As I made my full flip, my left foot smashed into the ground with such force, it tore open my skin and exposed my Achilles tendon. My spiraling flight came to an abrupt conclusion as I landed on my rear end and slid down the road with my shorts providing the only protection from the rough asphalt. It takes a while to stop when you are going ninety-five miles per hour, and the only brake you have is your bum. Finally stopping, I immediately jumped up, staring face-to-grill with a semi-trailer truck. It had skidded to a stop no more than twenty steps away from me. Quickly, I ran off the road to let him pass, shaking my fist and cursing as he slowly went by. I was utterly unclear about the source of my anger since I also was happy to be alive and amazed I was not gravely injured.

I noticed the people in a nearby truck had watched the entire episode. I started waving my arms and shouting, "I'm alive! I'm alive!" They marveled at what they had seen as they drove me to a hospital.

The doctor examined me and reported his good news, bad news as he shook his head. The bad news was my ripped flesh had exposed my Achilles, but the good news was it suffered no damage. He stitched me up, and I returned to my life with no lasting injuries and only a small scar as a souvenir.

I had no relationship with any god or higher power, and this experience did not drive me to seek one. There was nothing my need-to-see-the-logic brain could do to explain how this was possible, so I tried to ignore the event for the next couple of years. I tried but failed. Erasmus, an ancient philosopher, is attributed with saying, "Bidden or unbidden, God is near." In retrospect, it would seem he was correct. The motorcycle accident and other unexplainable events kept coming into my memory and clamoring for an explanation. In addition to events, I began to notice, really notice the wonders of the created world around me. Glacier National Park brandished its majesty. The Northern Lights took ordinary particles of oxygen and nitrogen, which fill our earth's atmosphere and turned them into dancing rays of radiance in an awe-inducing display. Creation is quite incredible once you take the time to contemplate it. Once contemplated, it compels comprehension. I had to know, once and for all, nothing less would do. I did not know how or who might answer, if at all, but I had to know one way or the other if there was a Creator of some sort. In boldness, I asked the top Supernatural force to reveal itself. My requirement was the answer must completely and positively meet my specific criteria.

- The supernatural force or forces had to be revealed as I stated, "In a way that I know that I know that I know."

- The supernatural force or forces had to "Reveal in a way that I knew which one was truly the Head Honcho—King of the Hill" so that I followed the right one. One must rise above and forever silence the others. At that time, I had heard of many deity claims like Baal, Hindu, Allah, Hare Krishna, New Age, Jesus, etc.

- The last criterion was more of a disclaimer to absolve me from any error. If the "True or Top" supernatural creating force happened to be dozing, allowing an inferior to sneak in with an answer, then it would not be my fault for following the wrong one.

Let me encourage any of you who have decided you have a clearly defined image of a god who is not The One True God of the Bible to stay open to my premise. The only way to keep the devil from providing his supernatural deviously wrong answer is to ask for the Top God of gods, the top Lord of lords, to respond. Satan does not want anyone praying to the One True God for revelation, which is why man-made, man-focused religions specifically tell their followers to pray to only the god of their understanding for supernatural signs or wonders. Please think about that for a moment. If you keep doing what you have always done, you will keep getting the same answers you have always gotten. If you are reading this account, could it be you, too, have a pressing need truly to know the answer about God? Why not pray for the Top God of gods to show up and provide a sign. If the god you believe in now is, in fact, Top God, won't he be the one to show up? If you have been instructed to only pray to a certain god in a certain way, it may be to keep you from discovering The One True God. What is there to be afraid of if you pray to the Top God of gods and then see what happens? The One True God never forces our choices; He states the facts and lets us decide.

The intuitive One True God I now personally know never falls asleep at the wheel. He doesn't need to reveal His truth a second time, long after Jesus Christ died, in a brand new book written in 1830 called the *"Book of Mormon."* Be careful; you are saying the One True God was somehow dozing for about 2000 years and needed to fix His book, The Bible, when He woke up. Not only that, but how fair would that be to the millions of people who lived and died before the *"Book of Mormon"* ever came out. The One True God I know is more than all-knowing and powerful enough to protect His Word as He originally wrote it. Men will interpret God and the Bible many ways, but those looking for Truth will always find it in those pages and will not need to go elsewhere for Truth. That is what God's Holy Spirit does. We can open the Bible up in our quiet time at home, and God will teach us through His Holy Spirit. There is no need for any other book; we just need to have a willing heart for Truth. My willing heart led me on an encounter which resolved, once and for all, who God is.

For Further Study

To invite you to understand what is in your eternity, The One True God is saying to you:

> *"Call to Me, and I will answer you, and show you
> great and mighty things, which you do not know."*
>
> —JEREMIAH 33:3

- Daniel 4:1–2

- John 14:25–27

CHAPTER THREE

BURNED AT LAKE OF FIRE

It may be hard to believe, but this is the entirely true account of how Jesus changed my life forever. I was in my late 20's and was living out the "eat, drink, and be merry" dream of single life. Unexpectedly, I experienced a profound reflective moment. It was around Christmas, an understandably nostalgic time of year, and I began looking at my past. It was not a particularly bad life, but it seemed more than a tad, repetitive, and boring. It was certainly not wholly fulfilling, nor completely satisfying. My reflections prompted me to look ahead and contemplate what the rest of my life might look like. I saw a guy who would continue to do the same things until he died.

I wondered if what I knew was all there was to life? Was I to keep eating, drinking, and being merry? If I was not merry, then that must mean I was not eating and drinking enough. Really? Is that all there is to it? I decided I had to solve the eternity thing; put it to rest one way or another. So I set out my criteria and then proceeded to offer my prayer, which was more of a demand, that the One True God reveal Himself.

If there was something that created all I could touch and see, then I had to know. If creation was more than just some freak cosmic "big bang," where did I, a small fry, figure into the scheme of life? At that moment, I knew I was headed nowhere fast, aware it could be horrifying when my time on Earth ended. And so I asked.

I can be a strong-minded guy and not easily swayed, so the response would have to be strong medicine, or I would figure out a way to dismiss it in a heartbeat. I made my appeal only to the Top God. If indeed there was a Top God, then I was confident He would hear me and answer it in the way I had asked. If even one criterion were not met, my hands would be clean, and I would be moving on with my life as is. Anything less than the Top God was not worth my time. My request was for a slam-dunk in my face proof! It is rather funny now, looking back on it. The One True God could have "smote" me in an instant, but He didn't.

I did have to wait a couple of months for His response, and frankly, I forgot all about the whole situation. Perhaps there were small, subtle answers along the way increasing in intensity, but my thick head ignored or rationalized them away. The response as the One True God revealed Himself to me was strong medicine that I could not explain away. It was not a fun experience.

I was living in Montana when one night, I had a spiritual encounter with an angel who took me to the Lake of Fire. The direction was up into the outer darkness, and when I looked down, I could see it was in a northeasterly direction slightly over Canada. As we were ascending, I could see just on the other side of the outer darkness and became aware of a little orange-red speck getting larger and larger. I was about halfway into this trip before I realized this was the answer to what I had asked around Christmas time. I turned to the angel to ask about returning home, and another shock hit me. I received the answer telepathically while I was formulating the question in my mind. There were no audible words needed. The communication was utterly telepathic in both directions. This knowledge flooded my mind with the reality that the Creator knew every thought I ever had, as well as my actual spoken words and deeds. I knew the years of my life contained a lot of serious trash. The reality of that fact shook me, and for the first time in my life, I was scared, really scared. Before this experience, I had bad dreams at night occasionally, but they were nothing to me, and I would go immediately back to sleep. I had the motorcycle accident going ninety-five miles per hour with not even a twinge of fear. But this experience left me scared stiff, to the very core of my being, and it left me afraid to go outside in the dark the rest of that night. Without audible words, the angel answered back; it had to take me to the Lake of Fire. It reassured me it was following its orders down to the very last detail. There was no more communication after that. We arrived there, and unexpectedly I was burned only on the inside of my nose. Then I was taken back home.

Thankfully, I received a round-trip, not a one-way ride to the Lake of Fire. Folks, God wrote in the Bible that it was a real place, and I am here to tell you I received physical burns while there. I understand perhaps, it is a story that is a bit hard to believe, but honestly, I was taken to a real place. My burned nostrils became a constant physical reminder for three days, as I smelled a sulfuric odor every time I inhaled through my nose. Afterward, I walked around my house, went to work, played sports, and partied at night with a twenty-four-hour constant reminder from the burns I had received. Somehow, I was burned only on the inside of my nostrils.

Trying to get some sleep during those three nights was a severe issue. I would fall asleep and then breathe through my nose. As soon as I did, it felt like I was knocked out on the football field, and a trainer was jamming smelling salts in my nose. It was quite startling each time; it was like sniffing smelling salts hundreds of times, day and night. To no avail, I tried snorting hundred percent Aloe-Vera juice every half hour that first day. I learned an incredible amount of things from what seemed a very brief trip.

At first, I didn't understand why the inside of my nose had to be burned like that. The experience seemed to me to be a bit of overkill. Then I came to understand five crucial revelations given to me and saw them as the reasons why the angel had to take me there.

First, that incredible trip to the Lake of Fire was a unique and powerful way to answer my request that God reveal Himself in a way that would cause me to know that I knew Him. Secondly, it showed the Lake of Fire was tied directly to the Bible and conveyed the truth of the second death. Thirdly, during my trip, there was nobody there but us. That fact helped me understand the Lake of Fire and Hell were two different things, serving different purposes, at two vastly different locations. Reinforcing that was the fact the Lake of Fire was up above the earth and the other, Hell, was down. The fourth point was the most impactful. Because I had experienced the trip there, I now knew my eternal destination was going to be at the Lake of Fire unless I asked Jesus to come into my life. I knew the instant this all happened I had no argument to present that would keep me from that eternal destination. The fifth reason I had to go and experience it was to be able to silence the enemy. From time to time, Satan would try to convince me it was not real, or it had been just a bad dream. When he did, the memory of that burning sensation and smell in my nostrils would instantly come back to me. Those physical burns left a lasting memento of the truth of the trip. It was God's way of keeping me from rationalizing the entire event away. So, I became grateful for the whole experience, including the burned nostrils. I would have no excuse come judgment day, should I choose to reject the One True God.

I now know how important it was that I asked the One True God to reveal Himself, whoever He was. Satan or one of his demon buddies could have easily shown up. History shows this has happened multiple times over the centuries leading to the creation of many different types of religions. If that were not true, then there would only be one religion, and life would be simple and less violent. But we have many different religions, as seen in the *"Book of Mormon,"* the Buddhism Bible or Tipitaka, Zoroastrianism's Avesta, the Quran, the Hindu Bible, or Vedas, the Jehovah Witness Bible, and many others. Each religion has a little something for everyone, so step up to the smorgasbord table and pick one that appeals to you or keeps you from being persecuted by those around you. Atheism is itself a religious belief system. It seems oxymoronic, but it is a belief that there is nothing in the universe, a belief in no God or gods or deities. Whichever of the many religions you choose, only one can be right or is at least better than the others, depending on your personal point of view or situation.

If you are a believer in Baal, then lesser or evil forces are behind all the other choices, or at a minimum, all the different options are pushing a less fulfilling religion. If you're a believer in the Quran, then lesser or evil forces are behind all the others and promoting a less fulfilling religion. If you believe in Jesus, then you believe lower or evil forces are behind all the others. They cannot all be right, because the different teachings are at odds with each other. If another god had sneaked in a side door in answer to my requests, then the Top God wasn't very attentive and not worth following. I was not overly worried about following the wrong one, as I knew if there were a Top God, then He was one mighty dude who heard everything I had requested of Him the instant I thought it. Stopping an unwanted pretender from stealing His property, "me," was easy for Him to do.

Ignoring the possibility of the existence of a supernatural being does not mean anyone can walk away free and clear. On judgment day, the God I now know will show you all the times He revealed Himself, and you either rationalized it away, chose to pretend nothing happened, or you knowingly chose against Him. God doesn't force our choices. At judgment time, no man will have the ability to overcome the God of gods in His righteous judgment against them. How can anyone argue or negotiate with something that made the earth and all life on it? Why not ask Him today for proof of His existence? What can it hurt? The short version of my experience is that Jesus heard my plea and showed up.

After I encountered Him, I saw He had been knocking on the door all along. I now can see that and am grateful for all the opportunities to figure it out. Still, dealing with the eternity question was a tremendous struggle for me. I finally had experienced the Truth and had come to know I was trading a short time in the flesh for all of my future eternity. Yet, I could not choose Jesus right then and there. I knew the Truth, so this difficulty made no logical sense. There is an end to life as we know it, but there is no end to eternity. I called myself an idiot hundreds of times during the next one and a half years while I was trying to decide if I would follow Jesus or not. It was like the old cartoons where a good angel would pop up on the one shoulder and say something, only to have a bad angel pop up on the other and say the exact opposite, and that led to my spiritual paralysis.

My eternity hung in the balance, and meeting Jesus had taken away my excuses. This decision should have been as quick and straightforward as turning on a light switch in the house. Even knowing all that, I resisted giving up my whole way of "eat, drink and be merry" living. I did not realize it at the time, but there was an entirely different way of doing the "eat, drink, and be merry" theme. There is a healthy way of living, which does not require giving anything up. Bars, alcohol, and the nightlife were easily replaceable with things more fulfilling.

I was reading the Bible almost every day, and sometimes most of the day on weekends. My struggle didn't end in a day or month, but gradually things I once valued lost their shine as their luster dimmed. I stopped craving things producing no lasting satisfaction and developed cravings for profoundly fulfilling things with lasting value. While I was in the midst of the struggle, I could not see gradual change taking place in me, so the battle continued for over a year. Someday, I will spend my eternity having fun with my wife, kids, grandkids, and a whole bunch of other saints, most of whom have better stories than mine. How cool is that? Several years after asking Jesus to be Lord over my life, my wife asked me a thought-provoking question, "If you could choose any three people from throughout all of time to have dinner with, who would they be?" After thinking about it, I said, "Moses, Jesus, and you." She was a bit shocked that I included her and thought I had not understood the question, but I did. It would be great fun for me to have a meal with them and the person who means the most to me.

Like the old saying Rome was not built in a day, it took one to two years of gradual progress for me to accept Jesus into my heart. I did have a choice since I have free will. God didn't predestine my decision for me. However, He had predestined before the creation of the world a fail-proof system for those who chose for or against Him and His divine statutes.

Part of my struggle to accept Jesus was because I didn't know who to trust. Different churches taught different things that seemed to conflict. However, there is a difference in the term "church" when it refers to the local worship buildings you see around you and the term "The Church," which refers to something much greater than that. The Church refers to the universal group of all people who have come to know Jesus Christ, have invited Him into their hearts, and have acknowledged that He is their personal Savior. The Church is also referred to as the "Bride of Christ" because He has chosen those who believe in Him to be the ones who will be in a union with Him in Heaven for all eternity when it is time. We are now living in a time when He has prepared the place for His Bride, and the Church is waiting faithfully for Her Groom. The local, visible church is a place where Christ-followers and others who are seeking Him meet to worship, study, and grow in their ability to follow Him.

It is important to remember we are all imperfect this side of heaven and must extend grace towards those that teach differently than we think. There is a lifelong improvement process for us all. Besides, the enemy, Satan, with his thousands of years of experience, is good at what he does. He knows how to twist, sweet talk, manipulate, and control men. Unless we have the Holy Spirit working in us, Satan and his forces can easily influence us. Even then, we are vulnerable because we are imperfect until Jesus comes for us. I speak from personal experience and know too well why the Apostle Paul said he dies daily to his fleshly nature. When I am not intentional about dying to my naturally selfish ways, I am easy prey for the interminable wiles of the persistent devil. I am not perfect in my life-long battle, but experiencing a brief visit to the Lake of Fire solidified an eternal desire in my soul to make sure I won't spend my eternity there.

For Further Study

To invite you to understand what is in your eternity, The One True God is saying to you:

> *"Call to Me, and I will answer you, and show you*
> *great and mighty things, which you do not know."*

—JEREMIAH 33:3

- Revelation 20:14–15

CHAPTER FOUR

TRUTH AND TRUST

When the One True God gave me that first Lake of Fire vision, I had huge trust issues. When I first opened the Bible, I wasn't sure I could trust it to answer the questions I had concerning the Lake of Fire experience. I also wondered if it could provide answers to the scientific and social issues I could see all around me.

Although I didn't trust it, I read it daily to see if I could at least develop some trust. I asked the God I had just met to help me do this. The Bible is a large book and took a while to read several times from front to back. But I had to have something I trusted, and that was the only way that would work for me.

I had read many books by the time I was thirty and already had two college degrees. In reading all those books, it seemed I never opened one that didn't have a mistake or error in it within the first chapter or two. I found many different issues in those books. Sometimes there was an issue with an example problem or an incorrect answer to a question at the back of the book. Based on my experience, I figured there would be plenty of mistakes in a book as large as the Bible. When I discovered scores of men wrote the Bible over a couple of thousand years, I speculated it would be chock full of errors and contradictions. I was sure these errors and inconsistencies I found would also explain why many churches seemed to disagree on so many issues. Honestly, I was looking for ways not to trust the Bible. If I could discount the Bible, I metaphorically would be able to pick up my flipped apple cart tumbled by the Lake of Fire experience and put some of the apples back on it. However, I soon found out the Bible was surprisingly consistent. As I continued my investigation into it, my flipped apple cart became less and less relevant. I began learning about God, and I found He wanted to do some internal house cleaning in me if I would let Him. Reluctantly allowing it, He began to rid my life of its rotten apples.

In my opinion, critical thinking, the ability to weigh both sides of the story, is essential in life, but it seems to be a lost art today. Who teaches us how to do that? The world we live in seems to say we are supposed to believe the experts blindly. I was guilty as charged, but now had a burning desire to understand both sides of the story. It was especially important when considering eternity. I was determined to press on, and it didn't matter how much effort and time I had to put into it.

Keep in mind, even after discovering that Jesus was real, I was still unreceptive to the concept of the One True God. I had thought all this was a bad hoax perpetrated upon mankind, but I was seriously wrong. Fortunately, God gave me all the grace and time I needed to unpack all the lies and untruths I had blindly accepted over time. Because it is worth repeating, this was no longer a belief I based on entirely blind faith. Now I knew Jesus was for real because I asked, and God answered me directly. However, what I do accept by faith is that God will do precisely as He says He will do and has written everything in the instruction manual He gave us; His Bible. In this regard, I am no different than Adam, Cain, Enoch, Noah, Abraham, the Apostles, and a whole host of other people. They all saw or at least spoke directly with God or an angel like Gabriel. They all knew Him and believed He would do the right thing, no matter what, even though it may not have made much sense at the time. I know if I had been Noah and God told me to build that massive ark, I would have been scratching my head. My answer would have been, "You want me to do what?" While I do not know if Noah scratched his head on that, I do know he said "okay" and built it. God also told Abraham to pack his bags and move to where the nation of Israel now is located. However, God then told him that his descendants would be strangers in a different land, Egypt, for four hundred years and would be greatly afflicted by the people there.[7] Yes, I would be scratching my head on that one, too, and asking why I should do that only to have my descendants go through all the misery. Why not just stay put and then go four hundred years from now? Yes, it does take faith, a lot of faith, to trust that God has the best plan, indeed the right plan, despite appearances. So, all the more reason to put some extra effort into understanding what is in the Bible. After all, it is your eternity. Ask for the Holy Spirit to help you understand His instruction manual, so as not to rationalize things with your own limited understanding. I am not trying to insult anyone with that comment, but when compared to the unlimited abilities of God, we all need help to understand His Scriptures more thoroughly. Even then, we will only see in part.

Wherever you hear or see Truth in this book, it is not mine, it is God's, and He is asking me to share it with you. God does not need me or any of us to protect His Word, but He does want us to share with others what He has shared with us individually. That is what He does. If you want to know something, God will see it in your heart and give you an answer.

When I started reading the Bible in my late twenties, I bought

---

7 Gen. 15:13

a new spiral binder to document all the discrepancies I found in it. Many people may have trusted the Bible right from the beginning, but I was not one of them. After reading from Genesis through Revelation the first time, I was surprised I could only find about two dozen issues or discrepancies in such a large book. However, I now had a good understanding of the Bible and decided I should reread it, front to back. I was confident that I would now find many more issues and discrepancies.

Living my life as I pleased, and loving the "eat, drink, and be merry" dream, I wavered between wanting to prove what happened to me at the Lake of Fire had been bogus, versus wanting to be able to trust the Bible as Truth. It was a fight between my mind that wanted to continue what I thought was my American "eat, drink, and be merry" dream, and my heart's desire to know the Truth. What happened next really surprised me. On my second reading through the Bible, I started crossing things off my list when I fully came to understand the perceived discrepancies. A greater understanding of the context of the adjacent verses gave me a deeper understanding of the Scriptural Truths. When I finished reading the Bible the second time, I only needed a few fingers to count how many issues I had with God's Word and figured I would never completely understand the infinite ways of God with my small finite mind. I realized then how tiny and insignificant I was, so I came to understand there were things in the Bible I could not understand or explain. However, I did have something I could turn to in complete trust. I also knew I had to make a decision for or against Jesus now. I had all that I needed to know, and the spotlight was directly on me. Under that scrutiny, I admitted that my Eternity mattered to me and confessed I knew Jesus was the only way to the

Father.[8] So, I made my decision for Jesus and to follow the One True God as best I could.

After thoroughly reading the Bible through a couple of more times, I started to understand several side issues I had been pondering since my trip to the Lake of Fire. It had seemed odd that it was up above the earth, past the outer darkness. Hell is down or below the earth. Sometimes Hell is referred to as Hades, Sheol, and other things. For practical purposes throughout this book, I'll stick with the word Hell and try to simplify what the Bible teaches about it.

The Bible shows both Hell and the Lake of Fire have two distinctly different purposes and are at two separate locations. A comprehensive study of various translations of the Bible revealed Revelation is the only book containing a reference to the Lake of Fire. Hell, Sheol and Hades are in many other books in the Old and New Testaments. All four names refer to places of torment and flame, so it is easy to think of them as the same. But they are not. I have labored to understand the differences because, during my trip, no one was at the Lake of Fire except the angel that took me there. Not another person or being of any sort. I wondered why the place wasn't littered with guys like Hitler, Stalin, etc. since there are plenty of evil people over the ages to populate the Lake of Fire from top to bottom. I had not read the Bible up to that point in my life, but it sure seemed to me it must have been loaded with evil people. As I studied the Bible, I discovered the Antichrist and a false prophet were the first two sentenced to the Lake of Fire. God functions outside our space-time continuum and knows the end from the beginning. Those two entities still have not come into power, which is why nobody is at the Lake of Fire even today.

---

8 John 14:6

But do not worry. God will eventually make sure it is full of those who rejected Him and His plan for mankind for all eternity. Not by His choice as He would rather that none perish but because many will freely choose to go there rather than serve the One True God.[9] It is Your Eternity, your choice.

God is letting all of us know what the two choices are. It is either a yes for Jesus or a no against Him. A simple decision to join Jesus' team can change everything in an instant, do it now if you have not done that already. I want to see you when we all get there! Just ask Him, "Jesus, I am not perfect; I am a sinner who wants to be on your team." Then do your best to get into His Word the Bible, allowing God, His Holy Spirit, and His Word guide you for the rest of your life. God knows what to do to help you move forward. Remember that His Grace covers everything before and everything after that moment. We are still imperfect beings on this side of heaven, no matter how long we have lived our lives for Christ. Life can be a fragile thing, and something like a car accident can take anyone's life in an instant. Do not worry; Jesus is above all that. Like the thief beside Him on the cross, He knows the moment your heart changed, and your eternity will be with Him forever.

The Bible contains many insights about Hell, and one particular teaching from Jesus shows an essential understanding. Jesus gives a true account of a man named Lazarus and the rich man in Luke 16:19–31. In it, there are two parts to Hell. One is a good side called Paradise, which is also known as Abraham's bosom, and that is where Lazarus went when he died. The rich man went to the other side. I call that the bad side for people who reject God and His plan for mankind. As He

---

9 2 Pet. 3:9

relates the events, Jesus reveals that a "great divide" separates the two sides. Lazarus and the rich man can see and talk to each other, but they can't interact. Their bodies are dead, but their soul and spirit are not.

The purpose of the great divide is to keep those on the bad side from getting over and causing trouble on the good side. Additionally, it keeps those on the good side from going over and providing relief to those on the bad side. It is called Hell because of sin. It was not God's choice for us, but He knew, before creating man, that we would have free will and choose to sin against His divine laws. None of us are without sin. So, God predestined Hell to exist before the creation of the heavens and the earth. It is all part of a much bigger plan that we only know in part. The account of Adam and Eve sinning by eating from the forbidden tree reveals they caused death to happen. That was when Hell started to become populated with souls and spirits. It is still the destination for all mankind upon death until all things are made right by God. Bible readers know God will accomplish that with the Great White Throne Judgment.[10] In human years it is an extremely long process, which started with Adam and Eve and will end when all of Death and Hell is bundled up and thrown into the Lake of Fire upon the occurrence of the second death. It happens after Jesus' second coming and His completion of a one thousand year reign from Jerusalem.

It is essential to understand the point that sin is not entirely dealt with until Hell is thrown into the Lake of Fire over one thousand years from now. Hell is for the first death because the wages of sin is death. The Lake of Fire, reserved for the second death, is for those who chose against the One True God's divine statutes. Their final verdict is to

---

10 Rev. 20:11–15; 1 Cor.15:24–26

spend their eternity in the Lake of Fire. Their fate signals everything is finished, and eternity begins for all. Some will have their eternity with God in the New Jerusalem, but everyone else will be in the Lake of Fire. That should be motive enough to investigate the truth of things before death knocks. Yes?

"In the beginning, God created the heavens and the earth." These are God's first words in the Bible. Genesis 1:1 shows He left no stone un-turned before there was the creation. The One True God has not been making it up as He goes along or ad-libbing His way throughout time. It was all preplanned in advance so that no part of creation, angels, man, nor living beings, could ever state otherwise.

Believers in Christ live with generational curses because the Bible says we do. Consider "Exhibit A," which involves Adam and Eve. They brought death to all mankind. We all live with the original curse of their sin, which results in the death of the body. Ephesians 1 tells us that believers, who accept God's predestined provision for their sin, are adopted as His sons because of Jesus Christ. Upon death, we go to the good side of Hell as Jesus, and one of the two criminals next to Him did. Those rejecting God's plan go to the bad side of Hell, like the other criminal on the cross beside Jesus. Those who accept Jesus as Lord receive forgiveness and the assurance of eternal peace living with Him in a future incorruptible body. That does not keep us from sin and death in these fleshly bodies, as none of us are without sin.

While we may sin less by thought, word, and deed once we accept Jesus as Lord, we do not become perfect and cannot attain god-like perfection as some religions teach. The wages of sin are the actual death of our flesh, which still happens today.[11] It is essential to understand

---

11 Rom. 6:23

God is in complete control over both sides of Hell as well as over the Lake of Fire when it opens for business, starting with the Antichrist and False Prophet. The enemy has always been entirely powerless at those locations. Hell did not have to come into use, but it was established as part of the creation, should man use his free choice to choose against God's divine law. Mankind did choose to break God's law at the beginning of our history, and we still do today. No one is without sin.[12] Some of us have our sin covered by the grace provided by Jesus, but many do not. The road traveled with repentant people is narrow and few are saved. It is narrow because few use their free will to choose for God's predestined plan of Grace that has been provided by His Son Jesus.

Because I was taken specifically to the Lake of Fire, I knew this was the God of the Bible. I also knew the Lake of Fire would be where I spent my eternity if I did not change the direction in my life. I had to know more about that place, so on that day, I opened the Bible. The index of my Bible showed the Lake of Fire was only in the Book of Revelation, so I read it first. Then I reread it because I did not understand much of anything the first time through. Reading Revelation a second time, that same day, was not helpful either. I knew then this was going to be a much larger project than I had anticipated. It was then that I got the new spiral binder and started in the book of Genesis. In repeated reading of the Bible, I came to understand God is a supernatural being, and man is a natural being. While that is a big "No Duh," moment, it seems that most of mankind has missed that point.

The more diligently I studied the Bible, the importance of critical-

---

12 Rom. 3:10; 1 John 1:18

ly considering both sides of the story started to spread to other parts of my thinking. Ideas and theories all around me won my trust only after I spent time in deep, critical thinking. Things from inventions to politics started changing before my very eyes. You see, natural man cannot build a piece of equipment out of natural materials capable of measuring something supernaturally created. So, concepts like evolution should be considered a genuinely bad hoax by any who believe in the supernatural. Pick any religion you want; they all, except atheism, have a supernatural element to them. By definition, anyone who believes in a supernatural being cannot believe in evolution, or that life just magically emerged from primordial ooze over billions of years. Natural man is incredibly limited compared to the supernatural. Anyone giving credibility to evolution is saying to others that there is no God or a supernatural force of any sort. The data supporting their findings often comes from faulty man-made things that cannot measure, quantify, or define supernatural activity. Most, if not all, do not talk about this since because they would lose money and followers. Either of those points should raise a huge red flag, at least to anyone trying to understand both sides of the argument.

The primary assumption held by evolutionists and others behind the big bang theory is that there is no God or any other supernatural force. They don't publically say that because it blows up all their work. They know they cannot measure and quantify the supernatural. Some Christians unwittingly have been duped into this way of thinking because they don't realize people are the apple of God's creation, and created in His image. He carefully, with meticulous detail, formed the earth and the heavens as the perfect place for man to live.

Consider the workings of this Earth He made. When our planet gets too hot, God has created a way for it to cool off. Volcanos erupt and spew ash over one hundred thousand feet into the air, thus, reflecting sunlight away from the earth. This effect, similar to reflective sunglasses, lasts for several years as those minuscule particles of ash slowly fall back to earth. Much like the human body sweats to cool off, the ice caps melt to cool the earth. Global cooling, in simple terms, happens as more clouds and moisture in the air reflect and limit the penetration of direct sunlight. The majority of the earth's heating comes from sunshine. Man's contribution to global warming is incredibly small. It is a component, but not the "major" component people present it to be. The One True God already knew warming would occur and predestined a proper fix for it using volcanos and the polar ice caps.

Unfortunately, there is another potentially damaging activity threatening the global climate nobody is considering. The fact that man is knowingly seeding clouds or the upper atmosphere with different types of chemicals requires more consideration and critical analysis. I do know this sort of thing has been going on for decades. But, why would any country do this? Perhaps, to increase rainfall in drought areas, or to cause drought in foreign countries to bring them to the bargaining table. While I do not have in-depth knowledge of how this works, I became aware of it when my wife and I were vacationing in Los Alamos, New Mexico. That city has a much-storied history of nuclear weapons development, spy rings, and intrigue. The atomic bombs dropped on Hiroshima and Nagasaki ending WWII with Japan were developed there. It is also the site of many Top Secret research activities even today. During my visit, I was surprised by the level of attention paid to climate control. I expected the focus to be on nuclear research or how best to develop outer space. However, the current research and development are directed toward learning how to control the weather.

I was stunned by what was blatantly being done in the open for all to see. We are not talking about how to observe the weather accurately. We are talking about how to change and control the weather anywhere on planet Earth. Revelation 16:21 says hailstones weighing about one hundred pounds will fall on people. Is that going to happen because of man's misguided efforts to control weather patterns?

In the early 2000s, I read different articles from NASA reporting their research showed that during years when the earth had higher temperatures, Venus and Mars were warmer, too. Those articles were readily available then, but now seem to have been removed or filtered. Nevertheless, Venus and Mars receive most of their heat from the sun just as Earth does. Research into global warming on Earth without exploring the sun's effects on planets like Venus and Mars is, in my opinion, a serious error. There are no humans or life forms on either of those planets which impact their cooling and warming periods. Since those planets have temperature changes correlating to similar changes on Earth, we have to ask why? It is crucial to determine the arguments from both sides, but many of us will struggle with the so-called scientific facts. Since we all do not think like scientists and rely on scientific discoveries, we must be aware there can be biased scientific information on both sides of any given argument. Only one side is in the right, but if we don't think like scientists, how do we know which is correct?

If we look for it, eventually we will find something we all can understand. We know man has not been able to record the earth's temperature for very long. The first thermometer, which was known as a thermoscope, was developed in the late 1500s and was not very accurate.

For the sake of this argument, let us say that it was an adequate tool to measure the earth's cooling and warming trends. That would mean man would have useful data for about the last five hundred years. Those arguing for man's destructive influence in causing global warming will say the earth is about four and a half billion years old, while others say it is even older. Christians believe the earth is much younger. For this discussion, let's use the four and a half billion year figure. What are five hundred years of measurement compared to four and a half billion years of the earth's existence? I expect most everyone, including the scientists arguing for global warming, would say that five hundred years is not a valid sample size when compared to four and a half billion years. That is especially true when you do not have real data going back to the very first day. When five hundred years is divided by four and a half billion years, the result is the fraction of 0.0000001; or the size of a single speck of dust. Not only is that speck an incredibly small sample size of time, but it is also tainted by the fact that it is a sample of only the most recent period. Data from all the other prior four and a half billion years does not exist in our record books, so we can only guess as to what might have happened. Don't you think a lot can happen in four and a half billion years? Another way of looking at it is by recording a small sample at the end of your life. If you lived to seventy-five years of age, that 0.0000001 is less than five minutes of your life, and it is a recording of just the last five minutes of your life. That recording doesn't have anything from your birth up to that time. Not only that, but if you died in your sleep, that five-minute recording of your life would be of you sleeping. That is what the last five hundred years are to four and a half billion years. Therefore, we must think critically.

Be careful of theories, which are just ideas used to support a position, not based on a proven fact like the law of gravity. Consider the theory stating man is responsible for global warming. If that is a fact, then it would be impossible to have multiple ice ages and multiple global warmings. Instead, there should have been one continuous upswing in global warming, with no global cooling. Now the narrative has changed to say global warming is causing global cooling. Really? I do believe global cooling and warming happens. But there is far more to this than the single argument that man is bad, which generates all the hyperbole fear tactics used by global warming proponents. Scientists are saying there have been five or six ice ages, and only the last one was with man on the earth. So how is it four to five global warming's happened when man was not on the earth? Even if man sped up global warming, the earth obviously has a way to cool down and heat back up with or without man being on the planet.

Over my sixty plus years, I have noticed the advocate shouting the loudest or trying to control the conversation generally is a bully. Control and fear tactics come straight from the devil's hand. God is all about free choice and freedom. Jesus said He came that we might be set free.[13] When theorists attempt to bully people into accepting their ideas, they are threatening your freedom to think and decide critically. Another factor in observing situations is that the right path is narrow, and the wrong path is wide. In other words, beware of the herd mentality. In the world of investments, a popular investment technique is the "contrarian" viewpoint. If the herd is selling, then the contrarians are buying. When the herd is buying, they are selling. Finding peace with a solution is another way and can go a long way by itself. A fourth method or tool that I use is to determine which answer seems to be the wisdom of man, i.e., the wide path, versus the wisdom of God, the narrow path.

---

13 John 8:31–32, 36; Gal.5:1

Understanding what is in the Bible is what matters. It seems to me the wide path is the path that has the most screaming going on and doesn't like it when the God angle is brought up. Why? Well, the bullies have to control the narrative and will do it any way they can. They have to control or shout the loudest because the facts are not in their favor, and they cannot handle being wrong because they usually have ulterior motives. Control has many forms and enticements, such as money, drugs, promotions, advancement, etc. Those are Satan's tactics that work well and are used repeatedly. Controlling the narrative, like the media does today, is a very useful tool against anyone who thinks differently. Doing whatever it takes to manage the storyline is especially effective against those who do not have enough "oil" in their lamps to resist. Hitler was able to do what he did because he controlled the narrative through the media. I am not saying all media is corrupt, but I am saying to be aware of who is governing the account of what is happening. I see very little in the mainstream media today that brings any glory to God the Father. Critical thinkers have two benchmarks for evaluating the narrative. It must show both sides of the issue, not one perspective in its presentation. Additionally, the narrative must align with the Bible.

Bible-believing Christians must know how to provide more light in the darkness around us. We are told not to fear man who can only kill the body, but rather fear God who can destroy our soul for all eternity. That is not always easy, and many have died as sheep led to the slaughter. But we have God on our side, and He alone will judge all things in His timing. Because of God's promises, many Christians over the centuries have willingly become martyrs for their faith in God. I am certainly willing to die and become a martyr for Jesus. Easier said than done perhaps, but that is my free choice to make. When I refer to being a martyr, I am not talking about the kind of death where you kill others and also die in the process. A martyr is a person who suffers persecution and death, at the hands of others, because the martyr advocated and refused to renounce their religious beliefs. A martyr is an innocent sheep minding their own business when the bully shows up. Blowing yourself up to kill others is not martyrdom.

I ask a lot of people this question, "Are you willing to die for your beliefs?" That question applies to everyone alive today regardless of their religion. For example, it is your choice if you want to remain an atheist until death. But the question before you now is, "Are you really willing to believe there is no life after death?" Are you willing to die believing there is nothing else out there? If there is even a hint of doubt, let me encourage you to stop reading right now and ask the One True God to reveal Himself to you in the way that you will know that unequivocally He exists. He is above all things and heard your concern the second you thought it. He will answer you in His time, not yours, but He knows when and how to respond. You will then know the truth. Like me, you will still have a choice to make for or against God, but it is your free will to choose.

Another issue requiring further investigation and critical thinking is the "Big Bang Theory." This theory essentially says the cosmos originated over a billion years ago from a single point explosion—a "singularity" as it is known scientifically. Creation is still expanding today from the explosion's center point. The central premise of the big bang is that before the explosion, everything was in the same spot. This theory posits the earth is billions of years old, and there isn't a God or supernatural force behind it. Ironically, we cannot prove the big bang since it is just a theory to explain something we cannot prove. What we can observe is light from stars tens of thousands of light-years away.

That means the earth cannot possibly be the biblical account of about six thousand years old, because we could not see the light from a star that far away, right? Well, let me suggest one immense flaw with that.

The flaw is the big bang says everything started from a "single" point. So, stars, planets, the universe were created at the same time and from the same location. From that exact location, everything exploded or expanded out from there. In this scenario, the light and stars were right next to Earth and everything else at the explosion.

The stars we see today are tens of thousands of light-years away because of the big bang explosion. When it all started from one big bowl of soup, though, they were all glowing right next to our planet. On the first day of the explosion, the earth and everything else had direct light from the stars. That light then followed those stars as they traveled away from each other and the Earth. We cannot say the Earth has been here tens of thousands of light-years based on the fact that any star we see today is now tens of thousands of "light-years" away after the explosion. Why? Everything was in the same spot when it happened. When this hole in the theory was exposed, some decided the stars traveled out to the locations tens of thousands of light-years away first; then "magically" turned on and gave off light when they got there.

That sounds a bit silly, but that is precisely what some are saying today. Some will say whatever it takes to keep the old theories alive and help great thinkers save face. They use any ideas they can to deny that God, or any supernatural force, is responsible for everything. Another troubling fact is they cannot explain how "something" like stars, moons, and the planets, came from "nothing."

God allows free will, and we can each decide for ourselves, just do not be too quick to dismiss any explanation, including God.

Some readers think God may be another of many theories like the big bang. His existence is one hundred percent fact to me. I asked Him to prove He was real, and He did. So, do whatever is needed to "know," because, in the end, you alone are responsible for your eternity. As I see it, these stars were emitting light from the very first instant of creation, were giving off that light right next to the planets, and continued shining as they traveled further and further away from each other. That means the earth, as we know it, really can be about six thousand years old, not billions. I am not saying you have to believe either of those numbers, but rather that no man can measure or quantify, through our natural man-made devices or electronics, something supernaturally created. Which gets us back to the point that scientists who do not believe God created all things do not tell everyone their base assumption is there can be no supernatural force, of any sort, for their theory to be valid. Can you imagine how things would go if they started a presentation to a stadium filled with one hundred thousand Christians or Muslims, or Hindus, or Baalists by saying that for their principles to be valid, there can be no such thing as supernatural beings? I suspect that most everyone would start to file out because their manmade theories become meaningless immediately. It doesn't matter if the talk is about the big bang or climate change.

When there is a great deal of hyperbole, histrionics, and hysteria around a topic, there is an emotional frenzy. When that creates fear, it takes our eyes off of God. Critical thinkers find and weigh all sides of the issue, and the Bible is a handy tool in that process. You can go to the New King James Version and consider it all by reading what is said in Galatians 5:19–26. This Scripture contrasts the things of the flesh and the things of God's Holy Spirit. Whether you believe in God or not, it is worth reading to consider what the two different viewpoints say. For example, bad actions in verses 19–21 include discord, jealousy, fits of rage, selfish ambition, envy, and drunkenness. Good actions in verses 22–24 include kindness, gentleness, self-control, love, peace, faithfulness. Reading these may shed light on the issues you are seeking to understand.

I have struggled to understand many scientifically based issues, as well as all the injustices I saw around me. It has also been challenging to explain my Lake of Fire experience adequately. Like dropping a stone into a lake, where many ripples come from the one stone, I had trouble believing I could trust the Bible to cover all the ripples of thoughts I had going on in my mind. It was not easy, but I put in the effort, and God knew that. He saw that in my heart, I genuinely wanted to find the truth of all things, not to justify my own reality or someone else's. One by one, He showed me the seemingly endless errors of my thinking. Some errors were deeply entrenched, and I have had to revisit them repeatedly. I am still far from perfect, but God's help is always close at hand.

He has shown me that truth and untruth battle on a horizontal and vertical axis, which is similar to the cross. At the top of the vertical axis is God, and at the bottom is Satan, who does not want us to see the battle going on upon the vertical axis because he is exposed. So, Satan does everything he can to keep us focused on the horizontal axis. That horizontal axis is set up to pit man against man, thus keeping all eyes away from the vertical God versus Satan axis. Many issues flood that horizontal axis; i.e., politics of the left versus politics of the right, or abortion on the left versus anti-abortion on the right, evolution on one side versus a well-planned and detailed creation on the other, country against country, one religion on the left versus another religion on the right. We could probably fill a book on all the different types of battles on that horizontal axis. It is the axis of distraction to keep us from truly seeing the works of Satan. Society is very polarized in all sorts of areas, and the more focused people are on the things of that horizontal axis, the less we see of the true fight going on at the vertical axis between God and Satan. If society could keep its eyes on the vertical, life would be more peaceful.

For Further Study

To invite you to understand what is in your eternity, The One True God is saying to you:

> *"Call to Me, and I will answer you, and show you*
> *great and mighty things, which you do not know."*

> —JEREMIAH 33:3

- Revelation 20:4–15 and 21:8

- Luke 16:19–26

- 1 Corintians 15:22–28

- Luke 23:39–43

- Matthew 7:13–14 & 21–23; Luke 13:23–25

- Matthew 25:1–4; Psalm 119:105; John 34–36

- Matthew 10:28; Matthew 16:26; Mark 8:36–37; Luke 12:20

- Ephesians 1

- Proverbs 8:22–23; John 1:1–15; John 17:24, Matthew 25:34; Hebrews 4:3; Hebrews 9:26; 2 Timothy 1:9; 1 Peter 1:19–20; Revelation 13:8; and Revelation 17:8

- 1 Samuel 28:13–15, Luke 16:19–27, Ephesians 4:9–10

CHAPTER FIVE

HEAVEN AND EARTH WILL BE REMADE

*F*or behold, I create new heavens and a new earth; and the former shall not be remembered or come to mind. But be glad and rejoice forever in what I create. These words come from Isaiah 65. Historically well known, Isaiah was a greatly-trusted prophet who lived about seven hundred years before Jesus was born. His prophecies regarding local matters came true, giving credibility to his gift of hearing from God about the future. Somewhere around seventy years after Jesus' death, John, the Elder, exiled on the barren island of Patmos, experienced an encounter with the One True God. He recounts, *Now I saw a new heaven and a new earth, for the first heaven and the first earth had passed away. Also there was no more sea.*[14] He recorded all he experienced, and this vision is in the book of Revelation.

In a world before the internet connected everyone with far-reaching information, the similarity held in one man's prophecy supported eight hundred years later by another man's vision is remarkable. They inform the Bible reader that God can create anything at any time He wants, and He will, in fact, do away with this heaven and earth and create new ones. If you are a believer in Jesus, who are we to argue against that. We know He has already done it at least one time, so there's no reason why He can't do it again. It is one of the many things

---

14 Rev. 21:1

He does. As a Christian, we can see the current Earth, stars and heavens are not going to be around forever. But we do know there are over one thousand years to go since Jesus has not started His reign from Jerusalem as recorded in Revelation 20.

God will destroy the earth and make a new one, and that will happen because He said He would. He will do this work in a way our limited perceptions can't imagine. God is not limited, but man is. When God finishes, the new Earth will not have any seas. God could create a brand new exact duplicate of all the life on this Earth, yet, it seems He plans to create a new world. God does not tell us much about the new Earth, other than there will be no seas, so we know there will be no sea creatures or sea life as we know it today. All of the existing animals, ocean plants, and vegetation will instantly be extinct. God may then create many other new forms of life because He can.

Only God has the knowledge and ability to save the Earth. Is there any need to even care about taking care of the earth? I am not saying there is something bad about taking care of the Earth as best we can. As Christians, my wife and I try to leave wherever we have been as clean as when we arrived. That includes places like picnic areas, parks, campgrounds, rented party rooms, and swimming areas. What I am saying is we need to be careful about the motivation behind taking care of the Earth. As Christians, do we have God as our motivation, or are we doing it based on our pride, guilt, or fear tactics from man?

Many will say God commanded us to take care of the Earth. But we must carefully consider what He said. In Genesis 2:15, God put Adam in the Garden of Eden and told him to, "Take care of it." In God's original plan, mankind was to tend and take care of Eden forever. As God created Eve as a companion for Adam, His original command was for them to never eat from the tree of the knowledge of good and evil in the middle of the garden. Their original sin was disobedience to Him, thus bringing sin and death into the world. Consequently, they were cast out of the Garden of Eden, lost access to the Tree of Life, and could no longer take care of Eden.

Eden was only a small patch on the Earth, not the entire Earth, and when they listened to the satanic reptile, they lost access to the Garden and the tree of life. Again, to be perfectly clear, the entire Earth is not the Garden of Eden, only a tiny portion of the planet was the Garden of Eden. God made Adam from the ground outside of Eden[15]; when Adam sinned, he was sent out of Eden to till that ground. When God removed Adam and Eve from Eden, He placed cherubic angels to ensure Adam and Eve could never return. God did not command them to take care of the entire Earth. Man does not have a green light to trash the planet, but God's command was to take care of Eden, and mankind failed. The good news is Jesus came to fulfill God's predestined plan, which was in place before all of creation.[16]

Before He created the Earth, God intended to reverse everything bad that eventually would happen should Adam and Eve lead humanity into death through sin. Adam and Eve sinned against God, as we all do today, but God showed us He had a plan to restore everything, as it was before sin entered the world. That plan is a rather long process in man-years for there are over one thousand years to go. It is written that Jesus will establish a reign of peace from Jerusalem. Afterward, Satan will be set free from the bottomless pit for a time.[17] After these events, God finishes judging everything and makes a new heaven and earth. Yes, Earth will be destroyed and remade by God, not man. Man

---

15 Gen. 2:7–8
16 Eph. 1:4–5
17 Rev. 20:6–7

may try to destroy this Earth, but God will not allow it. It is written that He is reserving the right to do that Himself. The existing universe with our current Earth, sun, moon, and stars will be utterly destroyed, giving way to a new heaven and Earth. As Christians, we must believe God has done what He says He has done, and God shall be doing what He says He is going to do.

To give proper consideration to our eternity, we must make a critical decision. Are we going to be loyal to the Earth and man, or God? We cannot serve two masters, as you will be faithful to one and against the other.[18] Isn't your "eternity" worth the time and effort to investigate?

He has made everything beautiful and appropriate in its time. He has also planted eternity, a sense of divine purpose in the human heart. It is a mysterious longing which nothing under the sun can satisfy, except God. Yet man cannot find out, understand or grasp what God has done or what is His overall plan *from the beginning to the end.* Solomon, the wise king, recorded this valuable insight in Ecclesiastes 3:11. Nobody knows how many times God has remade the heavens and Earth in the past, yet based on Scriptures like Revelation 21, we do know there are at least two times this happens, the current one and then the one in the future. There is a misunderstanding among church members about the account of creation in Genesis 1. The first question to consider is, does the universe have alternating days and nights like Earth does? If it does not have repeating nights and days like the earth, then what exactly is God calling a "complete" day in Genesis 1? Perhaps it is evident to some, but I have heard too many others claim different things such as God did not create the heavens

---

18 Matt. 6:24; Luke 16:13

and the Earth in six Earth days. They explain the account in Genesis is used to illustrate God's power to create, but He didn't do it in six twenty-four-hour days. Hmm, if the universe does not have a day and night to it, maybe it helps to consider the purpose of the Bible. Did God write it for Himself? Did God write it for Satan or some other of His created beings? If the answer is that Scripture is God's instruction manual for man, then the rest of this should be agreeable to you, unless you do not think God is all that powerful. If the Bible is God's instruction manual for man and the Earth he lives on has twenty-four-hour days consisting of both night and daylight, then it seems God did complete this creation in six Earth days. But there is more surprising detail in Genesis about His creation. There was only darkness until God created light, so there was no night-day sequence anywhere until God created light to alternate with the night. As it says in Genesis 1, first there was night, followed by daylight and that made one twenty-four-hour period of time. God repeats the night, followed by daylight sequence several times in Genesis 1. That sequence refers to back to back seven twenty-four-hour periods. What other night to day sequence could the Supernatural God possibly mean? After all, He is supernatural. He is not limited in what He can accomplish in seven twenty-four-hour periods. It is wise to read Scripture carefully, not adding nor subtracting to God's Word. An entire Earth day is not the same as other planets in our galaxy, so the age of the universe would be different depending on which planet was used as the clock. If we were on Mercury, a complete night-day would be around one thousand four hundred hours or fifty-eight Earth days, and a complete night-day on Jupiter would be approximately ten hours. The planets in our galaxy spin faster or slower on their axis than the Earth. Since the beginning of time, mankind has been tracking time using the twenty-four-hour

Earth clock. There was no other way to do it until recently, and I have yet to hear anyone start tracking time not based on a twenty-four-hour Earth day. The reasonable conclusion is God created the heavens and the Earth in six twenty-four-hour days and rested on the seventh day. Honestly, I think He could have done it in seven eye blinks, but God had other reasons to stretch it out over seven days. Part of this reasoning has to do with debunking ideas man would come up with like the big bang theory. If God had done it in an eye blink that would have given credibility to misguided theories, so, God stretched creation out over six days and rested on the seventh.

An area bearing deeper consideration is the fact God didn't create the sun, Earth, stars, and heavens all on the first day. Genesis 1 says God created only light, only part of a "Big Bang," but nothing else in the first twenty-four-hour day. By that, I am saying there were no separate pieces to the light. There was just one sizeable generic piece of light. Then on the fourth day, God breaks up the one big light into pieces we call the sun and stars.[19] So, on the fourth day, there was at least a second big bang that split up the light from day one into lights and planets from each other. It is not hard for believers in God to know He can do things this way. Especially since Scripture says God will indeed recreate the whole universe, the heavens, and Earth, after the Great White Throne Judgment, but the question is, why did He do it as written in Genesis?

Our omniscience God knew man would eventually come up with the big bang theory leading some believers to agree with that particular account. In doing so, they would not see God in His magnificent creation. Romans 1:19–21 states His creation speaks of His invisible

---

19 Gen. 1:14–19

attributes, and no one observing His creation will have an excuse. God is saying right there that even if a man has no Bible and no knowledge of the One True God, all of creation points to Him. Creation itself causes every man to pause and seek their Creator. Creation is too mind-boggling for any man to unbiasedly come up with something which explains how all of this "something" came out of nothing. Quite simply, only God, a powerful supernatural force, can make all of this "something" out of nothing.

All things with life are incredible and inexplicable. Scripture warns that if man exercises free will to reject the incredibleness of creation, their thoughts become futile, and their hearts become darkened. Darkened hearts happen not because God is upset with us, but rather because we have chosen against Truth, so God's light is not in our hearts the way it should be. Yes, unlimited God certainly could have done everything in one day, but He chose to do it differently, as Genesis describes, so those professing to be wise would become fools. Those are not my words; they are what God wrote. If God is who He says He is, then the foolishness of God is wiser than men.[20] Because God knows the intent within our heart, He knows whether an action is done to be seen and esteemed highly among men, or not. Luke 16:14–15 holds this admonishment, *"For what is highly esteemed among men is an abomination in the sight of God."*

The things of this man-made world will pass away when The One True God creates the new world. None of it will be missed or remembered. People who choose God will be glad and will rejoice forever in what He has created. Is that what is in your eternity?

---

20 1 Cor. 1:25

For Further Study

To invite you to understand what is in your eternity, The One True God is saying to you:

> *"Call to Me, and I will answer you, and show you great and mighty things, which you do not know."*
>
> —JEREMIAH 33:3

- Isaiah 65

- John's vision found in the Book of Revelation

CHAPTER SIX

THE WIRELESS GUIDE

T he God of gods has the original wireless communicator, called the Holy Spirit. The role of the Holy Spirit is multifaceted. But the primary function is to lead and guide us throughout our lives as we walk with God. People often mention the seven-fold Holy Spirit. That term comes from Isaiah 11:2, *The Spirit of the Lord shall rest upon Him, The Spirit of wisdom and understanding, The Spirit of counsel and might, The Spirit of knowledge and of the fear of the Lord.* This prophecy tells about the seven spirits of God resting on Jesus. It is the same Spirit with the same seven attributes which are available to believers today. They are the very Spirit of the Lord, the Spirit of wisdom, the Spirit of understanding, the Spirit of counsel, the Spirit of power, the Spirit of knowledge, and the Spirit of the fear of the Lord.

I had trouble understanding why two of the features of the Holy Spirit were knowledge and understanding. Were they not essentially the same thing? Over time, it became evident some people had knowledge, but lacked understanding of that knowledge and misapplied it. Another feature I didn't quite get was fear. Why was the fear of the Lord important? After several years, the Holy Spirit tied what was said in Isaiah 11:2 to what Jesus said in Matthew 10:28, *And do not fear those who kill the body but cannot kill the soul. But rather fear Him who is able to destroy both soul and body in hell.* God's Spirit is ever-present and all-knowing. He knows the intent of all hearts. Those attributes make it possible for God to judge all of us properly. Since He sees the intent of our hearts, you and I may accomplish the exact same action, but God may judge your action to be worthy and mine not worthy based on the intent, which was at the root of the action. A new activity, done the next day, may have the opposite results. Just because I have made my choice to be on Jesus' team, doesn't mean all of my motives are now good.

Unfortunately, some hold that against other believers and me, as if we are supposed to be perfect and bulletproof now, but Jesus does not hold anything against us on our judgment day. God knows that my human nature, while better than twenty years ago, is still flawed, and I cannot earn my salvation. The sevenfold Spirit of God comes and lives in and through believers to guide them into godly thoughts and actions and away from the old dark ways. Thankfully, my unworthy actions will burn in the refiner's fire, and I shall eventually receive an incorruptible body. Not because of what I have done, but because of what Jesus has done.

I have had far too much fear of man in the past, including those in the church, and not enough fear of God. Even now, that can present a problem. I know there is much fear today in America, and it is man-made. The more we allow the Holy Spirit to work in us, the more we become God-fearing and less man-fearing. That is what Isaiah 11:2 is telling us, concerning the Holy Spirit gift of fear. The fear of man has a very dark side, which was evident during the days leading up to WWII. The dark element influenced the media, which controlled the narrative in some locations allowing them to manipulate the German people and others. It should be no surprise to anyone that history is repeating itself through the media's control of the narrative today, but it is on a larger, global platform. There is nothing new under the sun,[21] and the two sides of the coin are the same today as they were in the days of old. The fear of God is on one side and fear of man on the other. Eternity has not changed either. Fearing God prompts proper behavior, which allows believers to store up ever-lasting treasure in heaven. Fearing man does not help anyone's eternity and holds no rewards in heaven.

Many man-made religions attempt to gain your faith and sway your actions to join in their activities. My journey solidified my faith in the One True God. He is a creator who cares about the quality of our lives. So, He produced a spectacular instruction manual to help us know His nature and character and to help us become more like Him. Unlike the enemy of mankind, He doesn't want confusion in our lives; instead, He has given a written guide book. The God of the Bible is the One True God. He is the God of all gods, and the Bible is correct precisely as originally written.

Without the Bible, a person has no reliable guidance concerning who and what to believe. Everything else presents conflicting information, even within particular belief systems. There are systems to suit every person's fancy, from Baal, Hinduism, Molech, Freemasonry, New Age, etc. or atheism for those who do not want to believe in anything related to eternity. Confusion is precisely what the enemy wants, and he has something for everyone. As for me, I asked for the top God of gods to answer, and I have personally met Jesus and Satan as a result of that. I know that I know the God of the Bible is the only correct choice. He is the God of all gods and has provided accurate and valid instruction for people through the Bible. The Bible describes

---

21 Eccles.1:9

real situations that actually happened and presents good advice to implement in our daily lives.

Some of the Bible may seem harsh, but if my heart has stopped beating, I want the paramedics to provide the necessary shock therapy. *Not everyone who says to Me, 'Lord, Lord,' shall enter the kingdom of heaven, but he who does the will of My Father in heaven. Many will say to Me in that day, 'Lord, Lord, have we not prophesied in Your name, cast out demons in Your name, and done many wonders in Your name?' And then I will declare to them, 'I never knew you; depart from Me, you who practice lawlessness!* This Scripture from Matthew 7:21–23 has harsh words, but they carry with them a warning intended to keep us focused on Him rather than empty outer acts of religion. God's free gift of grace must not be taken for granted. The context of this Scripture has to do with those whose hearts are not right. God knows the difference between who is playing or pretending and who has their heart in it. King David, like all the rest of us, was far from being perfect, but his heart was right before God. The intent throughout this book is to get the reader to start thinking about their eternity and start asking the God of gods for direction and answers, especially since the Bible, and indeed life itself, is confusing. He will answer. Sometimes faster than you think and other times much slower than you want. While God seems to hardly ever be early, He is never late.

For me, it all starts with the Word of God, the Bible, and a desire to know the Truth, no matter the consequences. Most people, including church-goers, don't understand what is in the Bible. That makes them easy prey for the enemy. Going to church on Sunday is good, but that is just a start. To know the character and nature of the One True God can come only through reading the Bible while asking God for help and understanding.

It is your eternity, and your life is your one shot at getting it right. It is vital to understand there is no second chance. Satan would have us believe there is a second chance through reincarnation. We are not the authors of life, nor did we give ourselves the physical and mental capabilities we have. We use what we have received, so we are not the authors in what happens after death. There is no new or second chance after death; however, as long as you have life, it is not too late to get focused on choosing your eternity. In His last moments on earth, Jesus told the man dying on the cross next to Him, *"Assuredly, I say to you, today you will be with Me in Paradise."*[22] This man, at the end of his life, encountered Jesus and believed. He was shown mercy and grace and received the promise of eternity.

The difference between God and the demonic angels that rejected Him is that the One True God is telepathic and knows every thought we have ever had and the intent in our heart behind those thoughts. Jesus, God the Son, understood the intention in that thief's heart. That is why God and only God can adequately judge us after our days on earth are done. God wants us to seek His Truth with all our hearts.

Mankind is very accomplished at twisting things to fit our circumstances. I have spent a lifetime rationalizing things to fit my way of thinking. The devil is more than ready to help. I don't even have to ask. Satan and his hordes can hear and observe actions, yet they do not have direct access to our internal thoughts or our heart. They have been practicing their craft over all mankind for thousands of years. If we live to seventy years of age, that is merely seconds relative to angels that have been around from before the creation of the heavens and the earth. So, when praying, many times, I do it without speaking, using

---

22 Luke 23:43

internal nonverbal thoughts only. I'm seeking an answer from God and do not want to get blindsided by a counterfeit response the devil has twisted into something that looks like the real thing. Then, to be sure of what seems to be a Truthful answer from God, I ask Him with internal prayers only for confirmation. True answers bring True peace to me. True answers will weigh on the side of the Holy Spirit. There should be a gentle calmness to it that does not contradict the Bible.

Think about all the random things that had to go right, at the same time, for a simple flower to exist. There had to be the right genetics for the flower, and there had to be dirt to hold it into place and grow. The soil had to have the right nutrients to feed the plant, and there had to be rain with the right atoms to provide water that the flower needed. There had to be sunlight at the right wavelengths for the flower to grow, and the Earth had to be located at just the right distance from the sun, so the temperature was neither too hot nor cold. There had to be carbon dioxide for the plant to inhale and then exhale oxygen. Those are just a few of the things that had to go right for a flower to have life.

Astoundingly, snowflakes are also unique in their design; no two of them are exactly alike. Really? I came to realize there had to be something behind all I could see and know. There are too many inexplicable situations in our lives, as well. They prompt us to know there really is something supernatural out there. As much as we might not want to admit it, something with intelligence does exist. Some of us have spent a lifetime rationalizing creation and supernatural events away, but they don't ever really go away. No matter how hard we try, they remain unexplainable and keep coming back to our remembrance.

Once I started reading the Bible, I came across a verse that contained the exact point which had caused me to wonder if there was a supernatural creator behind all that I could see. In Romans 1:20 I found: *For since the creation of the world His invisible attributes are clearly seen, being understood by the things that are made, even His eternal power and Godhead, so that they are without excuse.* I could now look up in the night sky and see the vastness of a creation that seemingly went on forever, and know who was behind it. God's divine nature and His invisible attributes were now very real in national parks like Glacier and Yellowstone. All the breath-taking features that caused me to shake my head in awestruck wonder now had meaning. All of creation, as well as the events of my life, had been screaming at me. I finally decided to pay attention rather than ignore them. I knew that as unique and creative as man was amongst life on Earth, we could not ever make what I saw as I looked up at the nightly sky at the Northern Lights. We could not create something like the sun, Earth, and all the sustainable life that exists.

Highly educated people may claim they are creating something, like genetically modified organisms, GMOs, crops, or cloning, yet nothing is being created from scratch. They are using genetics or materials already existing. We are a bit too lax in our use of the word "created." In my early years, I was quick to boast about anything I did to reveal my greatness, but now I know whatever I have, in terms of abilities, came from God, I am just using them. The real question has always been whether I would use what I have for my glory or God's. It is a constant battle to answer that question well, even today. Thankfully, God's gift of Grace covers me when I fail by attempting to bring glory to myself.

The God I have come to know can reach a person with the Truth anywhere on Earth. You must have a "want to know" in your heart. He is not constrained by geography or by cultures. He is telepathic and knows how to reach you. If you have not asked, don't you think it is about time you asked Him to prove Himself to you in a way you know? What do you have to lose? For me, I do not believe in the One True God based solely on blind faith, I have met Him and know that I know because I asked, and He answered.

What I do believe by blind faith is God will do exactly as written in the Bible. He is unchanging and responds no differently with me than He did with people whose lives are depicted in the Bible, like Noah or Abraham. God spoke directly to them, and they knew the One True God was for real, but they had to "believe by faith" He would precisely do what He told them, even if it did not make sense at the moment.

I am not trying to compare myself to any of the great figures spoken of in the Bible; I'm just saying that, like some of them, I have met other beings like Jesus and Satan. Adam and Eve met and talked with both God and Satan. They are every bit as real to me as my wife, kids, and grandkids.

I frequently refer to the Bible as being the Christian Bible because some people refer to their religious book as their "bible," but they are referring to something not written by the One True God. I have never thought of them as being deceitful when they call their book the bible. Instead, I see it as a quick, easy way to mention what they are quoting and indicating it is the book they use to guide their lives. During a conversation, it is essential to know what Bible or reference book they are referring to, as it helps in knowing what points and questions to discuss. I usually say, at least once, my Judeo-Christian Bible says this, which seems to contradict your bible that says something else. Sometimes it is another person talking about Christianity, and we may be trying to agree about what our Bible is saying. At least we have a common starting point. In these cases, it may seem like the Bible at twenty paces, but it's more about asking questions and understanding why we each believe differently about the writings of the Bible. Once we get to that point, it's relatively easy to reach a conclusion. We may still disagree, but that is not our problem. It is God's, and what better hands to leave it in, than His? The God I know is more than capable of crumbling nonsense to dust and then blowing it away with the wind. God causes the items that are Truth to keep coming back to a person's memory. God has written for us His instruction manual, the Bible, and the time to dig in and ask the Holy Spirit to help is now before you have taken your last breath.

My life experiences, pressing into the Bible, and seeking direction through God and His Holy Spirit, have shown me I can completely trust the Bible. However, you have to make that determination for yourself. I do not completely understand everything, but like Noah and Abraham, I trust God by faith. He will do everything exactly as He has said. He wanted believers to know Him, so He had men record and write everything down for future generations. You are a future generation, and He wrote it for you, too. You can have a relevant guide book filled with instruction and wisdom to help in your everyday life. It's a guidebook that comes with a personal guide (Holy Spirit) to help you know how to apply its teachings. It's yours for the asking.

For Further Study

To invite you to understand what is in your eternity, The One True God is saying to you:

"Call to Me, and I will answer you, and show you great and mighty things, which you do not know."

—JEREMIAH 33:3

- Isaiah 65:17; 2 Peter 3:6–7 & 10–13; Revelation 21

- Genesis 3

- Revelation 20:11–15; Revelation 21:1, 2 Peter 3:6–7 & 10–13; Isaiah 65:17

- 1 Corinthians 1:19–29; 1 Corinthians 3:18–21

- Luke 23:39–43

- Deuteronomy 10:17; Psalm 136:3; 1 Timothy 6:15; Revelation 17:14

- Luke 16:15, Acts 15:8, Psalm 7:9, Proverbs 21:2, Proverbs 24:12

- Psalm 112:1 & 115:13, Proverbs 1:7 & 8:13, Matthew 10:28, Isaiah 11:2–3, Luke 1:50

- Revelation 21:1, Isaiah 65:17, 2 Peter 3:6–7 & 10–13

- Romans 14:10; 1 Corinthians 3:12–16; 1 Corinthians 5:9

- Revelation 20:11–15

CHAPTER SEVEN

CHRISTIAN CHURCH UNITY

O ne of the last things Jesus prayed for before He left the earth was unity in the Church. He foresaw the division Satan would cause early in the life of the church. An example is when Apostle Paul called out the brethren concerning circumcision of Gentile's, an issue causing division in the young Church. Another time, Apostle Paul criticized Apostle Peter for not eating with the Gentile believers in Antioch, even calling him a hypocrite in front of everyone.[23] In Philippians 1:15–17, Paul says some preach of Christ from selfish ambition, not sincerity. Unfortunately, that is still true today. The Church was not perfect back then, and it is no more perfect today. Anyone thinking the Church has ever been perfected is deceived. It can't be perfect since people are not yet perfected, and they run the church. Be careful, learn to think for yourself. Nurture what you know by studying the Bible, praying, and talking with God. Seek clarity and understanding from the Holy Spirit, and discuss all things with the brothers and sisters in Christ around you. Be patient and wait on the Lord, do not manufacture something just because it makes sense. Listen, consider, and allow correction when it comes your way.[24]

The Catholic and Eastern Orthodox churches were originally one church. The Eastern Orthodox branch split from the Catholics in the

---

23 Gal. 2:11–13
24 2 Tim. 3:15–17

East-West Schism in 1054. The relations between the East and the West sides of the original church deteriorated until a formal split occurred. The Eastern Church became the Greek Orthodox Church by severing ties with the Roman Catholic Church. The Catholic Church had a second significant split about five hundred years later during the Protestant Reformation.

The Augustinian monk Martin Luther started the Reformation with his publication of the Ninety-Five Theses. The Protestant Reformation has brought its many variants, as well. Not all the Lutheran churches agree with each other, much less with the Methodists, Baptists, etc. There is a lot of good common ground to be sure, and I'm not trying to pick on any specific Church. It is the works of the devil causing division, so we each must take responsibility for Our Eternity. We must get into the Bible while asking for God's help. Despite our differences, all the true Christian churches are united as one in the teachings of Jesus as God, and the perfect final sacrifice He made for all time for our sins.

Many false teachings prevalent in the early church are still causing division in the Christian church today. Satan relentlessly attempts to divide the church. Revelation 2 and 3 confront the six of seven churches that had strayed away from God's ways. This Scripture warned them that sin was at the door, and they would fall if they did not heed God's warnings. They could all have survived, but they did not heed God's advice, and all are gone now. Despite everyone's free access to the Holy Spirit, churches and believers are not immune from the wiles of Satan. Double mindedness is rampant, and we are all flawed in the flesh. Are we listening to the Holy Spirit or something else? How often do we listen to the Holy Spirit versus our sinful nature? How are we doing when looking at the deeds of the flesh; versus acts of the

Holy Spirit as listed in Galatians 5? We all need to be walking the talk as defined in the Bible we are reading. If there is a deviation from that, then corrective action is required. Scripture is clear that there must be a loving correction given to those who are not standing on proper Biblical Truth.

Much of the New Testament deals with false teachings in the days of Jesus and the Apostles. In Matthew 24, Jesus warns there will be false teachings until the end of time. *Then if anyone says to you, 'Look, here is the Christ!' or 'There!' do not believe it. For false christs and false prophets will rise and show great signs and wonders to deceive, if possible, even the elect. See, I have told you beforehand. "Therefore if they say to you, 'Look, He is in the desert!' do not go out; or 'Look, He is in the inner rooms!' do not believe it.*

All people who trust God's Bible will immediately know when Jesus comes back. Whether you're awake or asleep, God's telepathic Holy Spirit feature will imprint the same scene into all our heads at the same time, and all who are alive will know. God does not need a phone, computer, or TV.

In a vision, I saw the Second Coming supernatural event. Jesus showed me His coming to Earth to reign for one thousand years. The sky went unnaturally dark with eerie cloud formations seemingly threatening a tornado at any instant. Then I heard a trumpet blast sounding like a single unified blast of many trumpets all at once. I'll try to describe it the best I can in human words. The blast sounded like one of those enormous pipe organs, not a piano or regular organ sound, and every key sounded at the exact same time. Then I saw Jesus appear in the clouds. He had a very fearsome and imposing appearance like Apostle John describes Him in Revelation 1. Because of God's telepathic nature and ability to give every man alive the same vision inside our heads, at the same time, we will all hear the blast and see Jesus the instant He comes in the clouds. No one will mistake that is Him when He comes again. So, if someone tells you they believe their leader or minister is Jesus, do not believe it and help them to understand when Jesus does come, there will be no guessing if it is or is not Him. The vision also revealed how Jesus would look in His one-thousand-year reign from Jerusalem. In that scenario, He had a more normal appearance of a man. As part of this vision, I saw my parents and one of my sisters accompanying Him. We saw the tremendous devastation from the Seven Seal Judgments upon all mankind, and the destruction caused by the antichrist and false prophet. My sister said to me, "We have quite the mess to clean up," and I said, "Yes, we do." The Body of Christ is composed of true believers in the church. Those believers came with Him to work with Jesus and the remaining men of the flesh to cleanse the land. Not because Jesus needed us to do it, but because He desired we would all work together and do it.

I was taken to a building in Jerusalem, where I joined with others to do accounting work during Jesus' one-thousand-year reign. While being happy to spend those years in Jerusalem with Jesus and doing accounting work, I remember thinking it was an odd job for me based on my skillset in today's world. Jesus knows best, though, and I am delighted to be doing whatever He wants me to do. Then I was shown the very end of time when Satan was let loose. There was a massive war zone outside the city.[25] While I was doing my job in Jerusalem, some-one came to me and said Jesus wanted to see me. So, I went to Him, and He handed me a sealed letter. He told me to hand-deliver it to Lucifer. I asked Him how, as there were many layers of defense around

---

25 Rev. 20:7–9

Lucifer, and there was just me. Jesus said any time someone stopped me, tell them I had a letter from Jesus to hand to Lucifer. He reassured me they would then let me through without any harm or harassment. So, off I went. Each time I was stopped, I said what Jesus told me to say, and they let me through to the next level. There was no argument or struggle of any sort. It was as if they had been told I was coming and were instructed to let me through. Eventually, I got through to the building where Satan was located and said one last time that I had a letter from Jesus to hand to Lucifer. He was close by and said, "I am Lucifer." I was surprised at how pleasant and gentle he seemed to be as I handed him the letter. That was the end of the vision.

This vision has been an important part of my Christian growth. It has also been a clarifying gift to help me understand how Satan has created division in the Church concerning Jesus' coming. First, when some are pretending to be Jesus already here on the earth, it causes division. Second, it is also important to be clear about what Jesus means since teachings by men on this vary. The third reason for the division is some people try to make God appear weak by saying, "He cannot reveal Himself to everyone at the very instant He breaks through the clouds. "Blasphemy! Hogwash!" Anyone who can make the sun, moon, stars, and earth can easily let us all know, whether we are awake or asleep on the other side of the earth, the very instant He comes to Earth to reign from Jerusalem. God is not limited in capability, and Jesus is coming back the same way He left. He is not coming to California or somewhere else outside of Israel. Scripture says he left in the clouds from the Mount of Olives, and Scripture says he will return the same way.[26] Zechariah 14:4–5 gives further detail

---

26 Acts 1:11

about when Jesus' feet descend from the clouds. He will touch the place of His ascent on the top of the Mount of Olives, and it will split in two. Instantly, when He does that, it creates a valley so those trapped in Jerusalem will be able to flee through it.

I, for one, do not believe the Jehovah's Witness writings or *"Book of Mormon"* are valid Christian writings. Both are examples of how the devil has successfully caused even greater division. God did not fall asleep for about 1800 years after the death of Jesus to then suddenly wake up in the 1800s and realize He had to write two new books because the Bible was not correct. In case someone missed it, both books contradict each other and the Bible. When you consider that, it would mean the infinite God has managed to write three books that do not agree with each other. The Bible warns us to beware of the wolves that come in sheep's clothing. Some may "look" Christian on the surface even better than most Christians. They can't look like wolves because we would all recognize them for who they are, and the devil would get no foothold. So, they have to look like Christians. We all need to be watchful for imposters, and the Jehovah's Witnesses book and *"Book of Mormon"* are two easy examples. Unfortunately, there are many different writings today claiming to be Christian, but they are not. Too many churches have leaders who claim to be Jesus Christ. A few recent ones that you might have heard of are Jim Jones, David Koresh, and Sun Myung Moon. We all need to be careful not to let our guard down, because they may look like the real thing, but are not. Pray and weigh all things in the balance of all Scripture. Try the New King James (NKJV), New International Version (NIV), The Living Bible or The Message versions of the Bible, or the approved Catholic Versions. Paraphrased versions are easier to read than direct translations from the Greek and Hebrew. But when it comes to Biblical prophecy, it is best to stick with a direct translation such as the King James Version. Use the internet to help you decide, as there are free online Bible sites with multiple languages such as www.biblegateway.com.

While I believe the original Bible is perfect as written, translations are frequently imperfect. Most do an excellent job, are consistent, and are worth reading, but the Holy Spirit is the key to helping us. Most of us do not speak Greek or Hebrew. My recommendation is to read a translation that makes sense to you. When you are doing an in-depth study, try other versions to get a broader picture of what Scripture is saying. As for me, I have pretty much settled on the New King James Version, but will look at many others from time to time. The paraphrased versions are easier to read, but a direct translation, like the King James Version or New King James Version, can make a difference when in need of precise details. Some of the latest Biblical updates are starting to fail under the pressure of political correctness. I would stay away from releases later than 2010. I say this because some adapt their Biblical prophecy to match their specific viewpoint, and others reflect today's political correctness. In the end, put all things in the hands of the One True God and remember what He said in Matthew 10:28: *Do not fear those who kill the body but cannot kill the soul. But rather fear Him who is able to destroy both soul and body.*

If you fear God more than man, you will be in good shape. It is best not to fear man at all. Today the list of Christian haters is growing. Are you willing to stand up for and possibly die for your beliefs? Are you ready to be martyred as a sheep led to slaughter?

Jesus says in John 14:6 He alone is the way, the truth, and the life. No one comes to the Father except through Him. If anyone is researching different religions, that single statement ought to catch their attention. If I were at the smorgasbord table contemplating the different religious options, the statement that He alone is the only way to the top would get my attention. Other religions may be more personally appealing, but why bet on one that may not work? When I was in my late twenties, I had been around that smorgasbord table more than a few times. Christianity was not even on the table. When I finally asked for God to show me which it was, the Holy Spirit showed up and led me to Jesus, who was the "only" way. That was not my preferred choice, so it took me some time to come to grips with that. Jesus was kind to me and gave me all the time I needed. Since asking Jesus to accept me on His team, being baptized by water and the Holy Spirit, I know now to try my best to take everything I hear to Jesus and His Word, The Bible. That does mean I have to read the Bible and ask God to send His Holy Spirit to help me understand Him and His ways. Going to church enhances our faith; however, it does not replace anyone's responsibility for studying, hearing, consuming Scripture, praying, talking, and cultivating your relationship directly with God. It is your relationship, your responsibility, your eternity. Nobody can blame anyone else at their judgment day. We all have to be actively vigilant. There is danger in "blindly" following others' teachings rather than doing our homework in seeking Truth through Scripture with the Holy Spirit's help. There have been many cults and false christs over the years that are wolves in sheep's clothing, causing discord in the Church. Be careful; some have watered down and or twisted God's Word so much their truth no longer matches God's Truth. It is your eternity, not anyone else's. Do your homework with the Holy Spirit's help, and do not blindly accept everything you hear. Find a church home that matches what Jesus is showing you in His Scripture.

I do not blindly trust my eternity to any other human being no matter how eloquent they may be in presenting their point, and neither should you. Like the Bereans, we should all pray for understanding through the Holy Spirit, dig into the Scripture to see what is Truth, and discuss with other trusted believers how they handle God's Word. But no man knows everything. The church consists of different parts of the body with a diversity of gifts and skills. Where one is weak, others are strong. Listening to each other is often the challenge. When Jesus imparts something into our understanding, it is worthy of sharing with others. Believers may not be on the same level of spiritual growth, but we can discuss and share without division if we hold to grace and have a heart for unity. Operating in the areas of personal giftedness and allowing others to do the same, we may all glean more than we would have done individually. Misunderstanding and misquoting are often the result of diverse interpretations. All believers make mistakes, but God does not. The key is that while I do not blindly trust my eternity to any man, I do entrust it to Jesus, who is the Word of God,[27] and sent the Holy Spirit to help all of us. There is no short cut. The Bible is not just another book; it requires time and attention, diligence, and Holy Spirit direction. The more we read it, the more deeply we understand it, thus allowing us to apply it in our lives.

God describes the value of Scripture. According to His word found in 2 Timothy 3:16–17. *All Scripture is given by inspiration of God, and is profitable for doctrine, for reproof, for correction, for instruction in righteousness, that the man of God may be complete, thoroughly equipped for every good work.* The New Testament recorded cases when Apostles and leaders filled with the Holy Spirit required correction, and they received it. My understanding is limited and flawed like all men, but

---

27 John 1:14

I hope my approach is closer to the Bereans who diligently examined the Old Testament daily. I recommend their approach to everyone. I have put the burden on Jesus to teach me through His Holy Spirit and correct me in whatever form He chooses. He prevents me from turning parts of His Word into nonsense and from having to pay the price for that on my judgment day.[28] I hope God will allow you to see into my heart through the words written in this book. If He has provided me with only one gift, then I want to utilize one-hundred percent of that one gift and not attempt to overstep my boundaries into someone else's giftedness. Only by following the guidance of Jesus through His Holy Spirit can I get one-hundred percent out of what He gave me. It is all about allowing Him to work through me, lest I have reason to boast.

It is imperative to note bad character and actions keep us from delivering on the gifts God has put into us at conception. The enemy knows our unique, God-given abilities and attempts to have us go down paths meant for others. If that direction is for someone else, we need to get out of the way and go where we are supposed to be going. Oddly, our greatest strengths can be our main weaknesses if we do not use our gifts correctly. I'm not trying to limit what God can do in me or anyone else. We must be good stewards over the few things we have been given, and He is faithful to provide us with more.[29]

I pray I will continue to allow Him to mold me with more understanding in the future. We must always be mindful we did not make ourselves, He did. He knew us before He formed us in the womb.[30] We did not give ourselves any ability; we had no input into our exis-

---

28 Matt. 5:18–19; Rev. 22:18–19
29 Matt. 25:21–23
30 Jer. 1:5

tence or abilities. We use what God gave us at our birth. What I do know is whatever we have is to be used to bring glory to God, not us. God works through His church to accomplish His master plan for the future. Unity comes to the church as we work together as one, following His guidance and letting Him work through each of us in our unique way.

For Further Study

To invite you to understand what is in your eternity, The One True God is saying to you:

> *"Call to Me, and I will answer you, and show you great and mighty things, which you do not know."*
>
> —JEREMIAH 33:3

- John 17:20–23

- Acts 15

- Matthew 7:15; Romans 16:17–20; 1 Timothy 6:3–5

- Ephesians 2:8–9

CHAPTER EIGHT

AUTHORSHIP OF THE BIBLE

Who wrote the Old Testament, the Tanakh, and the New Testament? The typical answer is men inspired by God. The only way to understand what God is telling us in the Bible is to use Scripture to interpret Scripture. This method takes away man's ability to deviate from the meaning of Scripture by using their own interpretation instead. When it comes to interpreting prophecy, Scripture is the preferred method. God tells us in 2 Peter 1:19–20, *knowing this first, that no prophecy of Scripture is of any private interpretation.* While nobody can lose their gift of Grace and eternal life with God, He warns us in several scriptural locations to be careful about what we say and teach because there is a price to pay for changing what God has spoken throughout His Word.

The Tanakh, also known as the Hebrew Bible, has the same content as the Christian Bible's Old Testament. However, it is formatted somewhat differently and has a slightly different number of books. As an example, the Poetic book combined Psalms, Proverbs, and Job, whereas the Bible has them in separate books. However, now modern versions of the Tanakh break them out and list thirty-nine different books, just like the protestant Bible's Old Testament. The Catholic Bible's version contains seven other books that are not in the Tanakh or the protestant Bible. Any descendants of Jacob considering Christianity must understand the protestant Old Testament Bible is the same as the Tanakh. If you unknowingly purchased a Catholic version, you will recognize the additional books, like First and Second Maccabees, so do not let that get in the way. Seek Truth and the Holy Spirit will get you where you need to be, regardless of which Bible you have in your hands. Yeshua, Jesus in English, regularly quoted the Tanakh and said He came in the flesh to fulfill what was written in the Tanakh.[31]

John 1 is an excellent place to begin the investigation into who wrote all of the Scriptures. In these troubled times, this chapter is incredibly important to understand. So, who wrote mankind's instruction manual, The Judeo-Christian Bible, from Genesis through Revelation?

In the beginning was the Word, and the Word was with God, and the Word was God. He was in the beginning with God. All things were made through Him, and without Him nothing was made that was made. John 1:1–3

And the Word became flesh and dwelt among us, and we beheld His glory, the glory as of the only begotten of the Father, full of grace and truth. John 1:14

And now, O Father, glorify Me together with Yourself, with the glory which I had with You before the world was. John 17:5

These five beautifully written verses describe Jesus as the "Word," existing before the creation of the world. Jesus, or Yeshua in Hebrew, created all things as we know it, and was God from the very beginning. Because Jesus as the Word, created everything, and then took on flesh, He is the author of the entire Bible.

To me, John 1 is the most significant one in the New Testament. The gospel of John was the last of the four written Gospel accounts,

---

31 Isa. 54, Matt. 5:17–20

and Apostle John wrote this chapter as an intense fight against heresy. That is why he started his gospel by explaining who Jesus really was. John does not begin with a lovely story of a baby in a manger. He does not mention the birth or anything else up to the baptism. Apostle John comes straight out, saying Jesus is God and was God before the creation of the earth. He added Jesus created you and me and everything we can see and touch. The heresy John was combating was that Jesus wasn't really God until His baptism, or He was not God until He was raised from the dead, or He was just a prophet, or because of how He lived His life he earned the right to become a "god," or you can fill in the blank with other reasons. With his very first words, John makes it clear Jesus is God; Jesus was God before creation, and Jesus created all things because denying the deity of Christ was a big deal back in Apostle John's day. From the tone of his words, we can see why he was named one of the "Sons of Thunder" by Jesus.[32] He came out swinging by emphatically saying Jesus was, in fact, God, since before creation. John also quotes Jesus proclaiming the same thing in John 17:5 ... the *glory which I had before the world was.* Many religions say Jesus was a "god" or just a prophet and deny the deity of Christ as God. However, both Apostle Paul and John wrote that Jesus was God before the creation and was, in fact, responsible for making the heavens and the earth.

It seems to me John started his gospel with a punch straight to the chops. Perhaps that's due to my ice hockey background, but it sure seems to be an "in your face" type of start, with no gray area. This is very black and white. What else can anyone say about the statements "Jesus was God before the creation of the heavens and the earth,"

---

32 Mark 3:17

"created the heavens and the earth," and then "took on flesh." Either you say "okay" and keep reading, or you walk away. Many perceive John as the sweetest Apostle ever. He was an example of Christ's love, but that doesn't mean he was a push-over when heresy had to be confronted. Jesus called him one of the "Sons of Thunder" for a reason. John calls people who deny the deity of Christ, a liar, and an antichrist; in fact, he used that term more times than any other writer in the New Testament. Too many people were saying Jesus was not the One True God, so the Apostle John was not going to pull any punches concerning Jesus.

Since mankind is created with a soul, body, spirit, and is created in God's image, then God has to have a Soul, Body, and Spirit. The Bible tells us God the Father is the Soul of God; God, the Son Jesus, is the Body of God; God, the Holy Spirit, is the Spirit of God. It is easier to grasp that man has three parts in one single package than it is to fully comprehend how God consists of those same three parts in one single package. We can see the concept, but how God comes together as all in one is a challenge.

Jesus, though, shows us this very thing in many Scriptures. Psalm 110:1 records David's words, "the Lord said to my Lord." That is quoted four times in the New Testament. There cannot be two Lords, as there is only One True God. Genesis 19:24 states *The Lord below called out to the Lord in the heavens to rain brimstone and fire upon Sodom and Gomorrah.* Before taking on flesh, the Lord Jesus called out to the Lord above, God the Father. These Scriptures illustrate how His triune identities are in fellowship with each other.

In the New Testament, Jesus is quoting Himself every time He says, "it is written," and that particular phrase exists sixty-one times in the New King James Version. While some of the Apostles, inspired by the Holy Spirit, penned "it is written" many times, Jesus is directly quoted as saying, "it is written" about thirty of those sixty-one times. The most famous of those was when Satan was tempting Jesus during the forty days in the wilderness. Jesus responded to Satan with "it is written" each time, quoting what He had already recorded in the Old Testament. Some New Testament readers tend to downplay the Old Testament, so it is essential to note the only "written" Scripture, at that time, came straight from the Old Testament. The Pharisees and Sadducees held Jesus accountable to the writings in their Tanakh. New Testament Scripture never contradicts the Old Testament. Since Jesus wrote both Old and New Testaments, Christians aren't just "New Testament" believers. How can anyone properly handle Part Two of the Bible Jesus wrote if you do not know and properly handle His Part One? This has often been a stumbling block for many Christians who think the Old Testament doesn't require much of their attention. They are missing a treasure trove of useful information and prophecies about the end times yet to be fulfilled.

In Luke 10, we are told Jesus himself ...*saw Satan fall like lightning from heaven.* Satan and one-third of the angels fell into sin before the creation of the Earth and the life on it. So how did Jesus do that unless He was there when it happened? Satan was in the Garden of Eden at the beginning of creation and led Adam and Eve into sin against God's divine laws. God has a much bigger plan in dealing with sin against His divine nature than we know since we see only in part. As a result of Satan's fall, he and his demonic angels have been tormenting man ever since, beginning with Adam and Eve. Revelation 12:3–9 gives a detailed illustration of Satan, *And another sign appeared in heaven: behold, a great, fiery red dragon having seven heads and ten horns, and seven diadems on his heads. His tail drew a third of the stars of heaven and threw them to the earth. And the dragon stood before the woman who was ready to give birth, to devour her Child as soon as it was born. She bore a male Child who was to rule all nations with a rod of iron. And her Child was caught up to God and His throne. Then the woman fled into the wilderness, where she has a place prepared by God, that they should feed her there one thousand two hundred and sixty days. And war broke out in heaven: Michael and his angels fought with the dragon; and the dragon and his angels fought, but they did not prevail, nor was a place found for them in heaven any longer. So the great dragon was cast out, that serpent of old, called the Devil and Satan, who deceives the whole world; he was cast to the earth, and his angels were cast out with him.*

Apostle Paul's writings in Ephesians 3:9 and Colossians 1:15–18 further strengthen the understanding that Jesus is God and created all that we know.

And to make all see what is the fellowship of the mystery, which from the beginning of the ages has been hidden in God who created all things through Jesus Christ;

and

He is the image of the invisible God, the firstborn over all creation. For by Him all things were created that are in heaven and that are on earth, visible and invisible, whether thrones or dominions or principalities or powers. All things were created through Him and for Him. And He is before all things, and in Him all things consist. And He is the head of the body, the church, who is the beginning, the firstborn from the dead, that in all things He may have the preeminence.

Before the foundation of the world, God predestined He would send Jesus in the flesh so we could be adopted as sons by Jesus himself. There are many places throughout the Bible, showing God wrote history before it happened. All of God's created beings other than man, including Lucifer, witnessed this particular event.[33]

Just as He chose us in Him before the foundation of the world, that we should be holy and without blame before Him in love, having predestined us to adoption as sons by Jesus Christ to Himself, according to the good pleasure of His will, to the praise of the glory of His grace, by which He made us accepted in the Beloved. In Him we have redemption through His blood, the forgiveness of sins, according to the riches of His grace. This is from Ephesians 1, you will find much to consider in that chapter, and I encourage you to read all of it. Verses here say God planned all this out "before" the creation, and He knew that man, when given a choice, would eventually choose evil just as Lucifer and a third of the angels had already done.

The term "adoption" used by Jesus identifies all whether we are an Israelite through Abraham-Isaac-Jacob or a Gentile. All men can be adopted into His team through Jesus' blood sacrifice. Jesus paid the price to redeem man and all of God's creation from sin introduced through Adam and Eve. This free gift is for all of us, yet, sadly, not all will accept it.

Many in the church misunderstand the Biblical usage of predestination. Predestination and prophecy are the same things. They are history written and recorded in advance. Jesus was predestined to be born to a virgin and become the blood sacrifice that would restore man to the Father. It was predestined that, like Jonah, Jesus would spend three days and three nights in the heart of the earth, and then be resurrected from the dead. All God has done to date or is still to do was predetermined before He created anything.

It is all history written before it happened. The misunderstand-

---

33 Rev. 4:6–8

ing about predestination comes from misguided teaching. It doesn't mean a specific person was predestined to be saved before they were even born. God did not create man as robots without choice and free will. God did predestine a system through which any person could be "adopted" by Jesus by freely choosing to accept this plan, God put into place before the creation of the world. The key is choice. It is written that few select the narrow gate that leads to eternal life, but many will reject it and choose the easy wide gate that leads to eternal damnation.[34] God has made provision for those who die in infancy or as a child. They die in total innocence since they never reached the age to understand the consequences of sin properly. Once a person reaches the age of accountability, they have free will to choose Jesus every day. Everyone's eternity reflects the choice each makes.

There is a common misconception that Jesus became fully God when the Holy Spirit descended upon Him at His baptism. Others thought He became fully God at His resurrection. What does God say in Scripture? Here are a couple of guiding principles that mean a great deal to me.

1. God has provided us with an understandable instruction manual—the Bible. The Holy Spirit leads and guides us through it into our understanding of God. We all have many ways to rationalize or twist things, so unless we submit to Holy Spirit's guidance, Satan can lead us astray. As we press in to study Scripture, our understanding will increase.

2. When reading it, if Scripture makes sense, then do not look for any other "sense," lest it gets turned into non-sense. If

---

34 Matt. 7:15–14; Luke 13:22–24

someone is saying it cannot be read as written, especially when it makes perfect sense, a red flag should go up quickly. I know people who stopped reading the Bible because a teacher they respected told them that what made perfect sense to them was not really true, indicating it meant something else. So, they quit trusting themselves. Let me encourage everyone in that situation to investigate what is said. If you do not have peace with it, there is a reason. Ask God to show you the Truth, search your Bible for context, and use other teaching sources as well. While I am not a big fan of commentaries, some are good when they stick to the gifting God gave them.

Should you investigate what I say? Absolutely! Dig in. That is what I want readers to do more than anything else. It is your eternity, not mine. Nobody has perfect understanding, but there should be easy to understand concrete evidence freely provided by the Holy Spirit. At times we must be patient and wait for the answer. In the end, the correct answer must always bring peace to your inner being. No peace, then keep searching.

Let me use one of my many misdeeds to illustrate. When I was about nine years old, I lacked the maturity level to understand the consequences of my sin. Back in the mid-1960s, where I grew up, young kids walked to and from school. Parents left keys in the car and house doors unlocked. Most people knew how to be nice. It was a safe time and place to be alive. One day my sisters and I were playing with the neighbor kids when we decided we would have a big squirt gun battle. Since all of us did not have functioning squirt guns, eight of us headed into town on a twelve-minute walk to buy what we needed. The cheapest squirt gun cost twenty-five cents; the exact amount

I had. Tax, however, added another penny, so the cashier explained I did not have enough money. Back then, you could buy gumballs for a penny, so a penny meant something. None of my friends would give me a penny so that I could buy the toy. Sadly, I walked back to the aisle to return it. However, in an instant, that little squirt gun made it into my pocket and out the door. If that was not bad enough, when we started the squirt gun battle, I was asked how I bought it and said I found a penny. So, I had managed to both steal and lie at almost the same time.

The point of this story is I no longer could have been the perfect savior. I could never present myself as the One Without Blemish. Was it before my age of accountability? Yes, but regardless, now I was blemished and could not be the perfect Lamb Sacrifice. Like Esau giving up his God-appointed birthright to Jacob and not being able to get it back, I could no longer save myself, much less anyone else. None of us can. Only someone that was God in the flesh at birth could do that. If Jesus were not God at birth, then He would have stumbled multiple times along the way as I did, and as all men do who are one-hundred percent human.

Some will use Scripture to point out that it seems to indicate Jesus was not fully mature or complete until the Holy Spirit descended upon Him like a dove. So, in their minds, Jesus was not fully God until then. However, I believe they are overlooking the fact Jesus was entirely God from the beginning, and that is what kept Him clean from the temptations of sin. That allowed Him to be the perfect unblemished sacrifice for all sin.

However, Jesus did have a human element, and His body of flesh had some growing to do. Most of us know the teenage years present challenges, and Jesus had to successfully experience all the things of the flesh, without sin. In simple terms, He was wholly God at birth but was not born as a fully mature adult in the flesh. He had to grow up and experience those years before He could begin His ministry and become the perfect sacrifice. Nobody, no matter how good they are, could have lived to thirty years of age without sinning somewhere along the way. Only the One who was God from the very beginning could do that. I have shared one of my real sin accounts, the squirt gun episode, to show it takes only one incident to become stained and need Jesus, the Savior, to reconcile us to God the Father. Matthew 22:41–46 explains Jesus was both a man of flesh through King David's lineage and also God. I like the question Jesus asks the Pharisees when he uses what was written in Psalm 110 to ask them how King David can call his descendant Lord.

*While the Pharisees were gathered together, Jesus asked them, saying, "What do you think about the Christ? Whose Son is He?" They said to Him, "The Son of David. " He said to them, "How then does David in the Spirit call Him 'Lord,' saying: 'The Lord said to my Lord, "Sit at My right hand, till I make Your enemies Your footstool"?" *[45]* "If David then calls Him 'Lord,' how is He his Son?" And no one was able to answer Him a word, nor from that day on did anyone dare question Him anymore.*

Jesus is saying to the Pharisees that if the Messiah were not God from birth, then He would have had David's DNA through His earthly father. But he quoted David's own words to the contrary, and the Pharisees had no response because it was apparent the only way to fulfill that Scripture was if the Messiah was both of God and flesh. Jesus was claiming to be exactly that. The Pharisees already knew David's genes had passed down through Jesus' mother, Mary. They also knew Jesus was perhaps the only male alive from Bethlehem's recorded birth census. Others had not survived Herod's slaughter of males two and under. The Pharisees were in quite a predicament and did not dare ask Him any more questions.

Satan told his first lie to humans in the Garden of Eden. He started the myth that man could become gods. Adam and Eve ate the forbidden fruit because Satan told them it was the way to become gods themselves. Another religion teaches this misconception today. Mormons teach Jesus was completely human and then earned his way up the ladder to become a god. They use that teaching to show they can make their "own" way to becoming a god as Jesus had done. It did not work for Adam and Eve; they did not become a god in any way. Neither will the lie work for anyone practicing Mormonism or other religious practices that deny the Deity of Jesus Christ from birth. Jesus was perfect from the very beginning, and that allowed Him to be the perfect, sinless sacrifice. He never told a lie, stole anything, cheated anyone, or anything else from birth to death. Why follow Him if He was not perfect from beginning to end? Biblical Scripture would have shown Him to be a fraud because the Messiah had to be without blemish. The One True God is, and always has been, perfect in every way and makes no mistakes.

While in college working on a second degree, I made friends with an Israeli who was on the same engineering degree path as I. He was a Christian, but his parents were both descendants of Jacob and were not. I asked him how he came to embrace Christianity. He explained it was because he could not resolve Psalm 110:1 any other way. That is a classic example of critical thinking for yourself. He knew he was the only one responsible for his deeds come judgment day, and took his eternity seriously. Despite his upbringing, he weighed his choices carefully and chose Jesus. That was what started his walk with the Messiah. Jesus repeats this part of Psalm 110 several times in Scripture, revealing this a very significant point for mankind. Why was it repeated? I believe it was so that every man would see Jesus was God from the very beginning, and also a man of flesh, as a genetic descendant of King David.

Many may be surprised at the amount of thought-provoking usefulness in the Old Testament writings. Of course, Satan wants us to believe those writings are ancient, outdated, and not worthy of reading, but they are very relevant today. My intent here is to show how relevant it is. To be clear, the Old Testament Covenant is the first of God's two-part instruction manual. The New Testament or New Covenant is the fulfillment of things written in the Old Testament.[35] By the way, not everything in the Old Testament has been fulfilled. There is much more prophecy yet to be finished. Jesus said He came to fulfill, not replace or change what had already been written. It is vital to note the New Testament does not change anything in the Old Testament. What it shows is the fulfillment of many previous prophesies, further defines the divine nature of God, and provides more detail about the future fulfillment of His prophetic words.

It is important to note Jesus never changed things like the Ten Commandments, festivals, or feasts. Some people in the Church imply the Old Testament is irrelevant, and only the New Testament matters. I believe that is changing Scripture because Jesus did not advocate writing new or different things. God is the same yesterday, today, and forever.[36] Jesus did not throw the Ten Commandments out the door. In Matthew 5:17–19, Jesus spoke strongly against anyone changing the Old Testament writings. Just because you are a New Testament Christian, have lying, cheating, stealing, and adultery all of a sudden

---

35 Matt. 5:17
36 Heb. 13:8–9

become acceptable? Jesus always quoted the Old Testament. He didn't change it or treat it as worthless trash, why would we?

Along the way, as we continue pressing in, our depth and breadth of understanding and trust will increase. We should understand better after thirty years of pressing in than when we were in year three or fifteen. Nobody is perfect this side of heaven, including the Apostles. No one person has a complete understanding of God's instruction manual. It is the role of the Holy Spirit to guide us, to illuminate and confirm, to communicate directly to us as we seek, read, and study God's Word with a pure heart. It bears repeating that it is a growth process over time, and we will never wholly comprehend the infinite God this side of heaven. The purpose of the Holy Spirit is to instruct and guide us along our journey of reading and studying Scripture. It is a lifelong process of learning which does not happen overnight.

You mustn't stop reading. Press on as there is something here for everyone. Similar to the uniqueness of a snowflake, each person is also different from all others. I remember going to a comedy show in the 1980s and was surprised at how the featured comedian "worked" the crowd. One part of the crowd laughed at specific types of jokes, while another group would laugh at others. We are indeed different from each other in many ways. God understands those differences because He created us that way. He has provided a perfect guide for every stage of life. If we let the Holy Spirit guide us as we study and share our understanding with others, it will always bring peace since the author is the Prince of Peace.

For Further Study

To invite you to understand what is in your eternity, The One True God is saying to you:

> *"Call to Me, and I will answer you, and show you*
> *great and mighty things, which you do not know."*
>
> —JEREMIAH 33:3

- 1 John 2:18; 1 John 2:22; 1 John 4:3; 2 John 1:7

- Matthew 22:44, Mark 12:36, Luke 20:42, Acts 2:34

- Matthew 12:40; Mark 8:31; John 2:18–22

- Revelation 22:18–10, Matthew 5:18–19, James 3:1, Proverbs 30:5–6, Deuteronomy 4:2, 12:32.

- Ephesians 1

- Isaiah 14:12–17; Luke 10:18; Revelation12:3–4 & 7– 9

- Romans 3:10 & 23; Isaiah 64:6; Ecclesiastes 7:20; Proverbs 28:13

- Matthew 22:44, Mark 12:36, Luke 20:42, Acts 2:34

- Matthew 5:27–28

- John 14:26, John 16:13–14, 1 Corinthians 2:12–14

CHAPTER NINE

STUDYING THE OLD TESTAMENT

I believe God has shown me how to illustrate Old Testament Scripture through current day examples. I hope these will promote an understanding of the validity and literalness of the entire Bible. I ask you to consider these examples with an open mind.

The Bible is to be taken literally unless Scripture identifies a passage as a parable or allegory. These parables and illustrative examples in Scripture say things such as "the kingdom of heaven is like." The usage of the word "like" indicates this is an example, not an exact literal account, but it is still the truth, with no exaggeration. It is every bit as true as the account of Jesus saying, "Stand up and walk" in John 5:8. A parable is a teaching tool God uses as He takes truth found in nature to reveal His character and shed light on man's ways.

A well-known parable, The Parable of the Sower, is found in Mark 4. In the agrarian culture of Jesus' day, this illustration of a man sowing seed to produce a crop was readily received and understood. Seeds mentioned in this parable represent God's Word. Some fall on rocks and some onto fertile ground. This illustrates that those who have an ear to hear, and a clean heart will better understand the kingdom of God. He always interprets the meaning; we just have to be paying attention. In this case, we are told the seed is the Word of God, and Satan comes to steal the Word from man's hearts. If the seed falls on stony ground, meaning a hard heart, it will not grow and bear fruit among men. Seeds falling on the fertile ground produce much fruit among men. It is not complicated. Everyone can take the seed literally as being God's Word because God said it was in that chapter, and then Jesus applied what happens to His Word to men with various types of hearts. Everything in the Bible is Truth from God; sometimes, we are just limited in our ability to understand it. When someone says they read the Bible literally, do not be quick to mock them. Maybe you are the one that does not understand what God is actually saying. We all understand only partially, and if your heart is right and you search for understanding, you will be rewarded with more.

Are the teachings related to life today? In the Old Testament, there is a teaching that it is unwise for a woman to go out alone into a field that is not her family's possession. Women going out in pairs today may seem like an old fashion approach, but there is safety in numbers. We should be careful about minimizing the Old Testament and the wisdom that comes with it. Many of today's news stories reflect situations that may have been avoided if Old Testament wisdom had been followed. Suffice it to say it is not an easy task to write a book like the Bible that is useful for all generations. Yet God has done it. Asking Him for clarity and a more in-depth understanding of what He wrote, rather than dismissing or rewording it based on our "superior intellect," brings greater wisdom than we have without His Word.

Upon occasion, I have had some people make fun of my essentially literal Biblical interpretation and say things like, "So, your wife wears skirts and dresses everywhere?"[37] My response is, "She dresses like most any other woman and wears woman's jeans, not men's clothes,

---

[37] Deut. 22:5

nor do I wear woman's clothes." The Scripture at issue is saying men should not look like women, and women should not look like men. God is telling us what to do in any era, and if we pay attention, then everything will be better for us. To me, the Old Testament is full of common sense words of advice but often gets a bad reputation for that.

Some people say they are New Testament Christians, not Old Testament Christians. My question to them is, "Do you believe it is okay to have other gods before God, to lie, kill, cheat, steal, or sleep with your neighbor's wife?" Those are all Old Testament teachings.

Be careful with God's Word; it is neither mine nor yours to change as we wish. The Divine law is His, and it is not changeable. If we follow God's instruction manual, then all will go well with us. The way we live our lives reflects on our eternity as seen in 1 Corinthians 3, *Each one's work will become clear; for the Day will declare it, because it will be revealed by fire; and the fire will test each one's work, of what sort it is. If anyone's work which he has built on it* endures, he will receive a reward. *If anyone's work is burned, he will suffer loss; but he himself will be saved, yet so as through fire.*

God knows that we all have problems, and we will all have quite the bonfire at our appointed time, but it would be nice if we all had at least one thing that survived the refining fire. While having something survive would be nice, that is not a requirement since God's Grace is a free gift. However, having something of value stored up in heaven that survives the fire would be a blessing. What God is saying is simple for me. He is saying there are results and consequences from the good and bad things we do. God says He is keeping track, and there will be rewards.

Yes, today, we are thankful for His Grace, which resolves the sin nature that exists in our flesh. However, concerning things such as adultery, there is a consequence in all eras. Today nobody in proper alignment with the Bible is going to stone someone to death for committing it. Yet, God is saying there will still be a consequence no matter when someone lived in this world. In Matthew 5:27–28, Jesus upped the ante by explaining that if you so much as think of it, you have done it. Abide by all of His Word, with the help of the Holy Spirit, and all will go well for you come judgment day.

There is a tremendous amount of Old Testament prophecy about the future that has yet to be fulfilled and is very relevant today. Consider and reflect on Zechariah 12–14, some of the beginning points to get you started are below.

- 12:9—God/Jesus will destroy "all" the nations that come against Jerusalem. As in not just "all" the armies, but "all" the nations.

- 12:7—God/Jesus will save the tents of the Tribe of Judah first, lest any of the other twelve Tribes of Israel try to claim they are more significant than Judah.

- 12:10—All of Israel will look upon Jesus, whom they have pierced.

- 12:12–14—All the land of Israel shall mourn every family by themselves.

These points barely scratch the surface of Zechariah 12–14. I will be covering some of my supernatural experiences in other sections. As I tell of those experiences, I cover many of these OT scriptures. As you read about them, keep in mind that they must stand up to all Scripture, or they are from the devil. Read my accounts as you would read anyone's, discerning the spirit as we are instructed by Scripture to do. It really is Your Eternity, so do not blindly accept someone else's interpretation. Do what the Bereans were commended for, pray, and then dig in.[38]

Real day experiences that I have had provide additional first-hand support of some of the Old Testament writings and may surprise you. Back in my unsaved days while on college summer break, I met a woman who said that she had been intimate with an angel. I did not know what to do with that other than to ask a lot of questions. She described a situation that was indeed real and very vivid to her. I forgot all about this until about seven years later, after I had my first supernatural experience, which prompted me to read the Bible for the first time, front to back. As I read Genesis 6, I found there were indeed giants created by angels who were intimate with human women. What she had told me seven years earlier instantly became more real than I could have ever imagined. Based on firsthand information from a woman who said she was intimate with an angel, I believe intimacy with angels is still going on today. The enemy may have improved his techniques over the centuries and is doing a better job of blending his offspring into today's society. The internet holds reports of current-day women reporting that they are intimate with angels, plus many pictures and news of giant human remains can be seen there. A simple internet search conducted on "largest skeletons" will produce stunning images showing large giants found in archaeological digs. Some of them make the Bible's Goliath look small. Who knows what else has been genetically modified by demonic angelic meddling? Wicked fallen angels are as busy as ever and, unfortunately, are very easy to contact for information. Obtaining evidence is as simple as calling

---

38 Acts 17:10–11

a psychic hotline or visiting a psychic or medium near you. But be careful where you turn for help. Do not jeopardize Your Eternity with a quick fix, ask the One True God, and then follow through. Your eternity is in the balance.

For Further Study

To invite you to understand what is in your eternity, The One True God is saying to you:

> *"Call to Me, and I will answer you, and show you great and mighty things, which you do not know."*
>
> —JEREMIAH 33:3

- Mark 4

- Ruth 2:8, 22–23

- Zechariah 12–14

- Matthew 25:34–40, 1 Corinthians 3:12–15

CHAPTER TEN

REVELATION 20 IMPORTANCE

In my opinion, there are two crucial Bible chapters for the church today. The first is John 1, which was covered in an earlier chapter, and Revelation 20. It is a book conveying understanding about the end times and biblical prophecy that is important to the church today. Man has made end-time prophecy very complicated, and hopefully, this chapter will help bring some clarity.

Prophecy is history written in advance. God has predestined, before creation, how it will all work out. Prophecy is the one thing that separates the Bible from all other books ever written. It is one of the reasons why the Bible is a living book that is as useful today as it has been for over four thousand years. With at least one-quarter of the Bible containing prophetic passages written in advance, it is essential to understand that to date, nobody has disproved any of them. That really should alarm people not yet connected to the One True God and what Jesus is currently doing. That includes what Jesus is going to do in the future, as well.

We can see in Revelation 20:2–6 that Jesus will rule on Earth from Jerusalem with total peace for one thousand years. Imagine not having to deal with Satan and his demonic army for one thousand years. Verse seven reveals after the one thousand years is over, God then lets Satan loose to roam the earth one last time. I know! I know! What is God thinking? Really! In verse eight, we see mankind is so fed up with true peace and quiet with Jesus and His reign, that men flock to Satan. The number of people who run after the devil is like the "sand of the sea." Only God can count the number of sand grains in the sea, but obviously, that represents large numbers of men and women who are going to war against Jesus, the saints and the beloved city Jerusalem. Many think that Armageddon is the final war with Satan, but it is not. This is the final war, and it is to make an end to "all" evil.

God recorded it this way before he created everything to prove the nature of man has never changed since the beginning of time and the original sin in the Garden of Eden. Once man listened to Satan, he never stopped. It doesn't matter that God talked directly with men like Adam, Cain, Enoch, Noah, Abraham, etc., used prophets, sent His Holy Spirit to all the Church, or shows up and rules for one thousand years from Jerusalem. The nature of man is corrupt, since the very first sin. That is the only explanation for why after one thousand years of true peace in Jesus' reign on Earth, most of mankind flocks to Satan and makes war against Jesus and the saints. The alluring draw of sin is tempting for men and women. We want to be in charge of our own destiny, with no thoughts of God. For those of us alive, eternity is being weighed in the balance. Some great thinkers consider themselves and our society today as far surpassing our ancestors. Revelation 20 is in the Bible to show how false that premise is. The nature of man is the same as it was in Genesis. To be entirely truthful, I felt I was reading the front page news of the paper when I read Genesis for the first time. There was lying, cheating, sleeping around, murder, war, and slavery, just to name a few of the transgressions. Ecclesiastes 1:9–10 states there is nothing new under the sun. I know many want to think that the nature of man is good, but God says it isn't. History proves it isn't.

That is why Jesus said the poor would always be with us. Our evil nature has caused history to repeat itself time after time. There has never been a "good" government lasting for any length of time that took care of the poor. They will always be with us until Jesus comes to reign for one thousand years. Today, even one day of real peace throughout the entire world seems to be impossible. While I am typing this, there may have been many murdered or even worse. Yet, Jesus will give one thousand years of true peace. Nobody will get by with anything because the telepathic nature of God will know before something bad happens and put a quick stop to it. Even so, human fallibility cannot tolerate one thousand years of peace. The moment Satan is let loose much of mankind will flock to him to make war against Jesus and the saints.

I am not perfect, my innate nature is evil, and if it is much better today, it is only because of what I have allowed Jesus to do in my life. However, my past is not all doom and gloom, because growing up, I learned how to toe the line between good and evil. I learned how to get by with certain things and not get caught. I weighed the risks involved, *"Hmm, is it worth a two-week grounding?"* Everything that was written in Genesis, exposing the nature of man, is still going on today. The only difference is we have more sophisticated toys and methods to do the same things written about in Genesis. Anyone who claims they can solve today's problems of poverty, depravity, slavery, sex trafficking, and create permanent peace is somebody to run away from as fast as you can. Recorded history over the last six thousand years has proven man is utterly incapable of resolving these issues. Man cannot change his sinful nature. God has shown us how to get there on the narrow road available to all. It is possible to all because of what Jesus is doing, yet few of us choose the path God has provided. We would rather do it ourselves even though we see our obvious shortcomings. None of us will ever be good enough to attain perfection. Jesus is our only hope; we cannot do it alone.

Revelation 20 conveys there will be one thousand years of peace when Jesus returns to Earth. How does He reign so long with total peace for all? Well, we are told Jesus has to rule with a rod of iron to keep mankind under control.[39] Why is a rod of iron necessary? Pretty simple, really, it's the only way to rule over the debauchery of men of the flesh who remain alive after Armageddon and repopulate the earth during those one thousand years.

The sinful nature of our flesh still exists in those who survive the Seven Seal Judgments and enter into Jesus' reign on Earth. To make matters worse, after experiencing one thousand years of total peace and knowledge of the world's violent history prior to that peace, it is written that mankind can't wait for Satan's release. Revelation 20 proves that no matter how much grace and mercy God provides, time and again, the enduring sinful nature of the majority of mankind rejects it. God is and always has been in control and will ultimately say that time is up forever, and completely defeat all evil by casting Death and Hades into the lake of fire, the second and final death.

---

39 Rev. 2:27, 12:5, 19:15

For Further Study

To invite you to understand what is in your eternity, The One True God is saying to you:

> *"Call to Me, and I will answer you, and show you great and mighty things, which you do not know."*
>
> —JEREMIAH 33:3

- Revelation 20

CHAPTER ELEVEN

KAI AS AND

The Book of Revelation requires close examination. Man has taken something simple and turned it into gibberish. Many imply it cannot be interpreted as written, yet it is very understandable when read this way. I believe the Bible is God's instruction manual for mankind, so, putting on my "critical thinking" hat, I have to ask why God would write something that cannot be understood as written. Perhaps that is a bit simplistic. Yet if Revelation was written so man cannot understand it as written, then why did God even write it? Why would any man even read it? God knew that Satan would play games with it, but He gave it to Apostle John anyway. It obviously is crucial for mankind to have it and read it. So, why do so many men disagree with each other concerning it?

Reading Revelation requires diligence and intentionality, so that "itchy ears" do not to lead us down the wrong path. Satan is very adept at seizing the narrative and providing misinformation. Like the hodge-podge of religions Satan has created, he has never stopped perverting the Bible. As a result, we have an array of end-time interpretations. Plenty to choose from, so, find the one that appeals to you, right? No, that's a bad idea. Since there is a great diversity of interpretation about Revelation, it is critical to ask God for clarity and to carefully compare it to all that is written in the Bible.

God writes Scripture that can be understood and will stand true throughout the centuries. The people of Apostle John's day accepted that when God wrote that a third angel blew the third trumpet, a star then fell from heaven upon a third of the rivers and springs of the Earth, causing them to become bitter. It is easy to understand, and it will happen exactly that way. One-third of the earth's rivers and streams become bitter, not one-third of them in the United States, or one-third in South Africa, or one-third in Sweden. Some claim the nuclear accident in Ukraine at the Chernobyl plant has already fulfilled Revelation 8:10. The man-made nuclear plant in Chernobyl, which exploded in 1986, is believed by some to be the "great star that fell from heaven." That would mean God needed a man-made structure residing on the earth, to become His star from heaven, and contaminated one-third of the earth's rivers and streams, and killed many people who drank the water. The Scripture says these people died from drinking contaminated water, with no mention of them dying from the nuclear fallout from the star. It was the nuclear fallout, in the air, that killed many in the city of Chernobyl. Only about one-hundred-thousand people were evacuated. They never got a chance to drink the water, and there were no reports of anyone dying from drinking the water. If Chernobyl was God's plan all along, would He not have written, "A great star from the *Earth*, burning like a torch, fell on a third of the rivers and springs of water *nearby*?" I only changed two words, from the NKJV, as italicized, because that is precisely what some men are teaching. The Chernobyl nuclear exclusion zone was only about nineteen miles, and there has been zero mention of any-thing remotely close to the contamination of a third of Earth's rivers and springs, much less killing many men. The total amount of waters around Chernobyl is incredibly small in comparison to the enormous Amazon River. The four thousand miles long Amazon contains only about twenty percent of Earth's freshwater supply. Even if the entire

Amazon were polluted, that event would not be close to one-third of the earth's freshwater supply.

The Chernobyl event was a terrible man-made disaster that did not have to happen. Regardless, it does not fit the description of the event God wrote in Revelation 8:10–11. Wrong conclusions like this show why it is essential to ask questions and think critically through the situation. In this case, does a man-made nuclear plant that exists on the earth sound like a "great star" from heaven? No, it was a man-made building on Earth that blew up. It was also incredibly small stuff compared to the man-made atomic bombs dropped on Hiroshima and Nagasaki. Why not pick one of them as the star that fell from heaven? However, the name Chernobyl means "wormwood," which is the name of the falling star in Revelation. Hiroshima and Nagasaki do not, so they do not fit the narrative some men were shaping. Additionally, a third of the earth's rivers and streams did not become undrinkable as related in Revelation. God's Word explicitly explains what he will do when He deems it is time, and the Chernobyl incident is going to be incredibly tiny in comparison.

The flood in Noah's day was God doing a huge event. He wiped out all of civilization, except Noah and his immediate family. One of God's angels killed one hundred eighty-five thousand Assyrians in a single night, which was a small, simple thing to God.[40] Of course, creating the heavens, stars, and the earth with all the life on it is well beyond huge from a human perspective. We know that anything entering the earth's atmosphere starts burning like a torch. Most of those objects are entirely consumed by fire before they reach the earth. This star falling from heaven will be like a large mountain and will still

---

40 2 Kings 19:34–36; Isaiah 37:35–37

have substantial mass when it finally hits the earth. It is going to be large enough to poison one-third of the earth's rivers and streams. This Scripture will be fulfilled precisely as God wrote it when He declares it is time.

Have any of Revelation's seals even been opened yet? While I think it is easy to answer "No," by using God's Word, many others believe and teach otherwise. The Chernobyl discussion was a first attempt to show the third trumpet has not yet been blown, despite what others are teaching. My simple answer is none of the seals have been opened, much less the trumpets blown, or vials poured out. According to Scripture, first, there must be a Seven-year Peace Treaty with Israel that allows for the third temple to be built and opened for sacrificing as in the days of old. Where are the two witnesses that live and prophesy from Jerusalem for the first three and one-half years of the Seven-year Tribulation period? Let's not be guilty of creating "private interpretations" in violation of 2 Peter 1:20–21 and of forcing a fit where there is none. The acid test is context and the nature of God, as shown throughout the entire Bible.

Another example of the importance of reading Revelation, as written, is found in Revelation 8:8. Where, at the second trumpet, God has a burning mountain thrown into the sea. The impact kills a third of the living creatures and destroys a third of the ships. Are we saying the God who created the heavens, the earth, and all the creatures cannot do these things? Has a third of all sea life ever died due to some disaster? This is a Revelation event that has not happened since it must be both a third of the living creatures and a third of the ships. You cannot accept one of them and ignore the other. If you happen to believe that a loving God would not kill one-third of the sea creatures, how do you explain Noah's flood or Sodom and Gomorrah?

Or explain Egypt's last plague in which, in one night, God killed all the firstborn offspring of men and animals of the families that didn't put the blood of a lamb on the lintel and doorposts.[41] Sorry, but I don't see items such as Revelation 8:8–10 as challenging to understand. It is not a question of if God can do all that He has written, because God can do whatever He wants with His creation. We need to trust that what He does is always in our best interests, even though it may not seem like it at the time.

Revelation and end times prophecy is made hard by all the different things written by men from their own private interpretations. No matter how credible some may seem, all are mere mortal men, not God, and we all need to be careful. As leaders of the Church body, priests, pastors, ministers, teachers, all are held to a higher standard than the rest of the body of Christ.[42] God says in 2 Timothy 4:3 that the time will come when they will not endure sound doctrine, but have "itchy" ears and be turned to fables or fictitious tales. God does what He says He will do. With that in mind, if this is corrective teaching, it is better to receive correction now than by Him later. Once it is read "as written" several times, it is surprising just how much sense Revelation makes. Be careful with God's Word, and all will go well with you.

Many times the only way to be sure that an interpretation of Scripture is proper is to look for the context from surrounding Scripture and also find it defined and supported somewhere else in the Bible. Jacob, the son of Isaac, can be referred to as either Jacob or Israel. Whenever the word Israel is used, it may mean Jacob specifically, the descendants of Jacob, or the land of Israel. The context from

---

41 Exodus 11:5; 12:7, 22
42 James 3:1

Scripture around it has to be examined. The Bible says Earth is God's creation, and He is the landowner.[43] When He says He has given a portion of it, the land called Israel, to the descendants of Jacob, and if nowhere in the Bible God says He has changed His mind and given it to someone else, then, according to the Creator, it still belongs to Israel. He is the one and only one who can make that happen. We can see that truth in Zechariah 12. *The LORD* will save the tents of Judah first, so that the glory of the house of David and the glory of the inhabitants of Jerusalem shall not become greater than that of Judah. It has been hard over the years for man to understand this. It is even more confounding to see how the people of Israel could have gone from enslavement in Egypt, wandered around in the desert for forty years, and then conquered a land with giants in it. As historical records show, we find they were conquered by Babylon and transported to Persia. Then seventy years later, they returned to their land and went back to Israel with all their possessions. Persia kept none. Really? But that's not the end of hard to believe things. The Israelite people were conquered again by Rome and expelled from Israel in 70 AD. Then they returned to the land again about 1,900 years later in 1948. How can that happen without God orchestrating it? That land keeps returning as their land again and again. In none of the cases, have the people of Israel ever paid for the land. Not only that, but in two of the three cases, it was given back to them, i.e., Persia after the seventy years, and then in 1948 by the British. The first was by conquest, but that too was by God's hand, starting with God taking down the walls around Jericho at the sound of the trumpets and the Israelite people shouting. They obtained the land because God made it happen.

---

43 Lev. 25:23

One purpose of giving the land to Israel was to fulfill God's promise to Abraham. Another was to bring judgment upon Egypt because of their worship of false gods in the exodus. A third was to send the Israelites out with great possessions, and a fourth was to show God had determined the depth of the Amorites iniquity had become complete.[44] While this may seem harsh to some men, remember what God did in the days of Noah, or Sodom and Gomorrah. When God moves in His Judgments, it isn't pretty. In the Seven-year Tribulation period, God's Judgments will kill fifty percent of mankind. If the world's population is seven billion, three and one-half billion will be dead after all the seals, trumpets, and bowls or vials are complete. If you think God is unfair, remember those people know they are in rebellion against God, and finally, He is saying time is up. By then, He will have given everyone a fair warning. All people could choose Him and be saved. But many won't.

This chapter has provided context to be able to address a fundamental question about the book of Revelation. Is it written in "chronological" order?" Some men are teaching there may be an order to Revelation, yet it is not necessarily in the precise chronological order as the text states. One of the confusing ideas taught today suggests that even if Scripture calls it the third trumpet, it does not mean it literally happens after the second or before the fifth or sixth trumpet in real life. As I study the Bible, I see there are multiple ways God preserved the proper order of "future" events in Revelation.

There are pieces to Revelation which have nothing to do with the chronological order of the end-time events, such as the letters to the seven churches that existed back then but are no longer here today.

---

44 Gen. 15:13

Those writings were about the present day and conditions, not the future end times events. The chronological order applies specifically to the future "Seven Seals" end-times judgments from God. The first three chapters are the chapters not chronologically involved. Chapter 1 announces Jesus is the one delivering the message. Then words of instruction for six of seven churches being rebuked for their shortcomings and encouraged to do what God has always said to do. Those words spoken to the churches are still useful today to remind churches of God's desire for them. The rest of Revelation holds explanatory writings, the Seven Seals, and other details to assist in our understanding. Study with the Holy Spirit leading prevents us from turning the teaching of Revelation into nonsense.

Reading through Revelation, as written, makes it extremely difficult to see the need to reorder any of the events. For God to put the fifth trumpet event before the third or second trumpet, out of chronological order in time, does not seem logical. God invented numbers and is not only perfect; He is the master mathematician holding the entire universe together. Are we then saying that God somehow has confused His numbered events? Do we think He wrote them out of order to see if we could figure it out? Even worse, was He trying to trick us? What other explanations can there be for a fifth trumpet event happening before the third or second, unless perhaps all seven trumpets were sounded at the same time allowing an out of order appearance? Is it possible they are listed in order of importance, instead of chronological order concerning time? Is there Biblical support for any of these possibilities? When do we stop and say "what if" and search for a better answer? Is there a way to be one hundred percent sure about the order and sequence of the Seven Seal Judgments as written in Revelation? Did God use multiple techniques to preserve the proper order of events besides using numbers?

In trying to find other Scripture to help understand if what is said is consistent with the ordering of Revelation Scripture, we can examine the Egyptian plagues under Moses of Exodus 7–12, and also the order of kingdoms in Daniel 2. Both the plagues and the kingdoms happened sequentially as separate events. None of them occurred at the same instance in time but ensued in the exact order, as God stated.

The Seven Feasts of Israel are Passover, Unleavened Bread, First Fruits, Pentecost, Feast of Trumpets, Day of Atonement, and Feast of Booths. Jesus is fulfilling each of them in precisely the order written in Leviticus. Christians can see Jesus fulfilled Passover first. He was the lamb without blemish and sacrificed so that we might have everlasting life. He was without leaven, a term meaning sinless, so Jesus was the Unleavened Bread. Jesus was the very first to be resurrected from the dead with a body that can't age or decay, so when He rose again, He became the First Fruits in fulfillment of the Feast of First Fruits. The next feast fulfilled was Pentecost, which was the day Jesus sent the Holy Spirit to His Bride-to-be, the Church. The last three Feasts are not yet fulfilled, but we know the final Feast; the Feast of Booths or Tabernacles will be achieved by the one-thousand-year reign of Jesus on Earth as documented in Zechariah 14. Some in the Church disagree about how the Feast of Trumpets and Day of Atonement will be fulfilled. I do not think, however, anyone puts those fulfillments out of the order God has presented them. Using all of the Scripture God has given us, there is nowhere God has reversed His written order. While that fact alone doesn't conclusively prove God has written Revelation in a way that preserved the written chronological order as is, it adds credibility. These small points add evidence and will help many understand the book of Revelation.

Seals, trumpets, and vials do not carry the same meaning. Some people teach all three are the same, but they are not by fit, form, or function. Seals keep things closed and guarantee the item stays closed until opened. In the world of defense products, we used test equipment sealed by quality assurance stickers or seals. A broken seal meant that particular piece of equipment could not be used for test purposes until it went through the established verification process. If it passed, it was sealed with a new seal and put back into the workflow. Seals do not make a noise like a trumpet and cannot be used to pour something out of them, like a bowl. God wrote and recorded many things before the creation and sealed them in front of the living beings and angels. When the time comes, Jesus will open the sealed writings of Revelation, and they will be explicitly executed, as stated.

Trumpets project a sound alerting people to pay attention. They do not seal anything but let out an audible sound. God commanded Israel to blow the trumpet to announce the beginning of a Feast, the new moon, the Sabbath, and giving signals of war as they did at Jericho. Trumpets emit a sound of alert ahead of an announcement or reading, and they do not seal writing or pour out something.

Vials or bowls are containers used to hold an item until it is time to pour it out. They do not seal anything or make a sound to alert or announce something. The vials in Revelation are the pouring out of God's final wrath judgments. They are listed after the seventh trumpet blast, not before, and there are no more trumpets listed in Revelation after the seventh one sounds. Vials, trumpets, and seals are not to be assumed to be the same thing. The first vial does not signal the same event as the first trumpet or first seal. The key understanding reflects; (1) the events are all written in a specific order; (2) they are written according to a numbering system; (3) they do not serve the same function in real life, i.e., sealing vs. audile sound vs. pouring; (4) the actual Scripture descriptions are not the same.

The first trumpet announces the burning up of just vegetation. Whereas when the first Vial is poured out, it affects just people, and a very select group at that, as it only falls upon people who have the mark of the beast and worshipped his image. There is no mention of vegetation in the first vial, and no mention of people in the first trumpet. God's Scripture is not to be rearranged. God did not write it that way; they are not the same event. The second trumpet announces the destruction of a third of the sea, a third of the creatures in the sea, and a third of the ships. In comparison, the second vial says, "every" living creature in the sea dies. Consider asking God for understanding as you read His Word. There is no reason for Revelation 22:18–19 to affect Your Eternity. Grace will cover you no matter what, but why not get His guidance. As for me, if it works as written, I'm okay with it. If it doesn't seem to work as written, I'm asking God to show me elsewhere in His Word what He means. That includes any dreams, words, or prophecies given to me. They have to hold up to Scripture. From my point of view, until God shows me in His Bible, talking about the matter is fruitless. Hopefully, this has cleared up some Revelation interpretation mistakes.

Let us reflect on a final important question. How can anyone be one hundred percent certain of the chronological order?" God has supplied this answer in His Bible, the only written source for Truth. In John 16:13, the Apostle John cautioned, *Let the Holy Spirit, that leads us and guides us into all Truth and understanding, provide the appropriate conviction in the heart of the believers seeking Truth.*

The clarifying answer to the question of order is in a small word. The book of Revelation, originally written in Greek, contains the word "kai" in crucial places. It is a simple word carrying a lot of power. Older Bibles like the King James and American Standard translate "kai" into its English word as "and." Newer translations tend to omit the original usage of that Greek word.

While I had many ways of proving God meant for the Seven Seals Judgments to happen in the exact order He wrote them, I felt like I was missing the key to solving this dilemma. In keeping with His Supernatural capabilities, God gave me the key in an unexpected way.

One day, during my lunch break, I was reading the electronic Bible from the computer on my office desk. I turned from the computer to take a bite of lunch and distinctly heard a voice say, "The key to understanding Revelation is in Chapter 12." I knew I had just heard God speak, and whether it was audible or telepathic, I do not know. But hearing those words, I immediately spun around in my chair to face my computer and quickly went to Revelation 12. Before I had even begun to read the text, the voice then asked me, "What do you see?" So based on a quick scan of the verses, my response was, "I see a lot of "and's." It was an obvious response when 16 of the 17 verses start with "And." I rarely have the old King James Version open for reading, but on this day I did, and there seemed to be the word "and" everywhere. The voice said, "Yes." When I heard that, I immediately knew "and" was the answer to proving the chronological issue I was stressing over.

God captured my attention by downloading information about the entire chapter that day, information you will find in the next chapter. But after I had written that information down, my thoughts turned again to the use of "and." I went straight to Revelation 12 and began to scan for the word "and." I immediately understood why it was so important. All the verses in that chapter started with "And," the Greek word "Kai," except one. I found sixteen of seventeen verses start with "And." Open a King James Version, not the New King James Version, and look for yourself. Briefly, I wondered how God could be so sloppy in His writing and start so many sentences and verses with "And." English teachers everywhere teach us never to begin sentences with "And." God is incredibly precise, so I knew there was a perfectly good reason. Then I remembered, God did not use punctuation. The original books of the Bible were essentially one long run-on sentence with no chapter numbers, verses, or punctuation. Men put those things in much later, after the death of Christ, and it certainly made things simpler for us.

Focusing on "kai" made it easy to see the inordinately high number of times God used "and" in the book of Revelation. Not just to start a verse, but multiple times in many verses, as well. I decided to check other chapters in Revelation and saw the same trend. Taking a quick look at the Gospels and other books in the Bible, it was easy to see the usage of "and" was extraordinarily high in Revelation. It was unique in this particular way, perhaps because it was a book filled with prophecy. Preserving the proper order of events was critical. I am sure God knew some of us would try to modify the order of the Revelation events, so He took care of that with "kai." It is impossible to change the order when there are all those "and" words in the way.

Now I knew the seals, trumpet blasts, and vials or bowls were going to be fulfilled in perfect order, exactly as written. Why? God designed a specific order to the book of Revelation to prevent man from tampering with it. Somehow I found it hilarious that God did it using the simple word "and" or Greek word "kai."

Of course, Satan has been trying to twist God's ways and Word since the days in the Garden of Eden and has been quite successful. I am sorry for implying men are gullible and can fall prey to the guile of the adversary Satan, yet, I know how naive I can be. My sixty-plus years of life and reasoning powers do not compare with Satan, who has been corrupting mankind for thousands of years, so he should be pretty good at it by now, don't you think?

I can imagine the responses to that statement. "Wait a minute! Are we Christians not born again? The devil has no power over us! Satan can't wrongfully influence the Holy Spirit-filled Christian in any way."

Let me ask you to give an honest answer before the Lord, not before me or any other man. Do you still have flashes of improper thoughts? Ever get off the path the Lord has set before you? Do you still sin from time to time, or are you now perfect in the flesh? My answer is no one in the flesh is immune from the wiles of the devil, which is why we need to die daily in the flesh and put on the full armor of God to help us. We do not shed the corrupt flesh permanently until the Rapture event spoken of by Apostle Paul in 1 Thessalonians 4. Consider how many church leaders have fallen. If they can fall to the wiles of the devil, all of us can. There is a reason why Scripture warns us to beware of the wolf in sheep's clothing.[45]

No one can wrap more into one sentence than God, and when He moves, there are ripple effects we will see when we are aware. Consider this example of what any man can do with a single sentence. If I were to state, "I drove to Hats R Us and purchased a hat," at least four things become clear in that one sentence.

1. Hats R Us and hat are linked to each other by the word "and." They are not independent of each other. I had to be at Hats R Us to purchase the hat at Hats R Us.

---

45 Matt. 7:15; Acts 20:28–30

2.   I drove to Hats R Us before buying the hat. There is a specific sequence; it is inferred I did not buy the hat before going to Hats R Us; it is misleading if the order happened the other way around; remember that misleading is the nature of the adversary, not God.

3.   I bought the hat while at Hats R Us, not some other place after I went to Hats R Us.

4.   There is only one event and sequence being described, not multiple events occurring at the same time. I did not buy the hat while driving to Hats R Us. In today's electronic age, we can now do that over cell phones while driving to Hats R Us, but the words chosen were that I drove to Hats R Us and bought the hat there.

There may be more "ripple" effects from that one sentence, but we can see there are at least four possibilities. God does not provide us with partial truths as man often does. The four statements above are to emphasize the point that when God says something, it unerringly is what He says it is. We may not completely understand, but God is not trying to be tricky or deceitful. That is not His nature, and we must be careful about reading things into His Word. He does want us to put effort into understanding Him and His ways, and that takes a lifetime.

When looking at the original Greek text used in Revelation, there are many "kai's" used. I can be somewhat of a skeptic, and I started asking questions and seeking His help. Questions like, "What if that is Apostle John's unique writing style?" Yes, God told John to write down what he saw and heard, and I'm quite sure John did exactly that. I was on a mission to prove Revelation was different than any other

Bible book when it came to the use of "and." Because Apostle John was used by God to write other books besides Revelation, I began my comparison with those books. I started with the Gospel of John using the King James Version and found there were 867 occurrences of "and" in a total of 879 verses. So, 867/879 is slightly less than one in each verse. Also, only 73 verses started with "And/Kai" or just 8.3%. Generally speaking, God used "kai" so many times that when man began adding punctuation and verse numbers to the Bible, it was difficult to not start some sentences with Kai/And. That is particularly the case for those compiling a direct "as-written" translation, as opposed to a paraphrased version.

An electronic concordance of ASV or KJV makes it relatively simple to verify the numbers. When looking at 1 John through 3 John, those books also produced similar results with about one "and/kai" for each verse. Twenty-four of those 132 verses started with "Kai/And" (18%). The King James Version tends to translate the Greek word "kai" into "and," but kai can also be translated to other words like "then," "therefore," "also," "but," etc. Again, newer versions tend to leave the "kai/and" out or use a different word, but God put "kai" into His original Greek writing for a reason, and I believe the original Bible was written without error.

By comparison to the other New Testament books just mentioned, the entire text of Revelation had a stunning 1,172 occurrences of "kai/and" spread over only 404 verses. That is 2.9 "and's" for each verse in Revelation, or about triple the occurrences of the less than one each verse in Apostle John's other writings. Not only that, but 275 of the 404 verses in Revelation start with an "And" (68% vs. the range of 8.3% to 18%). So, a little over two out of three verses in Revelation actually start with "Kai" in the original Greek version. More than three out of four verses after Revelation, Chapter 3 start with "Kai/And."

These are the verses describing the events of the Seven Seals, Trumpets, and Vials and beyond into Jesus' 1,000-year reign.

It is challenging to start a new paragraph, thought, separate event, or to rearrange the events when "kai/and" lock-in each occurrence. God used "kai/and" as a technique to connect each one after the other to preserve the chronological order of their sequence. The event after the "and" cannot occur before the event in front of the "and." No other book in the Bible is written like this. Do not take my word for it; check it out for yourself. After all, it is Your Eternity. I am sure you will see Revelation is genuinely a one of a kind book in how it uses "Kai/And." You will have to ask God and decide for yourself why this is so. Once you cross that hurdle, I suspect understanding Revelation will become easier.

As you begin your study, keep in mind the New Testament was originally written in Greek. Free online Bible sources with multiple languages, like www.biblegateway.com, are available to use to check the Greek for "kai" at the beginning of sentences and throughout the sentences. Those seeking an in-depth study of the Bible no longer need to know Greek because of the many translation resources available. You can see how chapter twelve's verses start with "Kai" since the verses are numbered with the English numbering system. The first six verses to Revelation 12, in Greek, are below to illustrate how easy it can be to see "Kai," with the start of each verse shown in bold.

ΑΠΟΚΑΛΥΨΙΣ ΙΩΑΝΝΟΥ 12SBL Greek New Testament (SBLGNT)

12 <u>Καὶ</u> σημεῖον μέγα ὤφθη ἐν τῷ οὐρανῷ, γυνὴ περιβεβλημένη τὸν ἥλιον, καὶ ἡ σελήνη ὑποκάτω τῶν ποδῶν αὐτῆς, καὶ ἐπὶ τῆς κεφαλῆς αὐτῆς στέφανος ἀστέρων δώδεκα, **2** <u>καὶ</u> ἐν γαστρὶ ἔχουσα· [a]καὶ κράζει ὠδίνουσα καὶ βασανιζομένη τεκεῖν. **3** <u>καὶ</u> ὤφθη ἄλλο σημεῖον ἐν τῷ οὐρανῷ, καὶ ἰδοὺ δράκων [b]μέγας πυρρός, ἔχων κεφαλὰς ἑπτὰ καὶ κέρατα δέκα καὶ ἐπὶ τὰς κεφαλὰς αὐτοῦ ἑπτὰ διαδήματα, **4** <u>καὶ</u> ἡ οὐρὰ αὐτοῦ σύρει τὸ τρίτον τῶν ἀστέρων τοῦ οὐρανοῦ, καὶ ἔβαλεν αὐτοὺς εἰς τὴν γῆν. καὶ ὁ δράκων ἕστηκεν ἐνώπιον τῆς γυναικὸς τῆς μελλούσης τεκεῖν, ἵνα ὅταν τέκῃ τὸ τέκνον αὐτῆς καταφάγῃ. **5** <u>καὶ</u> ἔτεκεν υἱόν, [c] ἄ ρσεν, ὃς μέλλει ποιμαίνειν πάντα τὰ ἔθνη ἐν ῥάβδῳ σιδηρᾷ· καὶ ἡρπάσθη τὸ τέκνον αὐτῆς πρὸς τὸν θεὸν καὶ πρὸς τὸν θρόνον αὐτοῦ. **6** καὶ ἡ γυνὴ ἔφυγεν εἰς τὴν ἔρημον, ὅπου ἔχει ἐκεῖ τόπον ἡτοιμασμένον ἀπὸ τοῦ θεοῦ, ἵνα ἐκεῖ [e]τρέφωσιν αὐτὴν ἡμέρας χιλίας διακοσίας ἑξήκοντα.

The Greek "kai," translates to "and" as well as to "then" in English. Next, read Revelation 12 by placing the word "Then" in place of "And" at the beginning of every verse. While somewhat clumsy, in many cases, this very clearly identifies a sequenced chronological order to all the Seven Seal Judgments. So, verse 17 events cannot occur before verse 10, etc.

An even better exercise is to remove "Kai/And" entirely from Revelation 12 to see if it is now possible to rearrange the order of the verses. In this "acid test" it should be evident the woman must be pregnant before giving birth, Satan had to have lost in order to be cast out of heaven forever, the woman was persecuted first and then fled because of it. While it might be possible to rearrange some of this order, logically, it is challenging to take these events out of their written sequence. Who would say the woman gave birth, before becoming pregnant or fled and then was persecuted? But, just in case we humans get creative, God has added "kai/and" to preserve the order in yet another way to keep us from doing that very thing. Just sharing some "critical thinking" lessons that have worked for me, and hopefully, they might help others.

As evident as it was by comparing all the writings of Apostle John, I wasn't satisfied at stopping there. I checked other books by examining 1 Peter through Jude. There occurs less than one " Kai/And " in each verse, of those, only 11% started with a "Kai/And." By comparison, the entire book of Revelation has 68% beginning with Kai. However, as we might expect by now, the trend of higher "Kai/And" usage does apply to prophecy areas in the Bible, as evidenced in Daniel and Ezekiel. But the higher trend does not come close to comparing with Revelation. In Daniel verses beginning with "Kai/And" is 30%, which is much higher than other books, but is nowhere close to 68% for the entire text of Revelation.

Remember the ripple effect, like when dropping a single rock into the water. In summary, there are at least five biblically woven methods implemented by God to preserve the exact chronological order of the book of Revelation. We can choose to ignore these methods or put them in our chest of God-given tools moving forward.

1. Order preserved by the use of a numbering scheme: Seal 1 comes before Seal 2.

2. It is preserved by the actual order of the events as written through word placement. God did not write about the fifth trumpet events before writing about trumpets 1 through 4.

3. Use of "and/then," discussed in detail in this chapter, to preserve the chronological flow.

4. The events are also described in a fashion which infers chronological order. The woman must be pregnant before giving birth. The woman must be persecuted first, which then causes her to flee.

5. The use of different descriptive words indicates various events or sequences in time. Vials do not serve the same purpose as trumpets, or seals, etc. Simply put, it means that seals, trumpets, and vials have different uses and meanings and are not the same.

What significance does this have for you? Ask God; it is Your Eternity. Listen to what He places on your heart through the guidance of the Holy Spirit. Remember, the only way the devil can defile our hearts is through our minds with the five senses. Satan is on the outside, trying to get inside to ruin our hearts and negatively affect our witness to others. God resides in our hearts and is trying to move outward if we let Him, to make a positive impact around us. Satan is noisy and pushy; God is quiet and allows us to choose. Be careful because some believers have fallen over the years. None of us are immune. Listen to the calm, quiet, peaceful voice of God that speaks through the presence of the Holy Spirit residing in our hearts. God is telepathic, and the Holy Spirit is His wireless feature. As for me, any claim that Revelation is not written in exact chronological order; well, I just cannot agree with that.

For Further Study

To invite you to understand what is in your eternity, The One True God is saying to you:

> *"Call to Me, and I will answer you, and show you*
> *great and mighty things, which you do not know."*

—JEREMIAH 33:3

- Revelation 11–12 (explore Chapter 12 in a Greek Version)

- Revelation 8:8, 10

CHAPTER TWELVE

REVELATION 12 COMMENTARY

B iblical prophecy can be understood only by reading the entire Bible, considering the context, asking God for insight, waiting for His response, and seeking His confirmation. Prophecy of Scripture is not to be someone's own interpretation, but rather men moved by the Holy Spirit.[46] In the unity of fellowship with other Bible believers, it can be helpful to share insights gained by prayerful, Spirit-led time spent on a prophecy. Often these results will be the same but not always. Consistently testing everything against the entire Bible is crucial.

In the previous chapter, I related the incident when God began to show me the importance of the word "and." Initially, I didn't have much time to ponder this "and" thought because a flood of information immediately came to me about Revelation 12. This insight skipped over verses 1 and 2, but essentially everything else that I have written in this chapter was supernaturally "downloaded" to me. I had to ask God to slow down because He was outpacing my writing speed. He didn't seem to slow down much, but He did lock things into my brain, and I kept writing long after He had stopped His instruction to me.

I devoted hours of praying, fasting, and studying in an attempt to prove or disprove what I received. It had to Biblically support ev-

---

46 2 Pet.1:20 – 2 Pet.2:1

erything written in both the Old and New Testaments. In the initial download, though, I received nothing about verses 1 and 2. I sought God diligently through fasting while questioning everything about my life, wondering why this wasn't forthcoming.

About a year later, while I was at lunch, I was reading Genesis 37. As I read, a powerful presence of God came upon me, and I knew He had shown me the key in those verses. In an electrifying moment, I immediately determined the final piece to understanding Revelation 12 was in the first two verses. There are times when God shows up so powerfully; He doesn't have to speak to make His presence known. Once a fellow engineer stopped by my office, and we were talking about Scripture when he abruptly stopped and asked, "What is that?" I knew he meant the heavy peaceful, quiet presence that lets you know God is there. I immediately responded that it was the presence of God. Just like when I flew off my motorcycle going 95 mph and knew I was going to be okay before hitting the ground. There was a quiet, peaceful presence there that I cannot precisely explain. God is always here with us, but when you have these compelling experiences, you begin to know when there is something supernatural going on that has changed the atmosphere.

Using the Bible to interpret the Bible is a method of gaining a more in-depth understanding of Scripture and ensuring accuracy. The following Scripture illustrates using God's Word to explain His Word elsewhere and how uniquely God says things in the first book, like Genesis 32:28, which directly impacts the last book, Revelation.

And He said, "Your name shall no longer be called Jacob, but Israel; for you have struggled with God and with men, and have prevailed."

Note 1: God renames Jacob here, so, when God uses Israel in the rest of Scripture, it could mean Jacob, it could mean the twelve tribes of Jacob where ever they are, the nation of Israel, or the actual land given to Israel. The surrounding context in each text clarifies which it is. Israel was re-established as a nation in 1948, indicating God still has a plan for the descendants of Israel. It was hard for the Church to grasp this fact until 1948, but Israel has a significant part in Biblical end times prophecy.

Note 2: There are teachings concerning the "lost tribes of Israel." God knows exactly where all the members of the twelve tribes are; He hasn't lost any of them. He is God. While man may think the tribes are lost, God, who created the sun, moon, earth, and all the life on it, does not lose track of anything. It is heresy to imply God could somehow lose track of things or make errors in His instruction book to mankind, the Bible.

Genesis 37:9–10 records Joseph, who was one of Jacob's twelve sons, having this dream: *Then he dreamed still another dream and told it to his brothers, and said, "Look, I have dreamed another dream. And this time, the sun, the moon, and the eleven stars bowed down to me." So he told it to his father and his brothers; and his father rebuked him and said to him, "What is this dream that you have dreamed? Shall your mother and I and your brothers indeed come to bow down to the earth before you?"*

Note 3: By using the Bible to interpret the Bible, we now know Joseph's father is represented here by the sun, the moon represents his mother, and the eleven stars represent his brothers. The twelfth star represents Joseph, and the entire family bows down to him. Now we know when a statement further on in the Bible refers to twelve stars, it might be referring to twelve actual stars, perhaps twelve angels, or the twelve Apostles, or the twelve tribes of Israel. In this verse, God is tying the sun, moon, and twelve stars directly to Jacob, his wife, and twelve sons. Later in the Bible, it does not have to mean that, however, based on this text, it can. Context from the surrounding text clarifies the meaning.

This commentary includes the understanding He gave me. It uses the King James Version and is an invitation to consider and discern with God's help what you understand for yourself. Chapter 12 is near the middle of the book of Revelation. God paused here to identify and clarify the main pieces, people, and places in the Seven-year Tribulation period. Interestingly, He also identifies many of these things in Daniel and 2 Thessalonians. God establishes the actual participants in Revelation to make end times prophecy more easily understood. The following is a verse-by-verse study of Revelation 12, with what I received from God, including the "Kai/And's," and then notes for a more in-depth discussion on the material.

¹And there appeared a great wonder in heaven; a woman clothed with the sun, and the moon under her feet, and upon her head a crown of twelve stars:

This verse identifies the nation of Israel as the people who He is talking about in this chapter. The chapter is a high-level overview covering Israel's past, present, and future. Verses 1 through 5 are Israel's past. The pause is the present period of time where Christ is caught up to His throne (last part of verse 5) and is waiting for the Father to say it is time for Daniel's last week of years. There really isn't much about the present time because this chapter is about God's dealings with Israel, not the Church. Then verses 6–17 document Israel's future when God the Father tells Jesus it is time for the Age of Judgment and His reign with the rod of iron to begin.

Note 4: Once again, the sun, moon, and twelve stars are all tied together. This combination only happens twice in Scripture, and it was now easy to see this could be a direct connection of God's last book to His first. God is also identifying precisely who the leading players are as the Seven Seals are opened. The focus is not the church as we know it today. While we do need to look for context in chapter twelve before declaring all this to be accurate, the woman is about to be defined as a descendant of Israel in subsequent verses. Israel is God the Father's chosen wife. It is through Israel, the Father's wife, that a woman, Mary, is chosen and gives birth to God's son Jesus. The church is to be the wife of the Son, Jesus, at the appointed time, which has not yet occurred.[47] This woman is clothed with the sun, representing Jacob and with the moon representing Jacob's wife. A crown of twelve stars, which can be the twelve sons of Jacob making up the twelve tribes of Israel, is on her head. I am not saying anyone has to believe this, but using the Bible to interpret the Bible means this is at least one of the possible explanations. Genesis 37 is the only location, besides Revelation 12, where the sun, moon, and twelve stars are mentioned together. It is wise to understand them to be what God defines them to be in Genesis 37.

[2] *And she being with child cried, travailing in birth, and pained to be delivered.*

Note 5: She means Mary, who was a direct descendant from God, the Father's wife, Israel. Mary is pregnant with God's Son, Jesus, and she cried out, being in labor and in pain to give birth. So, we have the promised Christ child, as can be seen in the next set of verses in Revelation 12, and as predicted in Genesis 3:14–15, Genesis 49:10, and other locations.

When using the Bible to interpret the Bible, things like the sun

---

47 Matt. 25:1–13, Rev. 19:7–8

can be the sun, but we now know it can also be a reference to Israel. Given the context of this text, there is no other way of interpreting Revelation 12:1–2 as anything other than Israel. Why? Genesis 37 is the only place that spells out what the sun, moon, and twelve stars all together can mean. It is not plausible for those to give birth to children or cry out in labor during delivery. Genesis 37:9–10 provides the only fitting explanation for the "context" of the rest of the chapter. In simple terms, if the Apostles were the twelve stars, as some suggest, then the Apostles or the Church give birth to Jesus in verses 4–5, when in fact, Jesus gives birth to the Church. God's use of the simple Greek word "kai" is used many times to connect these events to keep anyone from purposefully changing the sequence and interpretation.

³ And there appeared another wonder in heaven; and behold a great red dragon, having seven heads and ten horns, and seven crowns upon his heads.

As Mary, from the tribe of Judah, is giving birth to the Child Jesus, Satan, the great red dragon appeared.

Note 6: By using Scripture to interpret Scripture, the great red dragon is defined to be Satan in Revelation 12:9, and he has ten horns in Daniel 7:24–27, and Revelation 13:1–9.

⁴ And his tail drew the third part of the stars of heaven, and did cast them to the earth: and the dragon stood before the woman which was ready to be delivered, for to devour her child as soon as it was born.

When Satan rejected God, one-third of God's angels followed him. He brought them with him to the earth and stood before the woman (Mary) to devour her Child, Jesus, as soon as He was born. Consider Matthew 2: *Then Herod, when he saw that he was mocked of the wise men, was exceeding wroth, and sent forth, and slew all the children that were in Bethlehem, and in all the coasts thereof, from two years old and under, according to the time which he had diligently inquired of the wise men.*

Matthew 2:19–20: *Now when Herod was dead, behold, an angel of the Lord appeared in a dream to Joseph in Egypt, saying, "Arise, take the young Child and His mother, and go to the land of Israel, for those who sought the young Child's life are dead."*

Note 7: The better we understand the Bible, the easier it is to use it to interpret Scripture in other locations like Revelation 12. The second chapter of Matthew records Joseph was warned by an angel that Herod would try to kill the child, Jesus. He was instructed to flee to Egypt. Joseph arose, and they immediately departed to Egypt. Satan had, indeed, hatched a plan to kill the Christ child, just as God says here in Revelation 12:4

⁵ *And she brought forth a man child, who was to rule all nations with a rod of iron: and her child was caught up unto God, and to his throne.*

Mary brought forth Jesus, who was to rule all nations with a rod of iron at a future time, but not yet. Her Child, Jesus, died to pay the price for the sins of mankind, was resurrected from the grave with a new body and caught up unto God the Father, and to His throne.[48]

Note 8: Mary, this woman from Israel, gives birth to Jesus, who is going to rule in the future with a rod of iron when He returns to rule "all" the nations from Jerusalem. The key point is that it says "was to rule" because He was not ruling in that fashion when the Book of Revelation was written years after Jesus died. He must rule with a rod of iron in His millennial reign because man will try to rebel. Many will worship their little "g" god during His millennial reign because their hearts are not right.[49]

---

48 Dan. 9:26
49 Micah 4:4–5

They cannot start trouble, but God does allow them free will to choose against His plan for mankind. This verse says her Child was caught up to God and His throne. Jesus paid the price for our sins and is now indeed in heaven on His throne. He is waiting for God the Father's command to end the Age of Grace or Church Age and start the Age of Judgment. There is a break in God's interaction with unbelieving Israelis during the Age of Grace.[50] It is a break that will continue until the Age of Grace is over. God will then turn His attention back to the twelve tribes of Jacob. There is no wrath of God poured out, or Revelation seals broken, or countdown of days to Jesus' physical return to reign on Earth from Jerusalem until the Father tells Jesus it is time. Satan is still allowed to go before the throne of God, continually accusing the believers in Christ of sins.[51] I know it is true, yet I still find it hard to comprehend man is so hard-hearted that Jesus has to rule with a rod of iron to keep self-seeking man in line. The nature of man's flesh is still sinful, and until God does away with all flesh, death and sin will remain, even during Christ's one-thousand-year reign on Earth. The rod of iron is a needed tool if every man truly is to live in peace under his fig tree.[52] There are examples of God telepathically knowing man's plans for no good, all the way back to Cain, who killed Abel.[53] God knew Cain's thoughts and talked with Cain about his plan to kill Abel. God cautions Cain telling him that sin is at the door, to choose correctly, and he will be accepted, but Cain decides his plan is better than God's and kills Abel anyway. Afterward, Cain whines to God that his punishment is more than he can bear. How typical of mankind.

---

50 Rom. 11:25–32
51 Rev. 12:10
52 Mic. 4:1–4
53 Gen. 4

⁶ And the woman fled into the wilderness, where she hath a place prepared of God, that they should feed her there a thousand two hundred and threescore days.

Before Jesus, the Messiah, returns to Earth to rule with His rod of iron, the nation of Israel will be protected for the first twelve hundred sixty days after the signing of the Seven-year Peace Treaty with many nations.[54]

Note 9: In verse 5, the Child, Jesus, was caught up to His throne was written in the past tense; it had already happened. In fact, all that has been told about has already happened. Verse 6 begins with "And" in the King James Version, but the New King James is probably a better interpretation of Kai by using "Then," because the next thing of significant importance has not yet happened. Nobody can place this verse before the others based on the fact God keeps using "and" to preserve the order. Also, the twelve hundred sixty days of protection has not occurred yet. Nothing has changed since Jesus went to His throne in verse 5. Verse 6 states the woman who gives birth to Jesus, Israel, is protected for the first twelve hundred sixty days of the Seven-year Tribulation period. We know this to be true because the Antichrist inspires a Seven-year Peace Treaty with all the nations, which allows Israel to build the Third Temple and sacrifice in that Temple in peace. They can until the three and one-half year point when the Antichrist will break the treaty. Revelation 11 informs us the two witnesses rule everything from Jerusalem for those twelve hundred sixty days. While that angers the Antichrist, he cannot do much while Israel is supernaturally protected by God and allowed to sacrifice and worship at the Temple during this period. It is clear Israel is the one protected

---

54 Dan. 9:27; Rev. 11:3–11

during the first half of those seven years. After those twelve hundred sixty days, the two witnesses are killed by the works of Satan. The next three and one-half years is referred to as the time of Israel's great trouble and will be very hard for them. If Israel is the one promised protection in the first half of the Seven-year Peace Treaty, then there is no promise the Church is protected. Of course, God's Word seems to indicate in many locations the Church will be Raptured before Jesus starts opening the Seven Seals Judgments, leaving only luke-warmers behind.[55] The Church Age has completed with the Rapture, and the Age of Judgment has begun.

7 And there was war in heaven: Michael and his angels fought against the dragon; and the dragon fought and his angels,

This seven-year period starts with a conflict, and as described by the prophet Daniel, it leads to the seven-year agreement with the nations. I know that this next statement is going to set somebody's hair on fire, but please read to the end of the paragraph first.

There was war in heaven over the Bride of Christ being raised up to God the Father's heaven. Michael and his angels fought against the dragon and his angels. As mentioned in Daniel 10:12–14, it took two of God's angels to deliver a message to Daniel. The angel Michael was required to hold off one of Satan's army, so the angel Gabriel could then deliver God's word to Daniel twenty-one Earth days later. Satan and his army will fight to the bitter end to stop the Rapture, for he knows he has only a short time left. Still, God has twice as many angels to neutralize Satan's forces, and those that are free escort the Raptured saints up to the Father's heaven before shutting the doors behind them. There is only one time in scripture that God will shut the doors to the

---

55 Rev. 3:14–16

third Heaven, and scripture shows us Satan has been shut out for good in three locations. One is recorded here in verses 7–8, and we can see that this war is before the seven-year Tribulation within the context of verses 7–14. Another is in Isaiah 26:20–21, where the doors are shut "before" Jesus comes out of His place to punish mankind through the opening of the 7 Seals, and the third is Matthew 25:10. All show that the closing of the doors/access occurs before the seven-year Tribulation/Age of Judgment begins. Satan and his demons will not be able to mess with the Bride of Christ's wedding that is about to take place in God the Father's House.

Note 10: The dragon is identified as Satan in Revelation 12:9.

Note 11: After thousands of years, things are finally getting exciting. Why is all this warfare happening? We know the participants, and this is the first time there is an all-out battle between all of God's angels and all of those who followed Satan. The pervasive use of "and/kai in Revelation 12, in addition to the order of the words, and the fact these words come after what was written in verse 6, place this war as either part of what happens with verse 6 or directly after. Up to this point, this chapter is all about the woman, Israel. Satan no longer has access to the third heaven, which is God's realm, so he can no longer accuse the Church saints day and night before the throne of God. I intend to show Biblical proof throughout this book that this huge angelic fight is over those being caught up or Raptured.

When Pharaoh finally permitted Moses to take the Israelites, he then chased them to the Red Sea. God opened and then closed the water's doors behind Israel, destroying Pharaoh's army. God's people were completely safe, and no longer had to worry about Pharaoh and his army. Similarly, when God accounts for everyone in His Rapture, He then closes the gates to His heavenly realm. Satan and his demons are now banned forever from the Father's domain in the third heaven. The Bride of Christ no longer has to worry about Satan and his army. The Church Age has ended, and the Age of Judgement with the rod of iron has begun.

Matthew 25 relates the story of five virgins who, without enough oil for their lamps, were not ready when the Bridegroom came, so they were left behind. The oil represents the Holy Spirit. If you end up reading this after the Rapture, there is no reason to fear. God said ten virgins, so, while the five left behind will suffer through the Seven-year Tribulation period, God always provides hope and a way through. All is not lost for them, theirs is a tougher path to be sure, but God would not have called them virgins along with the first group of five virgins without making a way for them. It is not over until God says it is over, and He will love on them as a child that was lost but has been found. It will cost them their life, but they will be raised at the first resurrection provided they do the things listed in Revelation 20:4–6. To understand this Scripture, Zephaniah 2:3 says a certain group of believers will be hidden in the Day of the Lord's Anger. Isaiah 26:20–21 says He will hide them in their chambers for a "little moment." This is when the first five virgins, which represent the Bride of Christ or the Church, are Raptured up to be married in God the Father's house. The "little moment" they spend up there is the Seven-year Tribulation when understood in light of verse 21. This verse says the Lord comes out of His place to punish the inhabitants of the earth. In the very next verse, Isaiah 27:1 says the Lord will finally punish Satan and slay the reptile in the sea. Moving to the New Testament, we find more Scripture concerning the first five virgins escaping His wrath. Luke 21:36 says those who are worthy will escape all these things. 1 Thessalonians 1:10 and 5:9 and Revelation 3:10 all say those who are prepared or worthy will escape His wrath that is to come through the Seven Seals. Those who are ready will escape God's wrath.

Take a closer look at God's Scriptures. Additional information about what is to come can be found by scrutinizing John 14:2–4, *In My Father's house are many mansions; if it were not so, I would have told you. I go to prepare a place for you. And if I go and prepare a place for you, I will come again and receive you to Myself; that where I am, there you may be also. And where I go you know, and the way you know.*

Jesus is telling the Apostles He will leave them and go to the Father's realm or third heaven. He assures them He will (a) come again, (b) receive them to Himself, (c) take them to where He is in the third heaven, and (d) will have many mansions for them in His Father's house. This is not referring to somewhere here on the earth or in the clouds, nor is it a reference to the New Jerusalem in Revelation 21. Nothing in this sequence indicates Jesus is taking the brethren, including those who are alive, only to the clouds, and then straight back down to Earth to reign and rule for one thousand years. When Jesus says in verse 3, "I will come again," that is the Rapture event, and He explains the next destination is not the earth, but rather, His Father's house where He is. Jesus is coming for His Bride, signifying a different purpose than actually setting His feet on the ground in Jerusalem to rule and live among men a second time. Post-Tribulation believers think that when the Rapture happens, those alive will only go up to the clouds and never get to spend any time in our mansion in the Father's house when Jesus comes for us. Why would some in the Church get to live in their heavenly mansions while others still alive do not? Consider if Jesus "comes again" for each of us in our own death, then over the past two thousand years, Jesus has already come back many billions of times since the days of the Apostles.

This Scripture precisely means what it says. When Jesus comes for us, we will all go together at one time to His Father's house, to our mansions He has made there. When this particular "coming again" event takes place, we will all go to the Father's house for the wedding. We are the Bride, and that is where we will be married, in the Father's house.

Revelation 19, with supporting Scripture in Jude, explains we will be in the third heaven and follow Jesus on white horses down to the earth for the wedding supper. Traditionally, wedding suppers happen in a different venue than the wedding. In Jesus' day, upon the command of the father, the groom would get his bride and take her to a private place, prepared ahead in the father's house to consummate the union. On the seventh day, the couple comes out from that place in the father's home to the wedding feast. It is the intimacy act that consummates the marriage before God.

The phrase "The Second Coming of Jesus" is often misinterpreted within the Body of Christ. Jesus has come back to Earth many times since his resurrection, as recorded in the Scriptures. But, only twice will Jesus come to stay and live among the people. When He came the first time, the Kingdom message was rejected, and Jesus was crucified on the cross for all sin. The second coming is Jesus' return to Earth to stay and rule with a rod of iron. There is nothing in the Bible that says Jesus cannot come and go as many times as He wishes in either the Old Testament days or today. He just does not stay here to start His reign, because it is not time yet. Understanding the purpose of His coming and going matters. Many people report Jesus has appeared in the Middle East over the past ten years, making believers when he visits. Theirs is a hazardous journey. But no matter how many believers are killed, Jesus will ensure there will always be more until God sends man a strong delusion on the earth.[56] Jesus will keep answering the prayers of those who want to know the Truth and coming and going as He wishes.

[8] *And prevailed not; neither was their place found any more in heaven.*

Satan and his fallen angels did not prevail, and their places in God the Father's heaven were forever taken from them, and the doors were shut.

Note 12: Sometime very near the signing of the Seven-year Treaty with Israel, which begins the Seven-year Tribulation period, Satan and his angels wage a massive war in the Father's realm and are no longer allowed there. The doors are closed and locked. This leads to a very "key" point concerning end-time prophecy. From here on Satan cannot accuse the brethren before God and His throne anymore. But Satan is not going to let Jesus come for His Bride without a fight. Either this fight in Revelation 12 is over the brethren being raised, the dead first, each in their own order, with the last caught up being those that are still alive,[57] or it is just Satan and his demons being kicked out of God's realm. If Satan is just getting kicked out, then there will be an even bigger fight later when Jesus comes for His Bride in the clouds. Imagine what an un-peaceful mess that wedding in the clouds would be if Jesus did not come for His Bride until the very end, and it was all done in the clouds just above the earth with Satan and all his angels there fighting with God's angels. Not much of a wedding environment, I would say. Scripture explains there is only one war in the heavens between God's angels and Satan's angels and Revelation 12 records it is happening before the beginning of the Seven-year Tribulation. There is a big war before Jesus comes to Earth to rule, and the "doors" in

---

56 2 Thess. 2:8–11
57 1 Thess. 4:14–16

God's part of heaven are shut because of it. Satan is cast to earth to prepare for the next war, Armageddon, that is not between angels but rather war between Jesus and his saints against the Antichrist and his armies of men on earth.[58]

Scripture records the Rapture occurring over some time, not in one instantaneous process. Apostle Paul says the dead, each in the order of the time of their death, are raised with their new incorruptible bodies. God will then, at the fullness of time, raise those who are still alive. Satan and his angels are not going to stand around and watch this happen. God's angels will powerfully hold off Satan's angels, allowing others of God's angels to take us up to our mansion in the Father's house. We do not know where we are going, but the assigned angel does. Next, the Bride of Christ is married and then returns to Earth at Armageddon on a white horse. Armageddon is not the only battle between God and Satan before everything is complete. There are three distinctly different wars to be considered. Working backward from the last to the first, the following are the key points to notice for each one.

Revelation 20 records the third and final war between God and Satan. It happens over one thousand years after Armageddon when Satan is let loose from the bottomless pit. This is the grand finale of the battles between God and evil. It ends with the White Throne Judgment by God that results in the second death. The three keys to this are (a) there are no more wars between God and Satan, (b) this war is on Earth, and (c) Satan is thrown into the Lake of Fire to be tormented for all eternity.

Revelation 19 details the second or middle war between God and Satan at Armageddon. The three keys to this war are (a) it is on the

---

58 Rev. 16:14–16

earth, not God the Father's heaven, (b) Satan no longer has any time left, (c) Satan is locked up in the bottomless pit for one thousand years.

Revelation 12 records the first war between God and Satan. The keys to this war are (a) Satan and his angels are locked out of only the Father's realm, (b) he still has some time left on Earth before banishment to the bottomless pit, and (c) Satan is allowed to be worshipped as God in the rebuilt Jerusalem Temple.

⁹ *And the great dragon was cast out, that old serpent, called the Devil, and Satan, which deceiveth the whole world: he was cast out into the earth, and his angels were cast out with him.*

Here Scripture is clarifying the identity of the great dragon. Among his many names are Devil, Satan, serpent, and his working title is the deceiver. He was cast down into the earth, and his angels were cast out with him. Satan is close to deceiving the entire world, but it should be clear the One World Order or New World Order has not happened yet. It cannot with the Bride of Christ still here working through the Holy Spirit. The following Verse 10 is powerful and locks this event into its position in the end times.

¹⁰ *And I heard a loud voice saying in heaven, Now is come salvation, and strength, and the kingdom of our God, and the power of his Christ: for the accuser of our brethren is cast down, which accused them before our God day and night.*

Now Satan can no longer go before God the Father to accuse the saints of the Bride of Christ. The doors of the Father's realm are shut, and Jesus has stepped out from His place to reign with His power over the earth.[59] The opening of the Seven Revelation Seals is imminent. His reign with the rod of iron has now begun, and He steps out from

---

59 Isa. 26:21

His throne to punish all the inhabitants of the earth who have rejected God's gift of Grace.

Note 13: This verse requires deep consideration. It is easier to start at the end and work backward to the beginning. It says day and night Satan "was" accusing the brothers in Christ before the throne of God the Father. Something causes Satan to be unable to do what he has done for thousands of years. At a minimum, this means Satan no longer has access to the third heaven. It is implausible to believe Satan, who was accusing the Bride-to-be day and night before God, was cast down to Earth and can no longer be their accuser; yet, somehow part of the Bride of Christ is still living on the earth through the Seven-year Tribulation period. If that were true, the Bride of Christ that is still alive would then be going through both the wrath of Satan's Antichrist as recorded in Revelation 12:17, and the Wrath of Christ poured out at the same time. God, then, would be treating some of the saints differently from others.

There are different dispensations for men over time. This verse uses "now" to mark the beginning of a different dispensation of God. He is now doing something different among men. God is treating His saints differently, depending upon the time period of their life. The casting down of Satan and the Seven Seals Judgments show that. It is now time for the Age of Judgment to begin and for Jesus to rule with a rod of iron. The Age of Judgment is also referred to as the "Day of the Lord," which includes the supernatural protection of Israel by God for the first three and one-half years and the two witnesses of Revelation 11. There is strong support in these verses of a Pre-Tribulation Rapture since God is now doing something different. He is not using the Bride of Christ with their Holy Spirit. Why? They are no longer on the earth.

The Seven-year Tribulation period on Earth is populated by lukewarm Christians and those against Christ. Those who catch on fire for Jesus and God's Truth, during this period will go through God's Wrath. Eventually, they will die for finally breaking free of the Antichrist and accepting Jesus as Lord. That outcome does not sound very kind, but God's eternity is very much worth dying for. God's final judgment is worse than we can imagine. The book of Revelation only scratches the surface of what will take place. For those who think Christ's salvation, strength, power, authority, etc. is already here, consider verses 10–12. It relates that will happen when Satan is cast out of God's heaven and down to Earth for a short time.

Scripture indicates Satan has already lost. However, his sentencing is yet to come and is not complete. Revelation 12:10 shows one more step in that process is now complete. *Now is come the power of Christ,* conveys Jesus finally is allowed to use His full Power. He uses it to cast Satan out of God's heaven to Earth. Jesus has had that full power since His death and resurrection. He cannot, however, do certain things until God the Father says it is time. When this happens, Jesus will come out of His place to exercise His wrath on Satan, the demonic angels, and all the men that follow them. God has stated His wrath during this time will be much worse; in fact, the worst ever. His wrath will be far greater than they saw in the days of Noah or Sodom and Gomorrah.

Jesus has completed the first steps in the salvation process. He is just waiting for His Father to say the keyword, "Go" to get His Bride for the wedding in the Father's house. That is when Satan will be kicked out of the Father's house forever and confined to Earth. The Seven Seals process begins, and Jesus is now reclaiming all that was lost by Adam and Eve in the garden about six-thousand years ago.

Revelation 12:10 also shows that when Satan is kicked out of

God's heaven, "Now Salvation" has come. Salvation, the deliverance from sin and its consequences is accomplished through the atoning sacrifice of Jesus. Christians have the fuller picture of God's Salvation for eternity.

A doctor, in the right place at the right time, can save us from death. As great as that is, it is only a temporary deliverance from physical death. God's Salvation is our eternal deliverance and destination. Eternal deliverance, the completion of God's salvation, is an act of God's Grace finishing what He started. He delivered His saints from their bondage to sin and condemnation, transferred them to the kingdom of His beloved Son Jesus, and has prepared new, incorruptible, perfected bodies to give them for their eternal life. Jesus' salvation is all about saving us from eternal death, a process to be completed when we have our new immortal bodies. It is a process that has a beginning, middle, and end. As an illustration, consider the process of placing an order for something online. It is a process with many steps. We do not instantly click the "Finish" button and have our package in our hands. All we have is the promise that the parcel will be in our hands, someday. That is just the beginning. The supplier has to pull the product from the shelf, then put it in a box, address the box, put it in the mail, and then it has to pass through the delivery system before ending up at our door. The process is still not completed until we open the box, verify contents, and make sure it is okay. Then and only then is the process one-hundred percent complete. Our salvation process is not through until we have received our new bodies.

Jesus' reign starts when Satan is cast down and has only a short time left. This salvation process for the Bride of Christ will not be completed before that time. The proof is found in the fact we do not have our new eternal bodies.[60] Once Jesus accounts for all of His Bride, His salvation for His Bride is complete, and a new dispensation starts with the beginning of the Age of Judgment. Those who live in the one-thousand-year reign of Jesus will not receive their new incorruptible bodies until the time of the White Throne Judgment. It is quite an involved process when viewed through man's eyes.

Since Revelation was written thirty-five to seventy years after the death and resurrection of Jesus, there was no reason for God to write Revelation the way He did if we were already in the time of Jesus' reign with a rod of iron. What is it then that triggers Jesus' reign with a rod of iron? Fortunately, God answers that question in Revelation 12:5–9. Jesus is caught up to His throne, and then the woman, Israel, flees to wilderness for three and one-half years. However, when Jesus was caught up to His throne, Israel never fled anywhere. In fact, they were still living in Israel and sacrificing in their Temple for about another forty years. Even when the Temple was destroyed, Israel was not protected for three and one-half years. They were overrun and dispersed until they became a nation again in 1948.

None of this has happened yet. We are all in a holding pattern waiting for God the Father to say "Now" and trigger Jesus' reign over the earth. None of us know the date and time of this event, but we do know the order of what happens. When the time comes, God, the Father, will tell Jesus to start. The process has many steps, during which Jesus directs everything piece by piece, during His rod of iron reign over the earth.

[11] *And they overcame him by the blood of the Lamb, and by the word of their testimony; and they loved not their lives unto the death.*

---

60 Romans 8:23; 1 Corinthians 15:52–53; 1 Peter 1:4–5, 23

The Bride of Christ overcame Satan by the blood of Jesus, who is the Lamb.

Note 14: They overcame Satan is in the past tense. So who are these who had overcome Satan? They are the Bride of Christ that just went up in the Rapture. They were the ones Satan had been accusing before God's throne day and night, and this verse talks about how they overcame Satan. Rather than living their lives for themselves, they had lived their lives for Christ by becoming fishers of men. The key to this verse is that it has to do with past tense believers, not future tense believers like those who will be coming out of the period of Jesus' one thousand year reign with His rod of iron. The very next verse, Revelation 12:12 confirms that the rapture has happened and the Church saints are rejoicing in the Father's house, but those left behind are in for a heap of trouble.

¹² *Therefore rejoice, ye heavens, and ye that dwell in them. Woe to the inhabiters of the earth and of the sea! for the devil is come down unto you, having great wrath, because he knoweth that he hath but a short time.*

Therefore rejoice, you saints, angels, and created beings in the heavens, but woe to those left behind on the earth and sea! The devil is sent down to Earth and is furious because he knows he has only seven years before being thrown into the bottomless pit for one thousand years.

Note 15: God devotes quite a few verses detailing the casting out of Satan to the earth in this chapter and gives more evidence of the time it happens and why. Verses 7, 9, 10, and 12 point out there was a war in the Father's heavenly realm, and Satan lost and now has been cast down to Earth to stay, although it is just a short time. During this war, Jesus is allowed to move in His power with a rod of iron, completing the salvation to His Bride. The Bride of Christ is complete with their new bodies and is rejoicing in heaven. The doors are shut behind them, so Satan and his demons cannot re-enter and cause trouble. While this verse says there is an enormous party in the heavens, it also warns, "woe" to those on the earth as the devil comes with great wrath knowing that he has a short time. That short time is the seven-year countdown to his "house arrest" in the bottomless pit for one thousand years. The time during those Seven Seal Judgments will be a rough time to be on Earth no matter who you are, and I do not wish that on anybody.

Note 16: Now, with the understanding of this unfolding sequence of events leading up to the Rapture, it is easy to understand there would not be very many nice people on the earth. That sets up the perfect situation for the Antichrist to lobby support from a group of likeminded individuals to get his New World Order in place. Those inhabiting the earth are now in the "Day of the Lord," which does not end until all powers and principalities are under Christ's feet after Satan's release from the pit and after the White Throne of Judgment. At that time, there is no more death, and Jesus can give the kingdom to God the Father.[61] We cannot know all the ins and outs of why God chose to do it this way. In 1 Corinthians 13:12, God reminds us we will only know in part until we see Him face to face.

[13] *And when the dragon saw that he was cast unto the earth, he persecuted the woman which brought forth the man child.*

When the dragon saw he was cast forever out of God the Father's heaven, unto the earth, he went to persecute the woman, Israel, who brought forth the Christ Jesus.

Note 17: Here, the Scripture tells when this dragon Satan saw he

---

61 1 Cor. 15:20–28

was cast down to the earth, he tried to persecute Israel. Because Jesus came from the Tribe of Judah, Satan hates Israel.

Replacement Theology, also known as Supersessionism, is the teaching that the Church has replaced Israel, so Israel has no place in future end times prophecy. It has been a tool of Satan's and used to damage believers' understanding of Scripture. Ideology like this happens when we do not read the word literally and use context around what is written to help our understanding. God has carefully worded Revelation. God knows the difference between Church and Israel, and never once does He say the Church has become Israel. Man has said that. Fortunately, since Israel became a nation again in 1948, churches have been unwinding the damages done by this wrongful theology. The Catholics started relaxing their position on this as part of the Vatican II, which closed under Pope Paul VI in December of 1965. There are hundreds of places in the Bible where God says He has not finished with Israel. Since Israel became a nation again, there has been less resistance to setting the record straight on the damages caused by Replacement Theology. Some of it still exists, so we must be vigilant and address it when we see it. Gentiles are grafted into the original Olive Tree and are not a completely new one that throws away the original.[62]

[14] *And to the woman were given two wings of a great eagle, that she might fly into the wilderness, into her place, where she is nourished for a time, and times, and half a time, from the face of the serpent.*

The descendants of the twelve tribes of Israel were given safety in her place, which is the land of Israel, where she is taken care of by God for three and one-half years, from the face of Satan, the serpent. The

---

62 Rom. 11:11–27

location of protection being Israel is confirmed by the freedom to worship and sacrifice in the Temple for three and one-half years, including protection provided by the two witnesses in Jerusalem (Revelation 11).

Note 18: A time, and times, and a half a time is another way of saying three and one-half years. It says here this woman, who is Israel, is taken care of for those three and one-half years. After signing the Seven-year Peace Treaty, Israel is allowed to rebuild the Temple and resume sacrificing to God there. The eagle, with its wings spread, is a symbol of protection as portrayed in God's Word. Recalling their rescue from Egypt, God tells the Israelites, *I bore you on eagles' wings and brought you to Myself.*[63] Where did God bring them in the exodus? The land of Israel. That is *her place*, and God is protecting them there for those first 1260 days. God didn't use anyone else then; He did it Himself. Only God can provide this sort of protection. As much as Satan and the Antichrist want them dead, they cannot be killed during those three and one-half years. Some teach the eagle represents America. While the eagle is a symbol for America, it has also been used for many countries, including the Roman Empire. Satan also knows what God wrote in the Bible, so he is going to do whatever he can to ensure the eagle symbol shows up and distracts Biblical readers from seeing what God is saying in Exodus 19:4. He is the one providing for Israel's protection. If that were not true, Satan would annihilate Israel and make a mockery of all Scripture.

Throughout history, only God has been Israel's protector. Hitler was being used by Satan to destroy Israel, but God moved, and Israel became a nation in a day, just as God had written long before He actually did it.[64] A pivotal point to understand is if Satan destroyed

---

63 Exod.19:4
64 Isa. 66:7–8

all of Israel's offspring, Biblical prophecy could never be fulfilled. It would also mean Jesus could not return and save the Tribe of Judah first, as recorded in Zechariah 12:7 so Satan would win. God will not let that happen.

Across history, Israel's, or Judean alliances with other countries never seem to work out very well. The time will come when Israel will not be able to count on the United States. This sobering fact is a future happening foretold in Zechariah 12:3: *though all nations of the earth are gathered against it.* All the nations mean "all." I get that Christians in the United States will find this difficult. Still, if you understand that the Rapture has already happened before the seven-year treaty with Israel, then it shouldn't be hard to understand why the U.S. is no longer standing with Israel.

15-16 *"And the serpent cast out of his mouth water as a flood after Israel, that he might cause her to be destroyed. And the earth helped the woman, and the earth opened her mouth, and swallowed up the flood which the dragon cast out of his mouth."*

God helped Israel, and the earth opened her mouth and swallowed up the flood which the dragon cast out of his mouth. Satan will try to harm Israel but will fail in the first half of the Seven-Year Peace Treaty, those one thousand two-hundred-sixty days as stated concerning the two witnesses. Yet, in the last half of the seven years, God will remove His protection from Israel, and it will be the time of Jacob's great trouble (Jeremiah 30). The Antichrist will break the Seven-Year Treaty in the middle of those years after the death of the two witnesses.

Note 19: Even though Satan knows God's written word, he persists in trying to come against God's plan. It is written that Satan has lost; he already knows it and is a sore loser. He made a valiant effort to stop the plan of salvation when he tempted Jesus in the wilderness. Just as that was futile, this attack against Israel will be pointless for the same reason, for "It Is Written" his efforts will fail. The two witnesses will be a daily reminder to Satan of this for that first three and one-half year period, but after that, Israel will be in serious trouble in the second three and one-half year period. This is similar to what happened with Jesus in the forty days of temptation in the wilderness. Satan saw it was futile to come against Jesus at that time, so he stopped trying and departed until an opportune time, which was a future Passover that ended at the cross. In Revelation 12, Satan tries to destroy Israel in those first three and one-half years, but it is written that he will fail, and he knows that, so, he stops trying and departs until the future opportune time. Scripture relates the opportune time starts with the death of the two witnesses in Revelation 11, as that marks the end of the three and one-half years of protection for Israel.

17 And the dragon was wroth with the woman, and went to make war with the remnant of her seed, which keep the commandments of God, and have the testimony of Jesus Christ.

The dragon was furious with Israel and went to make war with the remnant of her seed, who keep the commandments of God and have the testimony of Jesus Christ.

The one thousand two-hundred-sixty days of verse 14 very neatly dovetails with verse 6, the beginning of the Seven-year Tribulation events restating God will supernaturally protect Israel for that time period. There should be no mistaking that the verses in Revelation 12:6–7, address only the first three and one-half-year period of the seven years. The options are, either the woman being protected is Israel, or it is the Church. If Revelation 12:1–5 does not conclusively resolve which it is, Revelation 12:17 should.

While unbelieving Israel is protected from Satan during the first half of this period, anyone confessing Jesus as their Lord and grafted into the Olive Tree will not be protected during this time, as is stated in Revelation 12:17. This is additional strong evidence the Rapture of the Church, known as the Bride of Christ, has already happened, and they are in God the Father's house for the wedding. If this is not true, then God is not protecting the Church that would still be on earth waiting for the Rapture.

Note 20: Satan realizes he can't impact unbelieving Israel in the first three and a half years. He tries another approach by attempting to torment her offspring. Her offspring is a strange group, as they must have two precise requirements. The first is easy to understand; they have the testimony of Christ. This group also has to keep the commandments of God. That has never applied to the Bride of Christ; the Church, because they are under Grace.

Since the Bride has their new bodies and is in the third heaven getting married, then this group is a new and different dispensation in time. They are now in "the Day of the Lord" in the Age of Judgment. It is now when Jesus pours His wrath out through the Seven Seals upon unrepentant mankind. To put more weight on the side of the Bride of Christ being before the Father's throne for the Wedding Ceremony, you have to be married before you get to have a "wedding supper." So the Rapture crowd must be in their new bodies in the third heaven to be married. After the marriage, the wedding feast is held, usually in a different location. Mine was, and so it is with Jesus who comes to earth with His wife for the wedding supper. You do not have the wedding supper before the marriage, and this marriage is before the throne of God, the Father, according to Revelation 19. So Revelation 12:17 is a different group of people than those Raptured and married in the Father's house. A group that has to keep the "commandments" could apply to the one hundred forty-four thousand from the twelve Tribes of Israel, as listed in Revelation 7. All of them are descendants of Jacob, and God never said Israelites should stop observing the law as it applies to them. That includes the seven feasts we will all be celebrating as written during the one-thousand-year reign of Christ. It is comforting to know God does say most of the law should not be a burden to Gentiles.[65] He never once tells the people of Israel to stop doing what He commanded them to do. The Age of Grace ends with the Rapture, and the world enters the Age of Judgment. This point sheds light on why God is now saying this group is keeping the commandments.

In the Age of Grace, the people of Israel and Gentile believers are both covered by Grace. Nowhere in the New Testament does it say it is okay for Gentile believers to commit adultery, or kill, or lie, or cheat, or have something before God in their hearts, or take God's name in vain. All of these are in the law. However, Grace is above it all. Something which does not fit within the boundaries of the Age of Grace has been changed here in Revelation 12:17. These people have to follow the commandments of God plus have the testimony of Jesus. They must die for rejecting the beast and refusing to receive his mark on their foreheads or hands.[66] Those who live in the Age of Grace do not have any such requirements. Yes, it is good to do our best to follow what is written, but it is not a compulsory requirement. These are mandatory requirements for those raised up in the First Resurrection. If I died today, I would not fit any of the criteria of Revelation 20:4–6; neither would anyone who has died in Christ over the past two thousand years. The Scriptures give a strong warning not to add to or subtract from what God's Word says.

---

65 Acts 15:28
66 Rev. 20:4–6

The statement in verse 17 concerning the rest of the woman's offspring and the remnant of her seed is also very telling. Why is this not all of the woman's offspring? We know this remnant does have the testimony of Jesus. Why does it state this is just a remnant? Remnant means a small quantity of something much more significant. It is a residue of what it once was. For those that want to say the woman in verse 17 is the Church, then how is it the Church became a remnant? What happened to the rest of the Church? In the year 2015, the Church was estimated to have over two billion people, hardly a remnant or residue of anything. If the Church experiences the Rapture before the opening of the Seven Seals Judgments, then all that is left are the luke-warmers that were not ready. They would indeed be a remnant. Even adding the one hundred forty-four thousand from Revelation 7, this would still be a remnant.

In summary, this is about a time when the Church Age or Age of Grace is over. It is particularly apparent because the last verse of Revelation 12 addresses those "who keep the commandments of God." The Church is not under the law; it is under Grace. This verse reveals those in the Tribulation are keeping the commandments as stated in both Revelation 12:17 and 14:12. It is also clear they have additional requirements to be part of the first resurrection. Requirements no saint who has died in the past two thousand years can meet.

For Further Study

To invite you to understand what is in your eternity, The One True God is saying to you:

> *"Call to Me, and I will answer you, and show you great and mighty things, which you do not know."*
>
> —JEREMIAH 33:3

- Daniel 7:25; 9:25–27; 12:7; 11–12

- 2 Thessalonians 2

- The three wars between God and Satan – Revelation 12, 19, 20

- Revelation 12:8, 20:4–6; Isaiah 26; Zephaniah 2; Matthew 25; Luke 13:23–25; Luke 21:36

- 1 Thessalonians 1:10 and 5:8–10; Revelation 3:10; Isaiah 26:20–21; Zephaniah 2:2–3; Matthew 25:6–10; Luke 13:23–25, 21:36

- Revelation 19:7, 14–16, 19–21; Jude 1:14

- Revelation 12:7–17; 2 Thessalonians 2:4; Revelation 13:4

- 1 Corinthians 15:22–25; 1 Thessalonians 4; Revelation 21:1–5, 8

- Zechariah 12 – 14; Romans 11:25 – 29

- Luke 4

CHAPTER THIRTEEN

"THAT DAY" EXPLAINED

Two similar phrases used by the church today often can be confusing. The first, the "Lord's Day" refers to Sunday since it is the day of the week when Jesus rose from the dead. "The Day of the Lord," which sounds similar, refers to the day Jesus will come from His current heavenly position to start His Rule of Judgment with a rod of iron, and the nations will not be able to endure His indignation that is poured out. At that time, Jesus begins His rule over mankind. It starts with the opening of the Seven Seals and execution of the judgments, as documented in Revelation. It is a lengthy step-by-step process. Jesus' judgment and reign over man will never stop from that point forward. Men of the flesh, as we are today, still have free will to accept God and His divine plan for mankind, and evil will be dealt with swiftly. For the duration of His one-thousand-year reign from Jerusalem, it will be impossible for thefts, muggings, or worse to be perpetrated, because God knows the instant anyone thinks up evil and puts an immediate stop to it. There will finally be real and complete peace in Jerusalem. Many pray for the peace of Jerusalem, not realizing they are praying for the Messiah Jesus to return to Jerusalem and start His reign from there. Until then, there is no true peace anywhere, especially in Jerusalem.

Understanding the term "Day of the Lord" is an integral part of understanding end times prophecy. There are hundreds of places in Scripture identifying "the Day of the Lord" or "the Day of the Lord's

Anger" or "that day" as the time when Jesus comes out of His place to pour out God's wrath and start His reign over the earth. The Lord's reign does not begin when He reaches the Mount of Olives; it commences when He starts to open the Seven Seals as described in Revelation.

Studying Scripture with an awareness of the context will bring a deeper understanding of the time frame God is talking about when He says "the Day of the Lord," or in "that day," or "the Day of Wrath." Of course, "that day" could also reference a specific single day, so you have to look at the context around the verse to understand the intended meaning.

It is your eternity, but you must understand this if you are going to study and talk about end-time prophecy. Grasping what time "that day" usually refers to will make end times much simpler to understand.

> Alas! For that day is great, So that none is like it; And it is the time of Jacob's trouble, But he shall be saved out of it 'For it shall come to pass in that day' Says the LORD of hosts, 'That I will break his yoke from your neck, And will burst your bonds; Foreigners shall no more enslave them. But they shall serve the LORD their God, And David their king, Whom I will raise up for them. 'Therefore do not fear, O My servant Jacob,' says the LORD, 'Nor be dismayed, O Israel; For behold, I will save you from afar, And your seed from the land of their captivity. Jacob shall return, have rest and be quiet, And no one shall make him afraid. For I am with you,' says the LORD, 'to save you; Though I make a full end of all nations where I have scattered you, Yet I will not make a complete end of you. But I will correct you in justice, and will not let you go altogether unpunished."

In "that day" includes the time of Jacob or Israel's great trouble. Reading Jeremiah 30:7–11, the above Scripture, in context, reveals several things that are happening in "that day." First, there is a time of great trouble like nothing man has ever experienced. In the history of man, there was Noah's flood, and focusing just on Israel, there were the two destructions of Jerusalem and the Temple. Those were times of dire trouble, particularly for Israel. The last time, in "that day," will be even worse. Placing "that day" in time relative to the context of the verses around it means it is a future event. God says Jacob, or Israel, will be saved out of it, and David will be their King. David had been dead for hundreds of years when Jeremiah wrote his book. Obviously, there will come a future time when King David will be raised from the dead and be King over Israel again on *that day*. Not only that, but Israel will be returned to the land with total rest when God will make a "full end" of "all the nations." By combining all of these events, it becomes clear the particular "day" spoken of has yet to happen. "That day" also contains a time identified to be God's judgments coming down on both the nation of Israel and all the nations, yet this time will be a time of total peace, rest, and quiet for all. Somehow, both judgment and peace exist "on that day." To accomplish that, Jesus must have started His reign over the men of the earth with His rod of iron.

It is referred to as "the Day of the Lord" or "that day" since from then onward, Jesus reigns forever over all the affairs of man. Some teach He currently is reigning over all. Since sin still abounds untethered on the earth, He is not. In a sense, He is ruler over all things because He will judge all for what they have done in the flesh, but God is not yet "forcing" His rule on the earth with a "rod of iron."

From another perspective, when we pray the Lord's Prayer, *Your kingdom come, Your will be done on earth as it is in heaven,* we are praying for the day when things on earth will be like they already are in God's heaven. Evil is not allowed to happen there, but that is not true on Earth today. God says the time will come when evil will no longer happen on Earth. It is often a challenge to understand why Satan is still allowed to accuse the saints before the throne of God in heaven. Unfortunately, all saints are sinners, and Satan is repeating actual activity before God. While I cannot explain why God tolerates Satan in this way, I know Satan can accomplish no evil in God's heaven. God had written all of this in His plan before He created the heavens and the earth. His plan does tolerate Satan and his evil on the earth for a while. The good news is God writes that He shall eventually put an end to it.

God has laid everything out a specific way, and Jesus is not going to come for His Bride, nor open the Seven Seals until an explicit future time. It is a process happening one step at a time, and there is much more at play in all of this than we know. Scripture tells us Jesus has overcome death and Satan. Satan and his demonic beings, however, are still doing what they have always done. Additionally, Satan gets to be worshipped as God in the Third Temple that is about to be built in Jerusalem. If that isn't disturbing enough, consider that after Jesus throws Satan into the bottomless pit for one thousand years, God then lets him back out for a time to deceive those men of the flesh that have had total peace for one thousand years.

Someday we will know in full why God tolerated Satan for so long. In the meantime, we need to understand that all of this is a long process relative to the years of men, and it must happen precisely as it was predestined before the creation. Revelation 12:6–10 proves this point. Verse ten is particularly helpful, stating, *Now is come salvation, and strength, and the kingdom of our God, and the power of his Christ.*

172

It does not put Salvation-Strength-Kingdom-Power of Christ at his resurrection. Those all come together in perfect completion in "the Day of the Lord" or "That Day," which starts with the Seven Seals being opened. We know this because it is that time when Satan is cast out of God's third heaven to Earth, realizes he has but a short time, and can no longer accuse the brethren before the Throne of the Father. In this, it is revealed the process of bringing the Kingdom of Christ back on Earth has yet to be complete.

It reminds me a bit of the US judicial system. If a serious capital crime is committed, and the guilty person is eventually arrested, they do not go straight to execution. They are arrested and in time are put on trial. Eventually, they are found guilty, but then sentencing has to be determined. Once sentencing is determined, they go to "death row." They are still very much alive and can stay that way for many years. At some point, they may be executed, and then the whole process is finally completed. God's plan for dealing with man's sin is also a long process, and it is not yet complete. It will be completed after the Great White Throne judgment is accomplished. The Apostle Paul writes in 1 Corinthians 15:24–26 that Jesus must reign until He has put all enemies under His feet. As of today, Jesus has overcome, but not all enemies are under His feet. It is a process, and there are more steps to take. God doesn't miss any details.

Zechariah 13 reveals more details about "that day." *In that day a fountain shall be opened for the house of David and for the inhabitants of Jerusalem, for sin and for uncleanness. "Awake, O sword, against My Shepherd, Against the Man who is My Companion, Says the LORD of hosts. Strike the Shepherd, And the sheep will be scattered; Then I will turn My hand against the little ones. And it shall come to pass in all the land, Says the LORD, "That two-thirds in it shall be cut off and die,*

But one-third shall be left in it. Verse one identifies Jerusalem, and verses 7–9 state two-thirds of the people there will die. In this chapter, "in that day" is mentioned three times. It is mentioned sixteen times in Zechariah 12–14. God must have had a reason to write the Bible this way, through many different men over thousands of years. **If** not, then there is no reason to call out in "that day" as if it was something different. If it is different, we need to take note of it. It is unique that the references to "that day" either seem to mean that very day, a particular day in the past or future, or a specific period that relates to the Age of Judgment.

I know what many are thinking, that we are all one in Christ, and there is no such thing as different periods or dispensations. Please consider John 10:15–26, which records Jesus saying He will lay His life down for His sheep and that He has "other" sheep, which are "not" of this fold. Jesus is talking to His disciples and saying He has other "folds" of sheep, and that He will combine them all into "one flock" and He will then be their one Shepard. Why? Because it was written, there would be different dispensations over time, and the Bible does show us that. The Old Testament saints are the "wife" married to the Father. They are a different flock than those of us who have yet to be married to Jesus as part of the Bride of Christ Rapture event. After the marriage of the Church saints with Jesus, He will return to Jerusalem for the one-thousand years of complete peace on Earth. The people of the flesh who are alive when Jesus comes back will repopulate the earth during those one-thousand years. That is after the marriage of the Church to Jesus, so they too are of a different flock or fold. How can they not be different when they can walk up to and talk with Jesus directly? After the Great White Throne Judgment, we will all become one in Jesus just as John 10:16 proclaims. God's plan to deal with sin has never changed, and His plan includes Satan and the fallen angels. Mere men cannot comprehend the magnitude of man's sin or God's eternal plan.

Studying all the Scripture reveals there are different periods when God deals differently with people. Before Moses, there was a time where there was no Law. Then once the Law was given to Moses, there was a "different time," the Age of the Law. The Age of Grace or Church Age with the Holy Spirit was next. The coming "different time period," the Age of Judgment or Jesus Millennial Reign will begin when He comes from His place in heaven and reigns with a "rod of iron." This age will include the one-thousand years of peace from Jerusalem.

We gain a new understanding by considering where we go after death. In the Scriptural account of Samuel's spirit coming to speak to King Saul, it is related he was raised "up." He did not descend from anywhere.[67] If there is no such thing as different dispensations, then all men who die go down to the place of rest just as Samuel did. That means even Christians, in death, go down to where Samuel and the other Old Testament saints have gone. Nobody goes to the Father's heaven where Jesus is, because God never changes. This means anyone who believes in a Post-Tribulation Rapture, where we all go up in the clouds above the earth and come straight back down for one thousand years, never goes up to the Father's heaven to the mansions Jesus promised to make for us. Why? Because God never changes, and we are treated the same way the Old Testament saints were. I hope you can see the error in this. It is hypocritical to say there is no such thing as different dispensations and then turn around and say New Testament saints are treated differently than Old Testament saints and

_____

67 1 Sam. 28:11–15

175

get to go to the Father's heaven upon death. Yes, in death, we all go to be with the Lord, but please consider where that is.

Both Samuel[68] and Lazarus[69] went down to Abraham's Bosom. Jesus and one of the criminals that died with Him also went down to the same place, which is also referred to as Paradise.[70] God has complete control of both the good and bad side of Hell. So, in these three cases, we can see that when those on God's team die, we all go to be with God in Paradise until we are raised with our new incorruptible bodies. This explanation shows why Jesus did not raise all the saints with His resurrection from the dead in Matthew 27:52.

Discerning the difference in the "Lord's Day," and the "Day of the Lord" is huge when it comes to end times prophecy, and yet it is often misunderstood. The vital thing to consider in all of this is if the Rapture event really is the Pre-Tribulation version, our focus needs to be spending time and resources on getting the Good News out to all people, nations, tongues; not building and supplying compounds to survive seven years. I never understood the mindset to acquire and stock up a compound to make it through God's Seven Seals of wrath. God is going to provide for me and my house from "His wrath that is to come," as He states. Are we not supposed to turn to God, who has numbered our days, rather than act in fear of man and what is coming? As for me and my house, we expect God to provide manna and protection should we need it. We believe there is nothing He cannot do, and our trust is in Him, not man.

One last point on this is that I could spend all my money and time on building and supplying a compound to survive those seven years,

68 1 Sam.28:8–20
69 Luke 16:19–31
70 Luke 23:43

and God's Tribulation may not happen for one hundred years. What then does that say about me and how I handled what God gave me to help me be a fisher of men? My family has the basics for a few weeks of emergency needs but sees no need to work excessively, saving money to spend on a compound safe-haven, food, bullets, and other supplies. We are "all in," putting our time, effort, and money into being fishers of men every day. Getting the Good News out using the skills God has given us keeps us prepared and focused on "that day" whenever God sets it in motion. My wife and I are passing down this belief to our children and hopefully all our following generations, until "that day" does come. What if "that day" doesn't come for 50–200 years or more. What happens to that compound, food, bullets, and other supplies? A couple of qualifiers are that there is nothing wrong with having a thirty-day supply of items for an emergency or if you believe God has told you to store up certain things as Joseph did for the seven lean years in Egypt.

There is tremendous detail in Zechariah about what the end times, "that day" will hold. Jesus touches the earth first to save the tents of Judah at Jerusalem. The Word of God clearly shows Jesus will come back to the place of His ascension, the Mount of Olives, to save the tribe of Judah, not the Church or Ruben or Levi or Gad.[71] Jesus questions if He will "really find faith on the earth" when He comes back.[72] If the Church is still here, it must be in seriously pathetic shape. I cannot say this enough, "if it makes clear sense, do not look for any other sense, lest you turn it into non-sense." It's Your eternity, not anyone else's. Take the time, pray, and put in the effort. Whether God has given you one skill or five, God knows what He gave you,

---

71 Acts 1:9–11
72 Luke 18:8

and He is not asking you to do more than what He has given you. Be encouraged, and ask Him for help. He does not force the issue; He waits for us to ask, and to put in the effort. Waiting and patience are major traits of God. If we want to be more like Him, we should work on waiting and having the patience to receive His answers, rather than run off with "itchy" ears.

For Further Study

To invite you to understand what is in your eternity, The One True God is saying to you:

> *"Call to Me, and I will answer you, and show you*
> *great and mighty things, which you do not know."*
>
> —JEREMIAH 33:3

- Perform an electronic Biblical search for "that day" and "in that day"

- Isaiah: 19:23–34, 24:21–23, 26:21, 27:1–13, 65:19–25, 34:1–2, 8

- Zephaniah: 1:14–18, 2:2–3, 13:2, 14, 3:8

- Zechariah 12–14

- Luke 16:19–31

- Acts 2:20

- 1 Thessalonians 5:2

- 2 Peter 3:10

- Ephesians 1:10, 3:2

- Revelation 2:27, 12:5, 14:9–10 and 19:15; Isaiah 11:4, 26:21–27:1; Jeremiah 10:10–11

CHAPTER FOURTEEN

ANTICHRIST, RAPTURE, MILLENNIUM

There are some end-time traps to avoid and many vital elements to study and understand, including the terms "Rapture" and "the Millennium." However, a prominent question needing to be explored is, "Who is the Antichrist?" which for now, is an open-ended question. God wants us to be aware of him and gave Scriptures with great detail about his role and information about his background. We will begin by exploring his characteristics.

Some suggest this man could not come from one of the twelve tribes of Jacob. That is dangerous, in my opinion. I can hear the "powers to be" exclaim to one and all that the person who becomes the head of the "One World Order" is not the Antichrist because he is a descendant of Abraham-Isaac-Jacob. Therefore, they might teach it is safe to worship him as the Messiah and to take his mark, "The mark of the beast," on the right hand or forehead. There is no Scripture, to my knowledge, stating the Antichrist absolutely shall not come from one of the tribes of Jacob. However, there is sufficient Scripture to allude to the tribe of Dan. It is not my opinion the Antichrist has to come from the tribe of Dan; however, a study of these Scriptures does point to the possibility that it could happen.

I am come in my Father's name, and ye receive me not: if another shall come in his own name, him ye will receive.

This statement by Jesus in John 5:43 indicates His people will reject Him, but they will accept another. He was speaking this to His Israelite brethren; He rarely talked to any Gentiles. The original Church was of Israelite descent and did not go out to the Gentiles until Peter was sent to the Gentile Cornelius after Jesus' ascension.[73] Because they knew God's prophecies, the only way Israel would accept the Antichrist as God would be if he were able to prove he was, in fact, one of them.

The Tribes of Dan and Ephraim were part of the original twelve tribes owning land in Israel; however, in the New Testament, there is no mention of the Tribe of Dan or Ephraim. The only mention of Ephraim is of a city named Ephraim, not the tribe of Ephraim. The twelve tribes mentioned in Revelation 7 include Manasseh and Joseph as two of the twelve tribes that make up the one hundred forty-four thousand chosen by God to witness in the tribulation period. Neither Dan nor Ephraim are listed. Why has God eliminated them? Are they no longer considered to be part of the twelve tribes? What the Bible does say is they believed, early on, in idols. Dan, in particular, is called a serpent, and we know God uses that term for Satan. Dan is condemned in Jacob's dying prophecy over him, found in Genesis 49.

And Jacob called unto his sons, and said, Gather yourselves together, that I may tell you that which shall befall you in the last days. Dan shall judge his people, as one of the tribes of Israel. Dan shall be a serpent by the way, an adder in the path, that biteth the horse heels, so that his rider shall fall backward. I have waited for thy salvation, O LORD.

Several things are going on here. Jacob's prophecy deals with the last days, which are far removed from Samson. "Dan shall judge

---

73 Acts 10

his people," and the only time that might have occurred was with Samson. There are, however, problems with that. There was nothing subtle about Samson or his approach. He was not the cunning type, an adder in the path, nipping at the horse heels to cause the rider to fall. However, this description does describe the attributes of the Antichrist. I have never seen God use the term serpent as anything other than Satan or the evil works of Satan. So, the statement Dan shall be a serpent implies Satan shall lead this leader from Dan, and that does not fit the accurate account of Samson, either. He was a bit careless and carefree towards life, but he was not a follower of Satan. In his death, he called out to God to strengthen him one more time to pay back the Philistines. Samson's supernatural strength came from God, and Samson did not lead Israel into satanic worship. Because of Jacob's prophetic words over Dan, the flag of Dan included a serpent, whereas the tribe of Judah had a lion. Also, to consider is the prophecy found in Jeremiah 8:15–20 that is yet to be fulfilled.

We looked for peace, but no good came; And for a time of health, and there was trouble! The snorting of His horses was heard from Dan. The whole land trembled at the sound of the neighing of His strong ones; for they have come and devoured the land and all that is in it, the city and those who dwell in it. For behold, I will send serpents among you, vipers which cannot be charmed, and they shall bite you, says the Lord. I would comfort myself in sorrow; my heart is faint in me. Listen! The voice, the cry of the daughter of my people from a far country: "Is not the Lord in Zion? Is not her King in her? Why have they provoked Me to anger With their carved images - With foreign idols? The harvest is past, the summer is ended, and we are not saved! Key points in this piece are: (1) Israel looked for peace, but there was no peace. (2) The whole land trembled at the sound of the horses from Dan. (3) Dan came to devour the land and all that is in it. (4) God says He will send serpents, and Dan is the tribe of serpents. (5) God asks, "Why have they provoked Me to anger?" and we know the Seven-Year Tribulation period is God's anger poured out on mankind, and more specifically, the last three and one-half years are the time of Jacob's great trouble. (6) The harvest is past, and this group of Israelites has missed the harvest. This Scripture indicates the Rapture has occurred. If not the Rapture, then what harvest have they missed? (7) This sequence ends with "we are not saved!" which is quite an admission that something terrible from Dan is attacking them, and it is after the harvest they missed, and they are not saved because of that. This is a good description of Antichrist's behavior and the fulfillment of Jacob's prophecy over his son Dan from Genesis 49:16–18. God wants us to have enough information about the Antichrist that we can be watchful in the end days. The Antichrist will be a descendant of the people who destroyed Jerusalem and the Temple. He may or may not come from the tribes of Israel, as we have covered. Daniel 9:26 and Revelation 12:5 assert he will not put in an appearance until after Jesus is killed and raised to the throne of God.

Scripture recounts only two destructions of Jerusalem and the Temple. One was by Babylon and the other under the leadership of Titus, whose father was the Emperor of Rome at the time. It is plausible the Israelites would refer to Rome as Babylon back in the day of the Apostles and early church. In 1 Peter 5:13, Peter calls a city of his time, Babylon, but the original Babylon did not exist then. What city is he referring too? Peter says, "*She who is in Babylon greets you as does Mark my son.* Some versions translate "she" to "your re is more work to do here. ered "w Kingin fact something else, you can, but wlly back in the mid-1990s. Just went tundion sister church here in Babylon" or "the church in Babylon." This difference in translation happens because there are two slightly different Greek texts for the New Testament. The older versions, like King James Version, based their translations on the "Textus Receptus" while the newer versions used the "Nestle-Aland." One includes the Greek word "ekklesia" that is translated as "church," while the other does not. I claim no expertise in Greek, but in this case, it shouldn't matter as we see Peter has written a letter in which he is calling the place where he's located "Babylon." What city, other than Rome, could Apostle Peter have been writing from that would be worthy of being called "Babylon"?

The only city in Jewish history worthy of being compared to and called Babylon was Rome. Parallel events show their similarities. Both ruled over the twelve Tribes of Israel, and both destroyed Jerusalem and the Temple. Apostle, Peter, was not the only one to call Rome, "Babylon." Early church fathers like Tertullian, Irenaeus, and Jerome did, too. Why is this important? Well, the early Church fathers did their best to follow in the footsteps and teachings of the Apostles. They knew Peter and others referred to Rome as Babylon.

In the mid-1990s, I was discussing Biblical prophecy with someone over the internet. I had never met this person, but he accused me of parroting some of C.I. Scofield's positions and said to me, "Those positions were not what the Early Church fathers taught." I was caught off-guard since I had no idea who Scofield was and had never gone around reading commentaries or other's work. I was reading the Bible and getting visions along the way. I thought I was reading and saying things that were quite clear to anyone who read the Bible. I had no idea how confusing end times prophecy had become over the centuries, and I had no idea what the early church fathers taught. As it turned out, neither did he. He threw that out as a standard reflex action when he disagreed with someone. Of course, for me, it was game on. Who were those early Church guys, and what did they teach?

I started rummaging around the internet by asking who the early church fathers were and started reading some of their writings. Names like Josephus, not a church father but an early historian, Papias, Polycarp, and Irenaeus, came up. I was specifically looking for people who lived within one hundred years of the Apostles, as I know how quickly man can make stuff up and contradict the Bible. That was true in the days of the Apostles, too. Many of the New Testament writings were about dealing with false teachings in their day. The great thing today is the internet allows us to find information the average person otherwise could not access. Even back in the early 1980s, this would have been tough. Now it is easy to search, find, and sort through. I quickly realized the man I was communicating with over email did not know anything more than I did. Since iron sharpens iron, I began sending him writings from great men of the faith like Papias, Polycarp, and Irenaeus. He then began to do the same. We both learned a lot from that exchange. When we started, we just wanted to determine God's Truth as best we could. During our exchange of ideas, we reached a common ground; he now saw the Pre-Tribulation Rapture as I did. I am grateful for the exchange and how it helped me better understand God's Bible. Proverbs 27:17 encourages us with, *Iron sharpens iron, and so, a man sharpens the countenance of his friend.*

The lessons from the Patristic Fathers of our faith shed light on the mindset of the Apostles. In this instance, they identify Rome as Mystery Babylon. By using the Bible to interpret the Bible, Mystery Babylon can be interpreted as either the original Babylon or the city where Apostle Paul was. Since Babylon had fallen long before the time the Apostle Peter was writing this letter, he couldn't have been writing from the original Babylon.

Why would God call that city a mystery? After two thousand years, people no longer thought Israel would become a nation again. In 1948 when it was re-established, a mystery was fulfilled. Scripture referring to Israel becoming a nation again and sacrificing in their rebuilt temple was mysterious indeed. With the fall of the Roman Empire thousands of years ago, it seems that Rome becoming the hub for the start of the Antichrist's world rule is just as much a mystery.

The Antichrist initially starts from the city on the seven hills. However, there is only one place where the Antichrist can be worshiped as "God." That location has to be Jerusalem, where the Messiah, Jesus, will eventually rule for one-thousand years. For the Antichrist to claim he is God, people must worship him from the Holy of Holies in the Third Temple. So, the Antichrist will eventually move from Rome or Mystery Babylon. He will then establish himself in Jerusalem. When he does that, the Antichrist will turn his back on Mystery Babylon and shut it down. This will be necessary so all mankind will look to him at the Temple and Jerusalem. Satan knows he cannot rule and be worshipped by all as God from anywhere else. Competition from another city as the heartbeat of the world will not be tolerated, and the Antichrist will destroy Rome. Satan is a user, and when he no longer has a use for something or someone, he ravages them. It is at the core of his nature and what he always does.

Studying Revelation requires an understanding of the meaning of prostitution between man and God. We know what it means in purely physical terms. Between God and man, however, it has to do with whatever is first in a person's heart. The ideal is to have God and Jesus at the forefront of your heart. A person forsaking God in their heart has gone whoring after the ways of the world. Galatians 5:19–21 provides a list of the ways of the world; false gods, money, power, false accusations against God and His people, murder, selfish ambitions, sorcery, drunkenness. Believers can use this Scripture to take inventory of what is in their hearts.

The woman is referred to as the "mother" of many other harlots in Revelation 17:5. This woman is the primary harlot of the world's system that is against everything pertaining to God. The power of the beast fuels this lead city. When the mother, Mystery Babylon, is taken down, the world's system is also taken down. The satanic beast carrying and supporting the woman and her world system turns on the woman and destroys her. That action focuses all attention on the Antichrist being worshipped as God from the rebuilt temple in Jerusalem. That is the Antichrist's end objective. From Revelation 13:1–4, we know the beast is Satan's puppet. The merchants of the earth weep having lost their great riches, and they all see the smoke of that city burning. In our era, it is not surprising that everyone on Earth can see the smoke rising. TV news channels cover destruction and show the scenes over and over, making sure the world sees.

Key points:

- The woman, Mystery Babylon, is the lead governing city of that One World Order.

- The woman is the mother of harlots because absolutely nothing about her honors God.

- The woman has many cities, throughout the world, over many waters, not just the Atlantic or Mediterranean, following her lead and direction.

- Satan dwells in the beast leading the world.

- Eventually, through the Antichrist, Satan does what he always does and turns on his own, when he no longer needs them.

- The Antichrist must turn on Mystery Babylon since he is being worshipped as God from the Temple in Jerusalem. All eyes need to be on him at Jerusalem, and destroying Mystery Babylon accomplishes that.

Understanding that the woman is a great city running the world's anti-God trade system throughout cities around the world is a good start. Now we need to discuss the beast and its seven heads. He is described as being seven kings in Revelation 17:9–11. These seven kings are referred to as a beast because all of them are being manipulated and controlled by Satan. There is nothing good about them, and their reigns over the world system are beastly indeed. A few empires fitting the description found in the Bible are Egypt, the original Babylon under Nebuchadnezzar, Medo Persian, Greek, and Roman Empires. They all operate with complete control and power over multitudes, nations, people, and languages. While they were not as entirely global as we understand the world today, the next one will indeed be global.

The beast's seven heads are also referred to as mountains. To get to the top and rule their world, these kings had Satan's help to climb a mountain of obstacles. These seven mountains may or may not have a single city on top of seven mountains. Further investigation helps bring an understanding of what is meant. From Scripture we see the Tower of Babel, Abraham and Isaac on Moriah, Jacob and Mount Gilead, Moses and the burning bush; we know the Israelite Temple was built on Mount Moriah, and places of higher elevation are significant to God. Jesus ascended to heaven from the summit of the Mount of Olives. Mountains represent more than just mountains, and here in Revelation 17, we find they can point to a significant city, the ruling city.

There is also specific detail about the city he will come from in Revelation 17:9, 18. The place is described as being on seven hills. Interestingly, both Rome and Vatican City inside Rome seem to fit that depiction. The area in Revelation 17:9 is built or seated on seven hills. Many towns may have hills surrounding them, but they were not constructed on them. Any city discussed here must be built on the hills. This description seems to perfectly describe Rome, not a city built in a flat valley or plain that happens to have hills near. If you travel to Rome, you can even take the Rome Seven Hills Tour.

There are mountains, and then there are huge mountains. The mountains in Israel look like small hills when compared to the tallest peaks in the world, which reach up to twenty-six thousand feet. Mount Moriah is more like a small hill with a peak of around four hundred feet above the lowest point in Jerusalem and only about twenty-five hundred feet above sea level. The Greek word "oros" is translated as a mountain in this Scripture, and some get caught up in the fact that Rome's hills are not really mountains. The point is then made that Rome is not a city built on seven mountains. The lowest elevation in Rome is around sixty-six feet, and its highest point about four hundred and fifty feet making the difference between the lowest elevation at Jerusalem and Rome relative to their highest elevation about four hundred to six hundred feet. Using Scripture, we find God referred to mountains in this area, i.e., Mount Zion, Mount Moriah, etc., and they were no taller above the city than those in Rome. Who are we to question God concerning hills or mountains?

Using Scripture to interpret Scripture, Daniel adds content about the beast's seven heads and seven mountains by revealing these empires do not exist at the same time. The woman sits on them one at a time, and there is one yet to be fulfilled. She is also the ruling city of man's system, not God's. God is not the mother of harlots. The beast has seven heads that are mountains, which means heads and mountains are interchangeable. Satan will lead man into seven different world powers. The mother of harlots is the great city ruling over each of these satanically controlled empires which have kings. Also, verses ten and eleven say five of these seven kings have died, and the sixth king was in power at the writing of the Book of Revelation. Verse 11 is a bit confusing and may not make sense until the Antichrist is revealed, but we are told the last king is the eighth of the seven. We can speculate that hereditarily he is from one of the seven kings. It could be a reference to the fact the seventh king, ruling during the Seven Year Tribulation, dies but is miraculously brought back to life by Satan as recorded in Revelation 13. That would make him the seventh and eighth king unless he has a clone that is substituted for him. There is no definitive answer, and speculation is always discouraged. These are illustrative scenarios intended to get you to be aware and think for yourself.

God's wrath against false religion will reach all people no matter where they hide. God's Wrath is not the same as Satan's wrath. The church will face tribulation from Satan every day we are here on the earth, but we will be protected from God's wrath as it is released in Revelation's 7 Seals, Trumpets, and Vials. In Isaiah 2:2–3 and Micah 4:1–2, God states the Lord's House shall be established on a mountain and be head of all the mountains and exalted above all the hills. God equates the city of Jerusalem to the ruling mountain. Satan is set loose after the one-thousand years and leads one more rebellion against God and the Holy City, but Jesus is ruling the entire time with a rod of iron, and we know who wins. Revelation 17 is very consistent with God's terminology elsewhere in the Bible. In the Scripture from Isaiah and Micah, Jesus is the King ruling from the top of a mountain and the city of Jerusalem. He rules with a rod of iron, over the entire world, all the other cities on Earth, all peoples, nations, and tongues.

From Daniel 9:26–27, we learn the following about the destroying army of Jerusalem and the Second Temple in AD 70:

1. Those considered regulars in the army were Romans, but volunteers from nearby kings joined the regulars, as did some paid mercenaries.

2. The war orders came from Rome, and without these orders from Rome, there would have been no destruction of Jerusalem and Temple.

3. The fighting forces and plans were directed by the Roman Commander Titus, no one else. Titus eventually became emperor of the Roman Empire.

4. To minimize casualties, Titus sent the Israelite historian Josephus to calm down the Jerusalem fighters. Josephus' writings very clearly identified the Jewish rebellion was against the Romans. The enemy was Rome, and no one else.

5. All the spoils of war were carried off to Rome by the winner.

6. Nero died before Jerusalem, and the Temple had been destroyed, so, Nero is not the Antichrist of all antichrists.

   a. Nero committed suicide in AD 68 and was followed by Galba, Otho, and Vitellius before the accession of Vespasian in AD 69.

b.   Vespasian, who was emperor when Jerusalem and the Second Temple were destroyed by his son Titus, died in AD 79. He was succeeded by Commander Titus, his natural son

c.   No one stood in the Temple and declared themselves as God, much less made the entire world worship him as God. Keep in mind that Titus did not become emperor until AD 79, 9 years after his destruction of Jerusalem and the temple in AD 70. So, there is no way Titus could have done anything in fulfillment of Daniel's seven years of Tribulation.

7.   The Roman Emperor at the time of the Second Temple's destruction was Vespasian, the father of Titus, and he would have had to be in the Temple and declared as God from the Temple. Yet, none of this happened, and anyone saying this fulfilled prophecies in Revelation should reconsider their position.

8.   Peter spent much time at the Church of Rome and referred to Rome as Babylon.

9.   Bishop Irenaeus and other early Church Fathers identify Rome as the Mystery Babylon.

10. If you are wondering why Peter and others would refer to Rome as Babylon, keep in mind the people of Israel were forced to serve under two different nations. One was Babylon for about seventy years, and the other was Rome. Both empires destroyed Jerusalem and the Temple, the only two times in history that has happened. It is also quite probable that to openly

talk or write bad things about Rome led to a reprimand, arrest, or even death. So, it is quite understandable they used a code name, Babylon, meaning Rome.

11.   Daniel 2:31–45 records Nebuchadnezzar's dream of a statue representing four kingdoms, which were shown to be Gold, Silver, Bronze, and Iron. Nebuchadnezzar's kingdom was gold and the first. The fourth and last kingdom is identified as iron in verse 40. The four kingdoms start at the head and finish at the feet. The fourth kingdom had ten toes mixed with clay, so it was the weakest point of the four kingdoms. Verses 44–45 say the Messiah, Jesus, will strike the iron with clay and destroy it. His new kingdom shall never be destroyed, and it will consume the four kingdoms of gold, silver, bronze, and iron with clay.

a.   Studying Daniel 2 removes any debate about how many kingdoms will rule the world. Starting with Nebuchadnezzar, there have been only four kingdoms that have ruled over many nations, tongues, and tribes.

b.   I do not think there is any debate the Roman Empire is the statue's fourth kingdom. Interestingly, all four kingdoms are to be replaced in succession by the next; yet the fourth has not been replaced by the fifth kingdom. The fourth, the Roman Empire, was never destroyed and replaced by a new kingdom that ruled over all peoples, nations, tribes, and tongues. So, this fourth kingdom is somewhat of a mystery as it destroys Jerusalem and the second temple but is not succeeded by the next kingdom. We know it is to be defeated by "the stone cut without hands," which is referring to Jesus. Somehow the Roman Empire does not exist, but it will when Jesus returns to destroy it. This reminds me of Israel ceasing to exist around AD 70, and then (poof) it becomes a nation again in AD 1948. It seems the same will be true of the Roman Empire in these last days. Poof, it will resurface, only to be destroyed by the stone cut without hands and will be succeeded by the fifth kingdom, which is Jesus' reign from Jerusalem. That kingdom shall never be destroyed.

c.   In summary, we understand the fourth kingdom is the Roman Empire, which has not been destroyed and re-placed with God's kingdom, yet. The ten toes represent kings, and when this Roman Empire of ten kings is formed, it will be destroyed by God, who then sets up His kingdom that cannot be destroyed.

12.   Questioning where the Antichrist will come from is not nearly as crucial as recognizing him when he arrives. Fortunately, Scripture informs us in precise detail what the characteristics of the Antichrist are and what he will be doing. Those traits make it impossible to miss him when he does show up. Anybody who is paying attention will know. Apostle Paul, who died two to three years before the Temple destruction in AD 70, wrote 2 Thessalonians about forty years before John wrote Revelation, AD 96. Some adjust the date of Revelation's writ-ing to make it fit their view of end-time prophecy. However, Saint Irenaeus put the writing of Revelation at AD 96. It

should not surprise anyone that what Paul wrote before his death completely matches what Apostle John was given years later in Revelation. Starting with 2 Thessalonians, these are the readily identifiable characteristics of the real Antichrist:

a.   The Antichrist is revealed to all. No doubt about it, no debate needed, he "is" revealed.[74]

b.   He will orchestrate a Seven-Year Treaty with all the nations, another confirmation he has been revealed to all. Dan 9:27

c.   The treaty will allow for the rebuilding of the Third Temple.

d.   The Antichrist will allow sacrifices to restart. This is incredibly revealing about this man.

e.   The sacrifices have to be started for him to stop them and declare himself as God.[75]

f.   The Antichrist will stop the sacrificing in the Temple three and one-half years into the seven-year agreement, right after the two witnesses have been killed.[76]

g.   The two witnesses, protected for those first three and one-half years, control what is happening globally from Jerusalem. Then they are killed, the world briefly cele-

---

74 2 Thess. 2:2–8, Rev. 13
75 Dan 8:9–14, 9:27, & 12:11; Matt 24:15; 2 Thess. 2:2–4
76 Dan 9:27, 2 Thess. 2:3

brates, and then their resurrection happens three-and-a-half days later with witnesses having great fear.

h.　After the death and resurrection of the two witnesses, the Antichrist will then declare himself God and sit in the Third Temple as God.[77] The Antichrist will be doing unnatural, unbelievable things through Satan's powers and deception.[78]

i.　The Antichrist shall set up his image in the Temple to be worshiped by all on the earth.[79]

j.　The Antichrist does not "completely" destroy Jerusalem or the Third Temple.[80]

Not even one of these ten points has been fulfilled, much less all ten. None were fulfilled by Nero, Titus, or any other leader to date. Some claim the destruction of the Second Temple in AD 70 was the fulfillment or the start of these things and God's Seven Seal Judgments. No! Some point to Constantine, yet he never even stepped into the temple, let alone set up his image there, etc. A key point to remember is the Antichrist of all antichrists does not destroy Jerusalem or the Temple. We know Jerusalem is not utterly destroyed since God's word states in Zechariah 12:2–12, that Jesus returns and saves the Tribe of Judah first.[81] They are the ones defending Jerusalem when Jesus returns. It is written the Tribe of Judah is first to be saved so no other

---

77 2 Thess. 2:4; Matt 24:15; Mark 13:14
78 2 Thess. 2:9, Revelation 13
79 Rev. 13:14–15, 14:9–11, 16:2; Revelation 19:20, 20:4
80 Zech. 13:8–9, Zech. 12
81 Zech. 12:7

tribe or peoples can boast of their greatness over Judah. Jesus is of the tribe of Judah, making this rightly so.

Think carefully, study carefully, and let the Holy Spirit lead you into Truth as you consider the end times. You don't want to wander down one of those roads implying we are already in the Tribulation listed by the Seven Seals in Revelation, or that it started with the Temple destruction in AD 70 or other erroneous ideas. Stick to Scripture and ask God and His Holy Spirit for clarity.

You can do your research via the internet and with other biblical resources because the material is freely available to prove the points already made. We truly live in the times when knowledge has been increased as foretold through the prophet Daniel 12:4. To verify the context and timing of Daniel 12:4, verses 1 and 11 are critical as the Archangel Michael stands up for Daniel's people, Israel. When Michael does this, it is perhaps just days before Jesus returns to Jerusalem to reign on Earth for one-thousand years.

¹*At that time Michael shall stand up, the great prince who stands watch over the sons of your people; and there shall be a time of trouble, such as never was since there was a nation, even to that time. ⁴But you, Daniel, shut up the words, and seal the book until the time of the end; many shall run to and fro, and knowledge shall increase. ¹¹And from the time that the daily sacrifice is taken away, and the abomination of desolation is set up, there shall be one thousand two hundred and ninety days.* (NKJV)

A few decades ago, I was talking with my uncles about the fact we were living in the times when knowledge increased, as God said in Daniel. Mankind was primarily limited to animals pulling carriages and wagons around until the invention of trains in the early 1800s and cars around 1900. Then we went to the moon in 1969. There was very little increase in knowledge over about five-thousand eight hundred years. Then in about one-hundred-sixty years, we went from horse and buggy to landing on the moon. I said, "It makes you wonder what in the heck we were doing for fifty-eight hundred years." While I thought I had just stated a simple fact, my uncles reacted with jaw-dropping surprise. It was the first time they had seen things that way. I decided I would keep telling the same points to others.

My next target was my grandfather, who was born in 1907. I received an equally funny but different reaction. He did not believe we had flown to the moon. He thought it was just another money-making fabrication of Hollywood, similar to the 1938 Martian Invasion story created by Orson Welles. To him, landing on the moon was a hoax. As an engineer, I understood how advanced technology had become. I also believe there was wisdom in my grandfather's viewpoint. It is essential to weigh what you hear carefully, particularly what comes from Hollywood and the media. Unfortunately, the majority of people take whatever the media narrative is and believes it without genuinely seeking to understand the truth. My grandfather was not one of them. He needed more facts before he would believe anything appearing to be another Hollywood production. During the days of Hitler in the 1930s, too many in Germany believed the media slant. Unfortunately, they did not have alternative media sources like we have today. While not all Germans believed the Nazi media onslaught, the majority did, and the rest was controlled by force and fear. We all must work to get both sides of the story and make a clean, clear decision.

I do not think any of us have higher IQs than the men who walked the earth in the past six-thousand years. We do have access to more knowledge, but that is not the same thing as mental capability. I understand God can do anything, including controlling the spread of knowledge as He foretold us in Daniel 12. So, pulling wagons and buggies around with horses or oxen for about fifty-eight hundred years doesn't surprise me. I am happy to have grown up in an age of significant amounts of accessible, available knowledge. Having more information in my head, though, does not increase my God-given IQ. While I cannot say when Jesus will begin to open the Seven Seals of Revelation, and God's Judgment will fall upon mankind, I can see we live in the age where knowledge has significantly increased as foretold in Daniel 12:4.

Looking to one of the ancient men of our faith for insight about this topic, we find Irenaeus had the following to say about the characteristics of the Antichrist.

> *And therefore, when in the end the Church shall be suddenly caught up from this, it is said, "There shall be tribulation such as has not been since the beginning, neither shall be." For this is the last contest of the righteous, in which, when they overcome they are crowned with incorruption. And there is therefore in this beast, when he comes, a recapitulation made of all sorts of iniquity and of every deceit, in order that all apostate power, flowing into and being shut up in him, may be sent into the furnace of fire. Fittingly, therefore, shall his name possess the number six hundred and sixty-six, since he sums up in his own person all the commixture of wickedness which took place previous to the deluge, due to the apostasy of the angels?*
>
> *Such, then, being the state of the case, and this number being found in all the most approved and ancient copies [of the Apocalypse], and those men who saw John face to face bearing their testimony [to it]; while reason also leads us to conclude that the number of the name of the beast, [if reckoned] according to the Greek mode of calculation by the [value of] the letters contained*

in it, will amount to six hundred and sixty and six; that is, the number of tens shall be equal to that of the hundreds, and the number of hundreds equal to that of the units (for that number which [expresses] the digit six being adhered to throughout, indicates the recapitulations of that apostasy, taken in its full extent, which occurred at the beginning, during the intermediate periods, and which shall take place at the end), — I do not know how it is that some have erred following the ordinary mode of speech, and have vitiated the middle number in the name, deducting the amount of fifty from it, so that instead of six decades they will have it that there is but one.

These men, therefore, ought to learn [what is the state of the case], and go back to the true number of the name, that they be not reckoned among false prophets. But, knowing the sure number declared by Scripture, that is, six hundred sixty and six, let them await, in the first place, the division of the kingdom into ten; then, in the next place, when these kings are reigning, and beginning to set their affairs in order, and advance their kingdom, [let them learn] to acknowledge that he who shall come claiming the kingdom for himself, and shall terrify those men of whom we have been speaking, having a name containing the aforesaid number, is truly the abomination of desolation. This, too, the apostle affirms: "When they shall say, Peace and safety, then sudden destruction shall come upon them." And Jeremiah does not merely point out his sudden coming, but he even indicates the tribe from which he shall come, where he says, "We shall hear the voice of his swift horses from Dan; the whole earth shall be moved by the voice of the neighing of his galloping horses: he shall also come and devour the earth, and the fullness thereof, the city also, and they that dwell therein." This, too, is the reason that this tribe is not reckoned in the Apocalypse along with those which are saved.

We will not, however, incur the risk of pronouncing positively as to the name of Antichrist; for if it were necessary that his name should be distinctly revealed in this present time, it would have been announced by him who beheld the apocalyptic vision.

But when this Antichrist shall have devastated all things in this world, he will reign for three years and six months, and sit in the temple at Jerusalem; and then the Lord will come from heaven in the clouds, in the glory of the Father, sending this man and those who follow him into the lake of fire; but bringing in for the righteous the times of the kingdom, that is, the rest, the hallowed seventh day; and restoring to Abraham the promised inheritance, in which kingdom the Lord declared, that "many coming from the east and from the west should sit down with Abraham, Isaac, and Jacob."

There are many important points in this segment from Irenaeus:

- Irenaeus was born about sixty years after the destruction of the Temple in AD 70, and he clearly states in the first couple of sentences quoted above a Pre-Tribulation Rapture view. Many, hoping to protect their "private interpretation" of the end times, claim Pre-Tribulation believers are lured into very recent teachings of a Pre-Tribulation Rapture that started around the 1800s. We can see, however, that Irenaeus wrote about the Pre-Tribulation Rapture within one-hundred years after Apostle John wrote the Book of Revelation. Anyone claiming the Pre-Tribulation viewpoint as something new has not been doing their homework. Whether a person does or does not like Irenaeus, the fact remains he was preaching a Pre-Tribulation Rapture one-thousand eight hundred years ago. There is nothing new about it. Those are fighting words for some, but the first recorded Pre-Tribulation Rapture teacher was from the 100's, not the 1800s, like Darby and Scofield. Irenaeus was simply repeating what a literal interpretation of Scripture says.

- Greek and Hebrew are two languages, which have letters that can either represent a letter or a number. This explains why the letters in the Antichrist's name will total 666. Since Revelation was written in Greek, I believe his name, in Greek, will total 666, and that is what Saint Irenaeus also says.

- Irenaeus teaches the Scripture is literal and means what it says. That makes it very easy to follow. Irenaeus says anyone still here on the earth should wait until it is divided into ten kingdoms before looking for the Antichrist.

- After the ten kingdoms, look for someone to become the leader whose name will add up to 666 in Greek.

- Irenaeus, quoting Jeremiah 8, says this leader will be from the Tribe of Dan. He may be merely repeating what Polycarp received straight from Apostle John. Irenaeus is very matter of fact in his understanding and does not appear to deviate from what Polycarp told him. These are in-depth instructions about looking for the attributes of the Antichrist. Apostle Paul provides information on the Antichrist in 2 Thessalonians 2. If a man comes along who fits them all, then that man is the Antichrist. If that man happens to claim or prove he is from the Tribe of Dan, all the better. The fact the Tribe of Dan is not listed in the New Testament, gives credibility to the idea that the Antichrist comes from that tribe. The fact they are not in the twelve tribes in Revelation 7's one hundred forty-four thousand is significant. Nonetheless, if the shoe fits all the scriptural descriptions of the Antichrist, then the shoe fits, whether he is of Gentile or Israeli descent.

- Irenaeus says the Antichrist will reign from the Temple in Jerusalem for three and one-half years, or forty-two months. Then the Lord will come and throw the Antichrist into the Lake of Fire, not Hell. Then the one-thousand years of Jesus' reign will begin. Many will come and sit down and talk with people like Abraham, Isaac, and Jacob. King David as well, because God says in Jeremiah 30:9 that Israel will serve the Lord and David, their king, who God will raise up for them. In the end, all Irenaeus is doing is repeating what is written. When people are allowed to read the Bible as it is written, it becomes pretty simple.

While there isn't much variation in the Pre-Tribulation viewpoint, there are multiple variants to the three prophecy viewpoints on the one-thousand years of peace. In a basic study, the issues become quickly apparent and emphasize the importance of reading the Bible literally.

The only way to understand which interpretation is correct is to read the Bible as it is written while considering the context. Satan will have a field day with limitless private interpretations for those with "itchy" ears. As 2 Peter 1:20 cautioned us all, *"No prophecy of Scripture is of any private interpretation, for prophecy never came by the will of man, but holy men of God spoke as they were moved by the Holy Spirit."*

These three points explain what may be meant concerning the one thousand years of peace mentioned in Revelation 20:4–5. These points are not about the Rapture event.

1. The Amillennialism viewpoint holds there are not any one-thousand-year reigns, not of Jesus on Earth, or any other. It holds that Christ's reign is *spiritual,* and we are in it today. However, whenever God decides the end of the Church Age is done, Jesus will *physically* return in the final, Great White Throne, judgment, and establish the new heaven and new earth. I have no idea how they can get through the text like Zechariah 12–14 and believe that. My experiences are not the same as theirs, but my supernatural experiences make it impossible for me to interpret Scripture symbolically. When a person has personally met Jesus and Satan, as I have, there isn't any room for that sort of thing. A literal understanding of Scripture, written as is, starts to jump off the pages.

2. Post-Millennialism, which is not the same as Post-Tribulation, says Jesus will come after the one thousand years or after a long period is completed. The Church's role in transforming the earth to perfection dictates when Jesus' return happens. Jesus provides help from above, throughout this process as man becomes better and better. Once they achieve perfection, then Jesus will come down and take over. I hope anyone who reads Revelation 20:7–9 will understand why (a) Jesus has to rule with a rod of iron, and (b) the reason for the rod of iron is that man is a rebellious selfish creature that flocks to Satan as soon as Satan is set free for a time. The selfish nature of man never

departs from us. That explains why there has never been a utopia on Earth, and there never will be. At least, not until Jesus comes and reigns with His rod of iron. Revelation 20:7–9 and Zechariah 14:16–19 are proof enough for me that this train of thought is not from God, but you have to decide for yourself.

3. Pre-Millennialism is the viewpoint that after the First Resurrection, Jesus reigns for one thousand years from Jerusalem, we are not talking about the rapture event yet, and this is what most Christians today believe. It is also what the early Church fathers like Polycarp, Irenaeus, and Papias of Hierapolis (AD 70 – 155) in volume 6 of the Fragments of Papias taught. Jesus comes to earth to live and rule from Jerusalem after the completion of the Seven Seals judgments. In Pre-Millennialism, Jesus starts and finishes His one-thousand-year reign on Earth from Jerusalem. There is peace only because of His rule with a rod of iron. We saints in our new incorruptible bodies get to help, but it is not because of the Bride of Christ, or Church, that there is total peace on the earth. It is because of Jesus and what He is doing from Jerusalem. Man would rebel otherwise during those years and does after Satan's release from the bottomless pit.

Someone reading Scripture from a literal viewpoint will agree with Pre-Millennialism. If a person wants to interpret it symbolically, they can. It is their eternity. As for me, I have been shown something authentic, like Apostle John at Patmos. It was as real as your reading these words. I have no choice to see it any other way. Because of what I have seen, through a series of visions, they do not allow me to take anything symbolically or allegorically unless Scripture says to understand it that way. We all have the responsibility to search the Scripture like the Bereans did to discern if what we hear was from God or if it was from Satan. Additionally, we need to be sure we aren't merely parroting what another says. It calls for doing our homework, which includes prayer and a heart-motivation checkup.

If you have seen any Truth in this, it came from Jesus, who revealed it to me. It has nothing to do with my intellect or lack thereof. It came from Him. So, ask the One True God and wait. The One True God will answer. He is telepathic and knows everything about you. Do not assume anything, be fair-minded in your approach, search the Scriptures, and do your best to hear God's voice with a clean heart to discern both sides of what is said before making a decision. Wait on His answer as long as you need to, and that could be a long time. I have had to endure some long waits, so be patient.

I believe that Pre- and Post-Millennialism shows how quickly man can be deceived by the devil and get off course with God's Word. It doesn't mean anyone who believes that way will not be saved because the Grace provided by Jesus is sufficient to overcome our flawed thinking and errant actions, including mine. I suspect some may consider me judgmental in some of the things I am saying, but the devil gets us all confused with that. God is saying to us to discern Truth, but leave the judging to Him. While discernment and judgment seem to be two closely related things, there is a significant difference between them. If we do not understand this, then we will fall into one of Satan's two traps that exist on the opposite sides of Truth. There is an old saying that Christians are either too heavenly-minded to be of any earthly good, or, too earthly-minded to be of heavenly good. If we are balanced, then we will be in the middle of those two situations, and that is where God wants us. I have spent too much time on both of those extreme ends and not enough in the middle where God wants me to be. Satan has been using those two extremes for thousands of years with traps set and waiting for all of us.

The words from Matthew 7:1–2 are enough to scare anyone and are misused by many in the church. Jesus said, *Judge not, that you be not judged. For with what judgment you judge, you will be judged; and with the measure you use, it will be measured back to you.*

There is a very good "understand the context" lesson to share here. Satan would like for us to believe Jesus stops there, but He does not. As a reminder, I have met in person both Jesus and Satan. They are real, and Satan appeared to be very pleasant, which astonished me. He really is a wolf in sheep's clothing, but Satan is not a sheep, despite appearances.

To understand what Jesus is saying, we must continue reading in Matthew 7. Jesus provides the context in verse 5. *And why do you look at the speck in your brother's eye, but do not consider the plank in your own eye. Or how can you say to your brother, 'Let me remove the speck from your eye,' and look, a plank is in your own eye? Hypocrite! First remove the plank from your own eye, and then you will see clearly to remove the speck from your brother's eye.*

Jesus says to remove the plank from your eye "first," and then you will clearly see to remove the speck from your brother's eye. Jesus says to deal with your brother's speck is a good thing, but do not do it without dealing with your own issues first. When you deal with your planks or issues, then you can help the brother's situation through proper discernment and context. When we haven't dealt with our problems, we will be taking action out of our flawed judgment. When in doubt, check your thoughts, feelings, and motivations to understand where your heart is relative to what God has provided in

Galatians 5:16–22.

Where is Satan in the midst of this? He has two traps set on either side of these situations and can snare us if we are not prepared with scriptural understanding. One trap is to have a brother who is not equipped to help, attempting to help anyway, oblivious to the plank in their own eye (too earthly minded to be of any heavenly help). The trap on the other side of Truth is to keep a perfectly equipped brother or sister from providing the guidance needed. That person thinks they are judging and remembers well the statement about judge not or you will be judged (too heavenly minded to be of earthly help). Falling for either of these two traps is easy, but both are wrong. We all fail here and there, but pull the planks out of our eyes first and then help as guided by the Lord's hand. Be patient, check your heart, and wait on the Lord for His direction. His Grace is sufficient for us when we make those occasional missteps, and it helps us move forward in our walk with Him.

After mentioning a couple of end times terms above like Amillennialism and Post-Millennialism addressing differing views on the one-thousand-year reign of Jesus, we should cover a brief description of how they view the "Rapture" event spoken of by Apostle Paul in 1 Thessalonians 4. Here are some of the differing views of the "Rapture" event.

a.   One of the Amillennialism viewpoints of the Rapture event says we are living in the millennial rule of Jesus today through the Church. In this case, nobody receives their new incorruptible body via Rapture until it is time for Jesus' spiritual millennium to be completed. Jesus then is coming physically for the Great White Throne Judgment. If that were true, life on Earth today would be peaceful and undoubtedly different than it was in Genesis. I remember reading Genesis for the first time when I was about twenty-seven years of age, and thinking I was reading front-page news in the daily paper. There was lying, stealing, cheating, murder, sexual exploitation, etc. I believed we were so much more advanced and "better" than way-way back then. Then I realized we simply had more sophisticated ways to lie, steal, cheat, murder, and molest, but the nature of man was unchanged. That is a formidable thought calling for deep reflection. It is a thought which stunned me and upended my whole perspective. These were not symbolic or metaphorical events; they were actual events that are being proven through archeological finds.

The Amillennialism view was the most popular until Israel became a nation again in 1948. Then most people started taking a more serious "literal" look at Scripture as it applied to Israel and end-time prophecy. The incomparable Sir Isaac Newton, who independently invented calculus around the same time as Gottfried Leibniz in the 1600s, stated that just before the Rapture event, many believers would return to a literal interpretation of end-time events. This great mind was a Pre-Tribulation Rapture believer about one hundred thirty years before John Darby, who is credited with starting this teaching in 1830.

Shortly after Darby, C. I. Scofield appeared, and the two were blamed for starting the Pre-Tribulation belief system. It is easy to search and find there is nothing "new" about the Pre-Tribulation Rapture. It is found early in the church teachings. For example, Irenaeus is quoted as teaching: *"And therefore, when in the end the Church shall be suddenly caught up from this, it is said there shall be tribulation such as has not been since the beginning."*

b.   Post-Tribulation Rapture of the Pre-Millennialism view essentially states Jesus, at His second coming, will Rapture the Church into the clouds. Then it will immediately come back down with Him to Earth to start His one-thousand-year reign of peace. It is seen as one event with the Church remaining on the earth through almost all of the seven years. Warning, there are many different versions of this being taught, but they all somehow tie the Rapture event to the First Resurrection in Revelation 20 as being the same. I see that as impossible, because the Rapture has to happen before the Armageddon battle for the Wife or Church saints to come down with Jesus for that event and the wedding supper, with the First Resurrection written to be after the Armageddon battle ends. In this case, the Rapture cannot be imminent. Many identifiable events must happen, such as the two witnesses that die at the mid-point and are then resurrected into their new bodies. Of those who believe there is a Rapture event before Christ's 1000-year reign, this view is the least literal of them. Many of the prophetic passages have to be interpreted figuratively to mean something other than what is written. Be careful in your interpretation.

Mid-Tribulation Rapture of the Pre-Millennialism view states the Rapture of the Church happens at the mid-point of the Seven-year Tribulation period just before the time of Jacobs "great trouble." This does make some sense as it would happen at the same time the two witnesses in Jerusalem are raised up from the dead.[82] Unfortunately, this event occurs after the Seventh Seal is opened, and the sixth trumpet has already sounded. So, we are now deep into the wrath of God being poured out on mankind. Going back to Revelation 6, we see in verse one Jesus has opened the First Seal, and in verses 16 and 17, we see God's wrath has already started well before any of the seven trumpets were sounded.

c. Pre-wrath Tribulation of the Pre-Millennial view is similar to the Mid-Tribulation view as the Rapture event does not happen before the Seven-year Tribulation period. Like the Mid-Tribulation Rapture, it is a separate event from Jesus' second coming. The argument here is there are three kinds of wrath in those seven years. The wrath of man and Satan both persist up to and past the first three and one-half year point, with God's wrath only coming sometime in the second three and one-half years. To me, this view is playing games with when the phrase "God's wrath" begins, but then you have to search that for yourself or stick with "no comment" until you have decided. Be careful, because the Bride of Christ is promised deliverance from God's wrath. So, they teach the Rapture happens just before God starts pouring out His wrath near the midpoint of seven years. However, once again, going back to Revelation 6, we see that God's wrath has already started before any trumpets are sounded. This "wrath" viewpoint is genuinely a new view on the Rapture, and it was introduced in the 1970s by a man by the name of Robert Van Kampen. It gained momentum even more recently from Marvin Rosenthal. Wrath is listed in

---

82 Revelation11:11

Revelation fourteen times; the first two "wraths of the Lamb, Jesus" are in Revelation 6:16 and 17, occurring before the seven-year mid-point. The Seven Seals are on scrolls written by God before the creation ever happened, and Jesus is the one who will open and execute everything as listed in each scroll. God's wrath starts with the opening of the First Seal. Some want to change that somehow, but the fact is Jesus is opening the seals on the scrolls God wrote before the beginning of time. The first question to ask involves how is it that this is somehow not God's wrath being opened by Jesus starting with Seal 1? If you believe that some of the first seals are not revealing God's wrath, whose wrath is it? Is Jesus opening Satan's seals before He gets to His?

d.   God uses both sequential numbering, and the Greek word "kai" or "and," to preserve the order of events properly. With that in mind, God does not get to the halfway point of the seven years until chapter 11 with the two witnesses, who have already been prophesying and striking the earth with plagues for the first three and one-half years or twelve hundred sixty days. Whose wrath are the two witnesses executing in those first three and one-half years? Their own? Satan's? God's? There is no way these two people could survive the first half of this period, with today's spies, mafia, and weaponry unless God were behind them. Let us not be guilty of rearranging God's preordained order or rationalizing these things away, as if they could not possibly happen. Have you asked and searched to know for sure? The Book of Revelation is not all that complicated once we start looking at it "as written" and get rid of all the wrong information we have heard along the way. There will be hard sections to understand, but the more you comprehend the entire Bible, the easier it becomes to understand Revelation. God's wrath upon unrepentant mankind starts when Jesus the Lamb opens His first seal. God has promised the Church will be protected from His wrath. The Church will have tribulations from Satan over the years. Correction we will receive from Jesus, but His wrath, no.

e. The Bride of Christ is not made up of the same saints as those who are born in the one-thousand-year reign of Christ from Jerusalem. We already have our new incorruptible bodies; their bodies are still of the flesh. They will eventually get their new bodies at the Great White Throne Judgment. This point alone should single-handedly kill any thoughts against multiple dispensations, as there are clearly two different dispensations shown in Revelation 20.

f. Pre-Tribulation Rapture of the Pre-Millennial viewpoint believes the Rapture is imminent and can happen at any moment as there is nothing that has to happen before it. Once the Rapture occurs, the opening of the first seal of Revelation then becomes imminent as there will be nothing else that has to happen before it. The process continues through each seal. Pre-Tribulation believers will agree with Post-Tribulation believers that we are still at least seven years away from Jesus' return to the earth to rule with a rod of iron from Jerusalem. There has yet to be a seven-year treaty which allows the Temple to be rebuilt and sacrifices to begin there. The two witnesses that control world events for the first three and one-half years haven't come and then died to be resurrected and raised up to heaven. The defiling of the Temple hasn't happened. The mark of the beast that controls all buying and selling has yet to occur. Both sides are in complete agreement on all of that. We are at least seven years away from when Jesus starts to rule from Jerusalem. Pre-Tribulation believers understand that the imminent Rapture is an entirely different event than when Jesus returns to rule from Jerusalem for one thousand years. When Jesus comes for His Bride, He is not coming to rule on Earth; His feet never touch the earth, He is claiming His Bride the Church and taking her to His Father's house where Jesus has prepared a place for her. Then God can shut His heavenly doors to Satan and his demonic minions. When the Rapture happens, there is going to be one massive battle in the clouds as Jesus' angels lift us to the place Jesus has prepared for us in His Father's heaven.

Think carefully, study carefully, and let the Holy Spirit lead you into Truth as you consider the end times. You don't want to wander down one of those roads implying we are already in the Tribulation listed by the Seven Seals in Revelation, or that it started with the Temple destruction in AD 70 or other erroneous ideas. Stick to Scripture and ask God and His Holy Spirit for clarity.

You can do your research via the internet and with other tools because the material is freely available to prove the points I have already made. We truly live in the times when knowledge has been increased as foretold through the prophet Daniel 12:4. To verify the context and timing of Daniel 12:4, verses 1 and 11 are critical as the Archangel Michael stands up for Daniel's people, Israel. He is not standing up for the Church, and that should be very clear in the scripture from Daniel that follows. When Michael does this, it is perhaps just days before Jesus returns to Jerusalem to reign on Earth for one-thousand years. From Daniel 12:

> [1]*At that time Michael shall stand up, the great prince who stands watch over the sons of your people; and there shall be a time of trouble, such as never was since there was a nation, even to that time.* [4]*But you, Daniel, shut up the words, and seal the book until the time of the end; many shall run to and fro, and knowledge shall increase.* [11]*And from the time that the daily sacrifice is taken away, and the abomination of desolation is set up, there shall be one thousand two hundred and ninety days. (NKJ)*

Getting ready for those end times requires study, contemplation, and guidance from the One True God. He has written it all down because He wants His children to be well informed and ready. Friends who are believers can be invaluable resources for sharing the gleanings of Truth, which God reveals to truth-seeking hearts. The Holy Spirit wants to guide us in our study of God's word and connect us to other believers. When we are all connected, we can focus on encouraging each other to stand solidly on The Word and to be ever watchful.

For Further Study

To invite you to understand what is in your eternity, The One True God is saying to you:

> *"Call to Me, and I will answer you, and show you*
> *great and mighty things, which you do not know."*
>
> —JEREMIAH 33:3

- Study the teachings from the Patristic Fathers of our Faith.

- Daniel 7, 8:11–12; 2 Thessalonians 2; Revelation 11–13, 17.

- Genesis 49

- Exodus 34:13–17; Jeremiah 3:6; Hosea 4:13; Ezekiel 6:13,18:15, 22:9, 28:16

- Zephaniah 2:2–3; Isaiah 26:19–27:1; 1 Thessalonians 1:10, 1 Thessalonians 5:9, Revelation 3:10

CHAPTER FIFTEEN

RAPTURE VISION

Where do our soul and spirit go upon the death of the body? What does that have to do with what is commonly called the Rapture event? These questions require examination and searching so that the critical topic of the Rapture can adequately be understood.

The terms associated with destinations for the dead can be a bit confusing. Sheol, Hell, Hades, or Gehenna all refer to the same location; and are the resultant next place in the "first" death. I use the generic term "Hell" for all of them. Hell was created as a place for a man's soul and spirit to go when the physical body dies. Since man's soul and spirit do not die with the body, a place was created for them to wait until a new incorruptible body is issued. The body is buried, and the soul-spirit is taken by angels to a "holding" location where it rests, yet is very much alive. This is the place where Jesus' Soul and Spirit went upon his death.[83] The Lake of Fire is also a destination for the dead, but it is reserved to be used only for the "second death."

Initially, we will consider the first death as we ask, exactly where do our souls and spirits go? The Israelites described the happiness of the righteous at death as going to a beautiful place, such as: (1) they go to the Garden of Eden, (2) they go to be under the throne of glory, or (3) they go to the bosom of Abraham. Jesus gave us a fourth description of the place where the righteous will go when he told one of the

---

83 Eph. 4:8–10

thieves on the cross that they were both going to "Paradise" that day. We are told He descended into Hell in the heart of the earth for three days and three nights; then immediately rose in an incorruptible body. What exactly do the following Scriptures mean?

So we are always confident, knowing that while we are at home in the body we are absent from the Lord, For we walk by faith, not by sight. We are confident, yes, well pleased rather to be absent from the body and to be present with the Lord.

For to me, to live is Christ, and to die is gain. But if I live on in the flesh, this will mean fruit from my labor; yet what I shall choose I cannot tell. For I am hard-pressed between the two, having a desire to depart and be with Christ, which is far better.

Both 2 Corinthians 5:6–8 and Philippians 1:21–23 show when our physical body no longer is a living, viable place for our souls and our spirits, they go to be with Jesus.

If man had never sinned, there would have been no need for Hell. Since man did sin, the two parts of Hell were immediately put into use. The name Hell has a nasty sound to it, but sinning against God's divine law has a nasty consequence. The Bible clearly states the wages earned for any sin is death. Thankfully, Jesus has allowed us an opportunity to follow Him. He provided the way out of Hell to restore us to God, our Father. Hell was planned before the "foundation" of the world and was put into use shortly after creation because of sin by Adam and Eve. The curse of death brought on by their sin has been passed down through all generations. There will be a day in the future when Hell will be entirely done away with and dumped into the Lake of Fire. Until then, we all go the way our ancestors have gone, and that includes those who die much later in the future one-thousand-year reign of Christ.

The account of Lazarus and the rich man from Luke 16:19–31 helps show Jesus is in control of Hell. Each man was on a different side of the great divide there in Hell. And while they could see and talk to each other, they couldn't cross that divide. Satan should have been creating havoc in that place, but Jesus' reveals that it was very orderly there.

A critical point to understand is Jesus has complete control over both sides of Hell, and Satan has no power there, not even the bad side. When all of Hell is dumped into the Lake of Fire, Satan will also be sent. He will then be powerless for all eternity in a hot and awful place. He made the choice that determined his eternity, the fate of the demonic angels following him, as well as the fate for men who rejected God's plan. Jesus has complete control of everything that exists, including the Lake of Fire. As odd as this may sound, in Hell, evil cannot corrupt or interact with other evil there. Jesus makes and enforces all the rules, and everyone there is bound to follow them without even a minor violation. More importantly, Jesus says He has the keys to Hell and Death in Revelation 1:18 and is in complete control.

What is written here is in keeping with the statement by Apostle Paul when he said. *"To be absent from the body is to be present with the Lord,"* because the Lord is in charge of both sides of Hell. Apostle Paul also wrote in 1 Thessalonians 5:10 that whether we are awake or asleep, we live together with Him. Sleep is a term for the Paradise side of Hell, but not used when referring to the third heaven where the Throne of God the Father is. It is fine to disagree, but you have to find Scripture to support that there is a big group of church saints asleep up in the third heaven to believe that your soul and spirit will be going up there in death. I don't currently know of any, but I sure can find a lot of references tying asleep, sleep, and rest to the Paradise side of Hell.

Revelation 6 tells of a group that has died as martyrs in the Tribulation period after the breaking of the Fifth Seal. They are reported to be under the altar and will remain there until the number of martyrs is completed. Where is "under the altar"? Why must they continue to "rest for a little while longer"? Why are their souls and spirits not with Christ above the altar with the twenty-four elders and the saints there around the throne of God before the first seal was broken in Chapter 6? The answer is that they were not ready when the Rapture came and died later in the seven-year Tribulation period. They are still at "rest" in Paradise, waiting for their appointed time to be raised up with their new eternal, incorruptible bodies at the first resurrection.[84]

We know where Jesus' Soul and Spirit went upon death, and it was not His Father's house. He could not go up there until it was His time to be raised and be presented before the Father as a completed, three-in-one being in His new incorruptible body. We also know that when Jesus was raised, He raised up many of the saints, but not all of the saints. Matthew 27:52–53 recorded, *The graves were opened; and many bodies of the saints who had fallen asleep were raised; and coming out of the graves after His resurrection, they went into the holy city and appeared to many.*

Those raised up with Jesus were the Old Testament saints who were the wife of the Father. They could not be raised with their new bodies until Jesus had paid the debt for all mankind. The saints, who were there and not raised, are part of the Bride of Christ and will be raised at their future appointed time in the Rapture. If this were not

---

84 Rev. 20

true, then there is a verse in the Bible that is incorrect, and that would be Matthew 27:52–53. It says "many of the bodies of the saints" when it should have said all of the saints were raised. It should have said that Paradise was emptied to never be in use ever again because from then on, all the souls and spirits of the saints would go to the third heaven where the God the Father is.

The criminal that went with Jesus down to the Paradise side of Hell is still there waiting for the future Rapture event. This is revealed in the text of Matthew 27:52–53. When Jesus' soul and spirit were reunited with His new incorruptible body, the Bible says that He was the first ever to be resurrected from the dead. Jesus was the first resurrection of the Church Age, and the Rapture of the Bride of Christ will be another which will close the Church Age. Then opens a new dispensation, which I am calling the Age of Judgment, where Jesus steps out to rule with His rod of iron. Revelation 20:4–5 describes the first resurrection of that dispensation. There is a second resurrection later at the Great White Throne Judgment. These are more topics to contemplate for a deeper understanding:

1. Can an "incomplete" person, i.e., just a man's soul-spirit, be in the third heaven before God's Throne without their body? Jesus did not do this, and we are not above our master.[85]

2. Who is in charge of Hell, which consists of at least two distinct parts? God is in charge of both the good and bad sides.[86] If not, Satan and his hordes would have a heyday on both sides, assuring there would be no rest on the good side. Dozens of Scriptures portray Paradise as a peaceful place of rest.

---

85 John 20:16–17
86 Luke 16:19–31

3. The Book of Acts has instructions for us to teach in the traditions of the Apostles, but Satan has worked diligently from day one to pervert this. Many of the New Testament writings exist to correct false teaching in their day. Those arguments of Truth used then still hold firm today. When it comes to end times prophecy, I believe we, the Church, are not doing a good job of teaching in the traditions of the Apostles. If we did, there would be much more common agreement in the Church.

As my experience related in an earlier chapter shows, I have come to know it is always a good practice to return to the teachings from those closest to the source as the Christian faith formed during the First Century. To follow are the writings about Paradise from Polycarp. Polycarp lived just before the Temple's destruction in AD 70 to 155. He was appointed by Apostle John to be the head of the Church at Smyrna. He died at an old age around AD 155 and represented the link between the apostolic fathers and the Christian teachers of the second century. Polycarp was the last of those personally acquainted with and instructed by the disciples of Jesus. The second of the seven churches of Revelation was Smyrna, and Polycarp may have been appointed bishop within a few years after the time of the first reading of Revelation. At the end of his ministry, he was to be martyred by being burned at the stake. It is reported he was unharmed by the flames which formed an arch around him. His persecutors then speared him and let him bleed to death instead. Polycarp taught that God was in full control of Hell, and all who died would go to either the good or bad side of Hell, depending on the condition of their hearts towards God. His is an important voice to listen to because of the teachings he directly received from the Apostle John.

The Revelation of Jesus, given to John, broke through the prophetic silence, which had lasted for about six hundred years. The direct connection of Revelation to the Prophet Daniel's writings is undeniable. Unlike some, I believe that John clearly understood the message because he "Swallowed the little book and described the taste as being sweet, but it turned sour in his stomach."[87] Apostle, John, consumed all the contents of the book. Then he was told he must prophesy again about many peoples, nations, tongues, and kings. The only book John wrote concerning prophecy was Revelation. He did not ask many questions, but when he did, they were answered in a way that showed he understood the answer. Apostle John did not fast and pray for clarification as Daniel did. Eating the book brought him understanding, so he didn't need an explanation. Some may claim that is hard to believe, but I see no purpose for having John eat the little book if it didn't provide him with the understanding he needed. Either eating the book had meaning, or Jesus would not have put it into Revelation. God does not go around inserting things into his Bible, such as visions and dreams that are meaningless or perhaps useless because we cannot ever understand them.

As I consume the Word of God, I obtain understanding. Perhaps I am nitpicking, but not all people try to absorb the Bible as they read it. They try to find things to discredit it; I know because I was one of them until I had my face to face encounter with the supernatural and was asked by Jesus to be on His team. Later, I told Him I was ready. I had a, "Put me in, coach" mentality! As you may have guessed, that did not work well. He was not going to put me in until I was ready. That took a long time, somewhere around twenty-five years. It is all

---

87 Rev. 10:8–11

about His timing. Looking back, I can see He eased me into things here and there along the way, but He couldn't trust me with bigger things until I matured the way He wanted me to.

Saint Irenaeus recorded Polycarp's teaching concerning what happens when a body dies. His purpose for the instruction is clearly to put down heretical teaching. As you consider the text found below, please keep in mind that it is not my writing; it is from an early church father who uses some strong words. I am not calling anyone a heretic for their beliefs, and I suspect he is not either. Instead, he is shouting out at those who are speaking untruth for their own benefit. He is addressing those trying to pull followers away from God's Truths. Satan's ways always start with something simple and small. With a little twist here and there, he pulls some people further and further away from the Truth. The father of lies uses one little lie after another to set his devious trap.

Polycarp was confronting anyone who taught we immediately go up into the third heaven where the throne of the Father is placed. We do go into the presence of the Lord upon death, but the location is wrong, and Polycarp was trying to fix that. The place is the Paradise side of Hell, which is below the earth as covered earlier. If Jesus weren't there, peace or rest for anyone would be impossible. Revelation 1:18 states Jesus alone has the keys for hell and death, and Satan does not. We can innocently believe a wrong thing, and His Grace covers that. However, that does not apply to a real heretic, who knowingly twists the truth for their own benefit. We can only understand the Bible up to the capability that God allows us. It always comes down to the condition of our hearts. What or who is number one in your heart?

To be open and forthright, I was completely caught off guard by Polycarp's teaching below. You may have to read this several times to grasp it. The resurrection of a "whole" man has to include the new incorruptible body along with the soul and spirit. I believe we have to be a complete three-in-one person, not partial, to stand before God the Father and His throne.

What does the Bible say? The Old Testament teaches everyone goes to Hell until they are raised up with their new bodies at the appropriate time. That was certainly true of the prophet Daniel who was told to go to the place of rest until he is risen up to his inheritance at the end of the days.[88]

Here are the teachings of Polycarp as reported by his pupil Irenaeus:

> Since, again, some who are reckoned among the orthodox go beyond the pre-arranged plan for the exaltation of the just, and are ignorant of the methods by which they are disciplined beforehand for incorruption, they thus entertain heretical opinions. For the heretics, despising the handiwork of God, and not admitting the salvation of their flesh, while they also treat the promise of God contemptuously, and pass beyond God altogether in the sentiments they form, affirm that immediately upon their death they shall pass above the heavens and the Demiurge, and go to the Mother (Achamoth) or to that Father whom they have feigned. Those persons, therefore, who disallow a resurrection affecting the whole man (universam reprobant resurrectionem), and as far as in them lies remove it from the midst [of the Christian scheme], how can they be wondered at, if again they know nothing as to the plan of the resurrection? For they do not choose to understand, that if these things are, as they say, the Lord Himself, in whom they profess to

---

88 Dan. 12:13

believe, did not rise again upon the third day; but immediately upon His expiring on the cross, undoubtedly departed on high, leaving His body to the earth. But the case was, that for three days He dwelt in the place where the dead were, as the prophet says concerning Him: "And the Lord remembered His dead saints who slept formerly in the land of sepulture; and He descended to them, to rescue and save them." And the Lord Himself says, "As Jonas remained three days and three nights in the whale's belly, so shall the Son of man be in the heart of the earth." Then the apostle also says, "But when He ascended, what is it but that He also descended into the lower parts of the earth?" This, too, David says when prophesying of Him, "And thou hast delivered my soul from the nethermost hell;" and on His rising again the third day, He said to Mary, who was the first to see and to worship Him, "Touch Me not, for I have not yet ascended to the Father; but go to the disciples, and say unto them, I ascend unto My Father, and unto your Father.

Some interpret "Touch Me Not" to support their end-times view, as one group will say this means Jesus went to the Father's throne and came back so He could then be touched when He encountered doubting Thomas in John 20:27. But going up to the Father and then coming back to Earth contradicts the argument of Post-Tribulation thinkers that say Jesus only comes to Earth twice. This cannot count as an ascension to God the Father since that would mean Jesus had then returned to Earth a second time for others, like Thomas, to touch him. So, they say Jesus did not really go up to the Father as Scripture reads. They say the real interpretation is Jesus meant you can touch me, but "hold me not" as that is for a future time. So, it was okay to touch Him, but not hold Him. This helped to preserve their Post-Tribulation teachings, and they were still safe in what they believed.

Now that we understand the different sides of this argument, what does that Scripture actually say? Many scriptural references show Jesus has already come to Earth to do something unrelated to reigning from Jerusalem for one thousand years. He has definitely come back to Earth since His ascension, as shown in the New Testament. One time is found in Acts 23:10–11, which states Apostle Paul, was locked up in the barracks for safekeeping, and that night the Lord "stood" by him and spoke to him. A second is when Jesus appeared to John at Patmos.[89] John is on the earth at Patmos and does not ascend until Revelation 4:1. These Scriptures are helpful as you do your homework, with the Holy Spirit's help, so you can decide what you believe. Please, think for yourself and consider both sides of the story. I am not going to put words into God's mouth, and Jesus really can come and go as He sees fit. What I do know is Jesus does come to Earth twice to reign. The word "reign" is the key, so be careful to apply "coming twice" within the context of Jesus coming to reign on Earth from Jerusalem. The first time Jesus was rejected at the cross as King of the Jews, and the second time He will come and reign by force with His "rod of iron." In the meantime, Jesus can come and observe or provide instruction anytime He wants, just like He did in the Old Testament.

Consider Polycarp's teachings about what happens after death.

> *If, then, the Lord observed the law of the dead, that He might become the first-begotten from the dead, and tarried until the third day "in the lower parts of the earth;" then afterward rising in the flesh, so that He even showed the print of the nails to His disciples, He thus ascended to the Father; — [if all these things occurred,*

---

89 Rev. 1:9–18

I say], how must these men not be put to confusion, who allege that "the lower parts" refer to this world of ours, but that their inner man, leaving the body here, ascends into the super-celestial place? For as the Lord "went away in the midst of the shadow of death," where the souls of the dead were, yet afterward arose in the body, and after the resurrection was taken up [into heaven], it is manifest that the souls of His disciples also, upon whose account the Lord underwent these things, shall go away into the invisible place allotted to them by God, and there remain until the resurrection, awaiting that event; then receiving their bodies, and rising in their entirety, that is bodily, just as the Lord arose, they shall come thus into the presence of God. "For no disciple is above the Master, but every one that is perfect shall be as his Master." As our Master, therefore, did not at once depart, taking flight [to heaven], but awaited the time of His resurrection prescribed by the Father, which had been also shown forth through Jonas, and rising again after three days was taken up [to heaven]; so ought we also to await the time of our resurrection prescribed by God and foretold by the prophets, and so, rising, be taken up, as many as the Lord shall account worthy of this [privilege].

Within one hundred years after the Temple's destruction in AD 70, church fathers like Polycarp and Irenaeus were confronting heretical teaching. This writing, by the early church fathers, addresses a wrong teaching. They are saying that we do not go up to the Father immediately after death. Some, out of innocence are teaching this today. I am not calling them out, but I am asking them to do their homework and challenging them to search these things out as the Bereans did.

Does this excerpt from Polycarp's writings help explain those above the altar versus those below it in Revelation 6? If we go straight to the Father's throne after death, why are those below not there with everyone else above the altar? Why are there two different groups, especially if there is no such thing as different dispensations? While I hope the turmoil surrounding dispensations have been put to rest, I do understand this may create more questions, but they will all fit together eventually. It's a lot of information, so patience and effort are essential. For starters, I say yes, Polycarp's response does answer the dilemma because:

1. If believers in Jesus are at rest down in Paradise, then since the days of Adam and Eve, He has been keeping total peace there. Revelation 1:18 informs us that only Jesus has the keys for both sides of hell. The word "keys" is plural, and if there are at least two sides of Hell, that will make sense as they are not opened at the same time.

2. The first group was before the Father's throne before the first seal was broken, so this group below the altar had to have died after the first group had been raised up in their new incorruptible bodies.

3. Because this group below the altar went to Paradise after the first group was raised, they were told to continue their "rest" at that location until their time had come to be raised.[90]

4. In particular, it is clear this group were martyrs "slain for the word of God."[91] This is a very limited group of people unless

90 Rev. 6:11
91 Rev. 6:9; 20:4–5

231

we add to God's word by saying it includes everybody who was not a martyr. I will not be guilty of that.

5.   This group of true martyrs under the altar has everything in common with those described in the first resurrection in Revelation 20:4–5. Most who have died in Christ over the past two thousand years did not die as martyrs.

There have been many martyrs from about AD 30 to today. Even they do not meet the complete description of Revelation 20:4–5. Nobody I have ever personally known fits the description of being "slain for the word of God." They have lived a normal life and died here in America. We cannot change God's word and slip extra things in there.

The same is true for the first resurrection; nobody fits that description except those slain in the Tribulation period as "martyrs" for refusing to worship the beast and his mark, etc. A person physically has to be dead to be resurrected. So what happens to those that were alive at the Rapture if the Rapture and first resurrection are the same event? You cannot resurrect a living person. They can be transformed, but not resurrected when they are not dead. I am getting a little ahead of myself here, but a person has to change God's word concerning the first resurrection to include those saints who are alive on the Earth in it. Perhaps just as bad is to ignore an early church father, Irenaeus, who says that any believers still on the Earth when Jesus returns will help to repopulate the world as stated in Jeremiah. These believers do not get their incorruptible body until the White Throne Judgment. Still, one of the many things I found in the early writings of Polycarp and Irenaeus was that those who were alive on the earth when Jesus returned, and had not accepted the mark of the beast, and had not worshiped him, were those that helped repopulate Earth since they stayed in their bodies of flesh. They did not get their new incorruptible bodies until the White Throne Judgment coming after Jesus' one-thousand years rule from Jerusalem.

Irenaeus continues with his teaching on this matter.

- *For all these and other words were unquestionably spoken in reference to the resurrection of the just, which takes place "after" the coming of Antichrist, and the destruction of all nations under his rule; in [the times of] which [resurrection] the righteous shall reign in the earth, waxing stronger by the sight of the Lord: and through Him they shall become accustomed to partake in the glory of God the Father, and shall enjoy in the kingdom intercourse and communion with the holy angels, and union with spiritual beings; and [with respect to] those whom the Lord shall find in the flesh, awaiting Him from heaven, and who have suffered tribulation, as well as escaped the hands of the Wicked one. For it is in reference to them that the prophet says: "And those that are left shall multiply upon the earth," And Jeremiah the prophet has pointed out, that as many believers as God has prepared for this purpose, to multiply those left upon earth, should both be under the rule of the saints to minister to this Jerusalem, and that [His] kingdom shall be in it.*

These are some of the highlighted points made by Irenaeus in his writings:

a. The resurrection of the just[92] comes after the Antichrist and after the destruction of all the nations under the

---

92 Revelation 20:4–6

Antichrist's rule. In other words, this resurrection is after Jesus comes to earth, saves the Israelites, and finishes off Armageddon and the Antichrist's rule. It is after Jesus throws the Antichrist and False Prophet into the Lake of Fire and after He jails Satan in the bottomless pit. After all of this, then the first resurrection finally happens. A Resurrection is not the same thing as the Rapture. Does anyone call the First Resurrection the First Rapture? If they are, in fact, the same thing, then they should be interchangeable with each other, but you decide if they are or are not the same thing.

b. This first resurrection happens after Jesus' feet touch Mount of Olives, and He has dealt with the Antichrist, so either Jesus comes back to Earth without His Bride of saints or the Rapture of the Bride has happened well in advance of what is called the first resurrection. Those Raptured saints then are the ones coming with Jesus as He comes to save the tribe of Judah first so no other tribes can magnify themselves against or above the tribe of Judah.

c. To further drive the correctness of points (a) and (b) home, Irenaeus says *"[with respect to] those whom the Lord shall find in the flesh, awaiting Him from heaven, and who have suffered tribulation, as well as escaped the hands of the Wicked one,"* that *"those that are left shall multiply upon the earth";* which the saints in their new incorruptible bodies cannot physically accomplish. Irenaeus then quotes the same from Jeremiah 30 by saying: *And Jeremiah the prophet has pointed out, that as many believers as God has prepared for this purpose, to multiply those left upon earth, should both be under the rule of the saints to minister to this Jerusalem, and that [His] kingdom shall be in it."*

When I first started looking into the specifics of the Rapture itself, there was so much contradicting and confusing information out there that I believed Satan was behind it. I wondered why was this was so important to Satan. Another point to consider is why Satan would even bother with it if the Rapture happened at or very near the end of the Seven-year Tribulation, as the Post-Tribulation believers think. Satan had nothing to gain by cluttering up the Rapture of the Bride of Christ, if true, as he will either be a brand new arrival to the bottomless pit for the next one-thousand years or just a few days away from going there.

The apparent conclusion was Satan had something to gain by creating confusion around the Rapture event. Then my next series of questions focused on "why" and "what" is his twist on the event. Answering the "why" was pretty easy; he always wants fewer people entering into God's kingdom. The fewer going to be with Christ, the merrier Satan is. With that in mind, a Pre-Tribulation Rapture event raising over one-and-one-half billion "alive" people off the face of the earth is a serious threat to his plans for death and destruction of the remaining six billion humans still on the earth based on today's population. If the Bride of Christ is a Pre-Tribulation Rapture, and the six billion left behind know it, Satan will have to kill many more as martyrs. That must be a hollow feeling for him since martyrs will eventually go to be with Jesus. Even worse will be how many martyrs he has to kill unless he has a great explanation about where all those seemingly nice people went. Think about it for a moment. If you were left behind and found a lot of Jesus believing neighbors, relatives, and friends were instantly gone, wouldn't you be looking for a good explanation as to why so many have entirely vanished?

To prevent souls from defecting from his nonbelieving camp and believing in Jesus Christ, Satan has to have prepared something outstanding. Something has to be in the works today so he can take numerous men and women with him to the Lake of Fire at the time of the second death. This answers why a Pre-Tribulation versus Post-Tribulation Rapture is so dangerous to Satan's plans, and why he has come up with so much confusion concerning the Rapture and end-time events. What has Satan planned, and does that shed any light on the Rapture? Most church people pick the doctrine that fits their personality or make-up. That was not acceptable to me, so I continued to look for answers wherever I could find them.

To say that I was surprised at what I found next is putting it mildly. While the church's beliefs were many and all over the map, Satan's strategy was clear. Part one was all about creating that confusion with a smorgasbord of Rapture choices for Church people, pick your flavor. Part two can be found by looking at what the New Agers believed about the Rapture. They seemed to be the new thing with some Christian aspects to it, appearing as a wolf in sheep's clothing. If it didn't come with hints of Christianity, it could not be called a sheep; we all know how to spot a wolf. In the 1990s, I found teachings that I believe Satan will use shortly after the Rapture to persuade those left behind. To follow are the highlights of those teachings.

New Agers teach that millions upon millions of people are dysfunctional, have proven they cannot adapt to this new age of enlightenment, will cause life on Earth to cease in just a few years, and accuse these people of preventing others from "harmonizing" themselves perfectly with the earth and the cosmos around us. Think of positions on the wrong side of climate change and religious intolerance, as examples of not being able to adapt or harmonize.

a. So, before these many millions of Jesus believers ruined things for everyone else, they had to be beamed up for treatment and re-education. They had to be rehabilitated. Meanwhile, those still on the earth would get the earth back into balance.

b. As you might imagine, these people referred to Christians as "backward fundamentalists" who had to be immediately removed from the planet. There was little time left to save the earth and life as we know it, so, up they all went to the waiting space ships, better known as UFOs. Yes, I do see the physics-defying nature of UFOs as a tool of Satan's to use at the appropriate time to cloud the truth of the Rapture event. Those beamed up to these spaceships are then rehabilitated into higher states of consciousness before being reintegrated into society. Do you see the sleight-of-hand here? Most people will nod their heads and move on with their life. Some will scratch their head and look for the other side of the story. They will look into the do-not-look-there side of the story and find out what happened to all those faulty but genuinely Christian people. While this may sound a bit morbid, some may find a completely empty urn or grave of a loved one that they knew was a serious Christian. Their bodies will be gone.[93] Many of them will accept Jesus as their Lord and Savior and become

---

93 Isa. 26:19; Matt. 27:52–53

part of the First Resurrection in Revelation 20. Creating the illusion of spaceships has been practiced by Satan and his minions for a long-long time. We observe and call them UFOs, but we cannot put our finger on exactly what or who they really are. They can be seen and sometimes picked up by radar only to then disappear into thin air.

Before rolling your eyes and closing this book or moving onto another chapter, please consider man can alter the genetics of plants and animals. There are now genetically modified foods (GMOs) and cloning. Man is probably at the point where we can create our own alien beings from genetic modifications and implantable chips. It should not be surprising that fallen angels or demons working against the One True God have been practicing their versions of human genetic experimentation since the beginning of man. Genesis 6 relates the story of the giants which support this idea. We can't know what else those angels have been up to, but I do know we are about to find out, and the Bible tells us what it will be like in the last days. Matthew 24:37–38 says the times will be like the days of Noah. What we know about Noah's days is God destroyed all humans and hybrid humans, because of the genetic alterations occurring between humans and fallen angels. In Genesis 6:9, God was quick to point out that Noah was completely human, perfect in all his generations. If there had been genetic alterations with fallen angels in Noah's past, then God would not have saved Noah and his family. Hybrid humans, or giants, were why God caused the flood in the first place. Noah was both genetically perfect and believed God when He spoke to him. Because Noah spoke regularly with

God, He was as real to Noah as his wife and children were. Noah believed God was who He said He was and chose to follow Him.

The Bible says the time will come when Satan and his evil angels will be forever tossed out of the upper heavens down to Earth. They will then know they have only about seven years left. They have been preparing for this future event for literally thousands of years. The fallen angels know what has been written in the Bible, so what mankind will see in those seven years will defy comprehension. It seems we are almost there, are you ready? Start by asking Jesus to take you on His team, and He will immediately accept you and help you the rest of the way.

We can also see Satan, along with his demonic army of angels, has been working hard on the spaceship and alien front for many years. So, it is reasonable they have continued to play with human genetics and create alien-looking creatures like the ones supposedly reported in a UFO crash landing at Roswell, New Mexico, in 1947. Whether anyone believes this is true or false does not matter. Satan has been preparing to explain away the impact of the Rapture of the Church for quite a while. UFOs and the abduction of millions, perhaps billions, of defective humans is the only explanation Satan will have for the mass exodus of all those people at once. So, what exactly is the narrative Satan is projecting to convince men of this? It seems a schism is increasing among those who are pushing dividing issues like climate change, abortion, sexual orientation, and racism. I believe most people miss the point that the divisive narrative created today is to show that those on the wrong side are (a) defective thinkers, (b) will ruin the world, and (c) have to be removed. So then it becomes easy to say they were flawed and beamed up to UFOs to be retrained, while those still on the earth were chosen to bring harmony and restoration to the planet. That is the classic sleight-of-hand, "look over there, not over here" maneuver.

c. The New Agers still left on Earth will help everyone else understand what has happened and will help them cope with the "coming earth changes." As part of this indoctrination, the New Age thinkers will be touted as superior beings having superior connections. This is a strategy designed to put everyone under their complete control so they will follow their every instruction. In my opinion, their connection is to Satan.

d. Psychics, mediums, and channelers have long been prophesying earth changes, and these messages get more main-stream with each passing day. The New Age psychics, who say they are giving us communications from higher beings, have been consistent in their prophecies of significant earth changes. Of course, Christians were forewarned over two-thousand years ago by Jesus to recognize those as signs of the end times. It was written thousands of years ago, and Satan knows what was written. Satan knows what is coming next better than we do, and with his team of fallen angels, he is changing the narrative to look over there, not over here.

e. While the above information about the New Agers and others' ideas may seem a bit on the goofy side, what comes next is just as surprising. The daily news conditions and influences our thoughts and ideas about this next topic.

Earth changes, more commonly called "climate change or global warming," are considered such a high threat to humans worldwide that the US government formed a watchdog organization in 1970 called the Environmental Protection Agency or EPA. That organization's budget had grown to over eight billion dollars in the year 2016. There has been a lot of money spent since 1970 on this. The agency has birthed all sorts of rules and regulations to protect the earth, basically from humans.

While Satan is changing the world through the media and government reports, the New Age types are also saying cancers and pollution are from negative-thinking humans. At times they use the term "haters" to describe those contaminating the earth. Those who do not reform while on Earth will have to be evacuated in one fell swoop, as in the Rapture. Yes, I am smiling more than a little bit.

Project World Evacuation is what they call it. The rescue ships will be able to come in close enough and, in the twinkling of an eye, complete the beaming up operation. So, in just a small amount of time, the undesirables will be lifted up to smaller ships that feed much larger ships higher up. Supposedly, there is no need to worry; there will be ample space and proper provisions for all the evacuees.

I first read this sort of thing in the mid-1990s. I wasn't exactly shocked but was surprised by the amount of it in mainstream media and government reports, even in America. It seemed so obvious how well that twisted sleight-of-hand information directly ties with a Pre-Tribulation.

Satan very much seems to be preparing for the Pre-Tribulation version of the Rapture event and working tirelessly to obscure it. Of course, back in the mid-1990s, I was not aware of all the scriptural support I needed to understand this Truth. I could plainly see where Satan, the adversary of God, was coming from, but I could not piece together what God was saying. However, I was praying and fasting quite a bit. Eventually, I was given another vision where I was caught up, very much like Apostle John was in Revelation 4, and shown how things would be happening in the Rapture event.

I was naive, and at the time, I had no idea what a hot topic the Rapture event could be. When I was directed by my pastor to talk with a staff member about having a group Bible study on Revelation and end times, I was told we do not discuss end times Scripture. It was all about keeping harmony in the church, and the topic itself was not an easy one to address. Since then, when I have brought up short snippets of information, I know it seems to get somebody stirred up. Maybe a book is a better way to present the information and keep tempers down. The Rapture Vision recorded below was God's way of helping me understand.

I have enough substantiation to know what happened to me was not a dream. Something very real did happen to me, and it had an impact while I was awake. So, disbelieving or dismissing that it ever happened was not an option for me. The only two possibilities are that it was from God or Satan. When I have experienced a telepathic conversation, it makes it simple for me to know it is from God. Only God can read our minds and talk to us inside our minds without an audible voice. Of course, God can use an audible voice too, but Satan's only access is from the outside using our five senses to get to our minds. His final objective is always to defile our hearts and thus ruin our witness. God, on the other hand, is in our hearts trying to radiate outward to others around us when we allow Him.

As I explained previously, in my first vision, I was physically burned in a way that remained with me for three days. In this vision, I was awake and sitting at my piano at the end of the vision.

Rapture Event Vision: It was summer 1993, and as I often did, I walked the seven-minute walk from work and arrived home for lunch. Usually, my wife and kids were there, but they were gone on this particular day. As was my custom, after eating lunch, I was relaxing for around fifteen minutes before going back to work. Sometimes I would play the piano for a bit. Other times I read, thought, and prayed.

At the time this occurred, I was staying away from Rapture discussions since they seemed to be a heated conversation within the Church. Additionally, I felt I didn't have enough scriptural background to discuss it intelligently. My mindset aligned with the crowd of believers who "hope for the best and prepare for the worst." The vision started with an angel taking me up alive in the Rapture event. Going up in the Rapture brought me into a vast open area facing what looked like a large stage area going out forever, both to the left and right of me. The area was already full of people, so, there were not many seats left, and I could see angels showing other human beings to their appointed places. As the angel took me to my chair, I wondered why almost everyone was already seated. Then I remembered that those who died in Christ would be raised up first, each in their own order. I was alive and caught up, so that meant I was one of the very last to be shown a seat.[94]

When I arrived at my seat, I was so excited I turned to offer big hugs to the two men sitting next to me. As I did, I realized they were

---

94 1 Thessalonians 4:15–17

two people I did not particularly like. The angel tapped me on the shoulder to follow him out towards the back. As I walked, I stared down at the floor and saw it was as transparent as glass. I was not sure I was walking on glass, but it was a material I could see through. As I looked, I could somehow see that many types of war and chaos had broken out everywhere on the earth. I have no idea how to explain what it was I was walking on, what people seemed to be sitting on, or how I could easily see down on the earth. What I do know is that I could. As I walked towards the back, I thought to myself, *"Oh no, I'm going back to that mess on Earth."* The angel was telepathic and knew what I was thinking and responded: *"No, that is not what is written."* We eventually stopped in front of my new seat, which was very far in the back. As I stood before my chair, I looked to the front and saw what looked like a stage in a gigantic theater. It also had no end to the left or right side. I realized that what I saw straight in front of me was the exact same view everyone else had regardless of how far to my left or right they were. No turning of heads was required to watch what was happening. I knew then that we all could have had a front-row seat, with no rows behind us, as there is no limit to God. He would just expand the first row and what people saw in front of them. While this entire scene is beyond my ability to describe it well, I can say I knew we were all there because of God's Grace. There were consequences to our choices on Earth, which made it necessary to have many rows. I knew my work on Earth had produced lots of wood, hay, and stubble that would burn in the refiner's fire; however, because of Grace, I still received a seat I didn't deserve.[95]

Then I heard the opening worship song. The smallest, tiniest voic-

---

95 1 Corinthians 3:12–15

es I had ever heard were singing. It sounded like it was coming from young infants, yet the words were perfectly clear. The notes were not only in perfect pitch relative to each other, but it seemed they went from zero hertz to a million hertz. I know that is not possible as human hearing only goes up to twenty-thousand hertz, but we did have our new incorruptible bodies. The worship song's lyrics and melody were the most inspiring I had ever heard or could have ever imagined. Words here cannot describe it. Think of your favorite music, and multiply that by a million, it was that incredible. Repeatedly replaying them in my head, I immediately went over to my piano to play and record the words and notes. At that time, I was playing the piano regularly, and I had paper and pencil ready to write music. I raised my hands above the keyboard to strike the keys. As my hands moved downward, I heard a male voice behind me say, "Stop, that is for then, not now." As much as I wanted to play a few bits of the chorus, I stopped and rested my hands on the keys. Looking behind me, I could see no one there. After taking a few deep breaths, I walked away from the piano and went back to work. Even though that was well over twenty-five years ago, that experience is as clear to me today as it was back then. The worship song is still the most incredible I have ever heard. Even after all this time, it is still hard to capture the fullness of this vision.

Unlike some, I do not have very many of these visions, but I knew God had shown me the Rapture event for a reason. Following the example set by Daniel, I fasted and prayed for twenty-one days. I'm not sure why I had to wait a year for God to start showing me things about this in His Bible. Perhaps He was waiting to see if I had the patience to say nothing and wait rather than running off with "itchy" ears" at the first thing that made sense in my small, always-active mind. The first Scripture God showed me was in the Old Testament. I immediately knew why. Several years earlier, I had heard a panel of Bible experts talking about the Rapture. One of them took the position that since the Pre-Tribulation Rapture event could not be found in the Old Testament, it couldn't be true. That day, no one was there to dispute his statement. That really stuck with me as I was not near their level of understanding, but inherently I knew that if it was not in the Old Testament, it was a fabrication by man. Where did God take me? The scriptural support He showed me follows below.

Most of Zephaniah addresses the Rapture event, explaining what happens in what God calls *"In that day; the day of My anger or wrath."* I refer to this long period as the Age of Judgment, which extends from the opening of God's first Seal, goes through Jesus' one-thousand-year reign, then ends with the Great White Throne Judgment. The King James Version records that Zephaniah 2:2–3 admonishes believers to seek *"Truth before the Day of the Lord's Anger comes upon you, so you "shall" be hid in the Day of the Lord's Anger."* The Lord's anger is mentioned three times in these two verses, and those who seek Truth "shall" be hidden. I have emphasized the word "shall" because (1) that is what God wrote, and (2) it means what is written is mandatory and cannot be undone or changed. In the military world of products, where I worked for decades, a contract using "will have" instead of "shall have" created a goal to aim toward, yet was not regarded as something that absolutely must be achieved. "Shall" meant that it had to happen, or the company was in violation of the contract. God says in verse 3 that you "shall" hide, so it is not a question of believers perhaps hiding in the Day of the Lord's Anger. It is absolutely one-hundred-percent going to happen. Some of the newer Bible translations like the NKJV and NASV say something along the lines of "perhaps you "will" be hidden." To me, that is a big deal and why I tend to stick with the KJV as it applies to Biblical prophecy, rather than using newer translations that are easier to read. It is essential to pay close attention to the wording. In this case, it is saying there is something you must be doing. "If" you do what it says, then you "shall" be hidden. The "hidden" part is going to happen. The unknown is whether or not you will accept Jesus into your heart and become part of that "hidden" group.

For those Post-Tribulation believers who mock God's secret Rapture, be careful! In addition to Zephaniah, consider Isaiah 26. Read at least Isaiah 26:19–27:1. Isaiah's words clearly state the dead will rise up from their graves, enter into their rooms or chambers, and then the doors close behind them. They are to "hide" for a little moment or short time until the Lord's indignation and punishment are complete. The earth no more will cover her slain is a concise description of the Pre-Tribulation Rapture and the beginning of the Seven Seal Judgments. Isaiah 27:1 informs us, "in that day," the Lord shall finally punish Leviathan the twisted, crooked serpent. He shall also slay the dragon that is in the sea. Revelation 13:1 and Revelation 19:20 reinforce this part of Scripture. In those texts, we see a beast that rises out of the sea. That beast and the false prophet are then cast alive into the Lake of Fire.

All of this might have been meaningless if God had not said the same things in the New Testament as He mentioned in Zephaniah and Isaiah. Hopefully, you see the connection to things Jesus said. Isaiah 26 states they enter into their room or chambers; in John 14:1–3, Jesus says explicitly, *"in my Father's house, there are many mansions."* Continuing, He explains He will go to prepare a place for them, so when He comes for them, they will be where He is. Jesus does not say when He will come for them, just that He eventually will.

Isaiah 26:20 says to "shut the doors" behind them that are raised from the grave in their new bodies. Jesus says the same thing in Matthew 25. Five of the ten virgins are prepared with enough oil, and when He comes for His Bride, they go up with Him, and the door shuts behind them. The other five indifferent virgins, who were not prepared, will have to prove themselves worthy in the time of God's wrath during the opening of the 7 Seals.

More evidence supporting a Pre-Tribulation Rapture comes from 1 Corinthians 15:51–52.

Behold, I show you a mystery; We shall not all sleep, but we shall all be changed, in a moment, in the twinkling of an eye, at the last trump: for the trumpet shall sound, and the dead shall be raised incorruptible, and we shall be changed.

This raises the question, "The last trumpet of what?" Is it the last of the Feast of Trumpets? Is it the last of the Church Age? Is it the last trumpet, after Jesus' one-thousand-year reign? Does it mean the final trump forever because God will no longer sound a trumpet for all eternity?

Scripture does not support the idea that it is the last trumpet God will ever blow. God does not change, and He said feasts and other events are to be celebrated with trumpet blasts. Jesus, who is from the Tribe of Judah, states we will be celebrating the feasts during His one-thousand-year reign, including Passover. Jesus has fulfilled the first four feasts, and the next one is the Feast of Trumpets, I believe at the last trumpet of that feast, all of the church will have been raised up for the wedding that is to take place in the Father's heaven; in His house. When that happens, that will leave us with the last two feasts to be fulfilled, the Day of Atonement and Feast of Tabernacles.

Often Apostle Paul's writings require some homework and in-depth study to understand his message better. He was clearly an intelligent man who was more than adequately equipped to oppose the brightest of scholars. The fact that Apostle Paul's teachings can be hard to understand is a point confirmed in 2 Peter 3:15–16. God directs the blowing of the trumpet for all kinds of occasions. Apostle Paul's writing about the last trumpet is an opportunity to dig deep into Scripture and ask the Holy Spirit to shed light on the meaning here. We would be well served by giving Saint Irenaeus the last word on this, as he taught: *It is He who is Himself able to extend both healing and life to His handiwork, that His words concerning its [future] resurrection may also be believed; so also at the end, when the Lord utters His voice "by the last trumpet," the dead shall be raised, as He Himself declares: "The hour shall come, in which all the dead which are in the tombs shall hear the voice of the Son of man, and shall come forth; those that have done good to the resurrection of life, and those that have done evil to the resurrection of judgment."* We can see that Saint Irenaeus is referring directly to the second resurrection at the Great White Throne Judgment, where the last of both good and evil are raised up. It is the only time the evil are raised up with new bodies. That is the "last trumpet" spoken of by Apostle Paul in 1 Corinthians 15:52, and it marks the end of all evil, forever. It isn't about the trumpet; it is about the message announced from the trumpet within the context of scripture around it.

There are Scriptures stating the Body of Christ is protected. In contrast, other Scriptures warn we will suffer through tribulations. These require our attention if we are to reconcile the differences. There are many of these listed at the end of this chapter for you to study and prayerfully contemplate. As you do, a key point for understanding is there are two forms of tribulation. One is coming from Satan, and the other occurs as the Seven Seals are opened, causing the Lord's wrath to be poured out on earth. The Lord poured His wrath out upon

Earth in the flood of Noah's day, and Noah was protected. Lot and his family were physically saved by angels from God's wrath poured out on Sodom and Gomorrah in Genesis 19:15–16. God's wrath will be poured out, once again, in the Seven Seal Judgments, and God says the Bride of Christ shall be protected. The two tribulations are not the same thing; consequently, any teaching which theorizes they are should be questioned.

We have covered a lot of different yet interrelated pieces, and need to wrap up the discussion on Polycarp. What Polycarp says happens to our soul and spirit when our body dies does require looking at a few Scriptures to resolve.

> *We are confident, yes, well pleased rather to be absent from the body and to be present with the Lord.*
>
> *And since we have the same spirit of faith, according to what is written, "I believed and therefore I spoke," we also believe and therefore speak, knowing that He who raised up the Lord Jesus will also raise us up with Jesus, and will present us with you.*

These images Apostle Paul creates in 2 Corinthians 5:8 and 2 Corinthians 4:13–14 bring with them some questions. Why do they need to be "raised up" and then "presented" if they are already up there with the Lord as implied in verse eight? Paul says Jesus will raise "us" up and present "us with you." He is addressing this to people still alive. He is clearly saying "all" in the Rapture will be presented. While I need more proof than this, the apparent problem is the Rapture event results in "all" being "presented." That doesn't sound like us having a one-second party in the clouds and coming right back down to Earth in Jesus' Second Coming. What we do know, for a fact, is Jesus' soul and spirit were "raised up" from Paradise, and Mary was told not to touch Him as He had to be presented up to God the Father first.

These Scriptures bring forth more difficulties for those thinking our soul and spirit go straight up to the Father's realm, rather than going to Paradise to await their appointed time to be raised up. Further information can be gleaned through Ephesians 4:9–10 and Revelation 6:9–11.

> *Now that he ascended, what is it but that he also descended first into the lower parts of the earth? He that descended is the same also that ascended up far above all heavens, that he might fill all things.*
>
> *When He opened the fifth seal, I saw under the altar the souls of those who had been slain for the word of God and for the testimony which they held. And they cried with a loud voice, saying, "How long, O Lord, holy and true, until You judge and avenge our blood on those who dwell on the earth?" Then a white robe was given to each of them; and it was said to them that they should rest a little while longer, until both the number of their fellow servants and their brethren, who would be killed as they were, was completed.*

For a person who believes we go straight to the third heaven to be with the Father and Jesus, the problem presented in Revelation 6:9–11 is it doesn't happen with this group of people stuck under the altar. Why are they destined for more "rest" "under the altar"? Where is under the altar? Why are they not allowed with the others "above" the altar in Revelation 4 and 5? Some simple answers are:

1. God temporarily allows Satan limited power over the earth and the air, but Satan has no authority over everything else, including both the good and bad sides of Hell. Thus, we can

be in Paradise, the good side, and be present with the Lord who governs over it at the same time.

2. Satan also has no control over the bad side of Hell. They are not eating cake and ice cream over there, and they are not beating up each other. This is confirmed by the rich man in Luke 16:19–27.

3. Polycarp agrees with what the Bible says. We all, including this group under the altar, enter into rest until the appointed time of our resurrection.[96] They have not yet arrived at their appointed time to be resurrected, and they have to wait as others are still being added to their group. There is another group that is raised up over one thousand years after this. They are those that died in Jesus' thousand-year reign from Jerusalem and got their new bodies at the White Throne Judgment. The interesting point here is where do their soul and spirit go upon death? If they go to be with Jesus, does that mean their soul and spirit float around Jesus in Jerusalem because they have to be exactly where Jesus is at all times until they get reunited with their new bodies at the White Throne Judgment? No, their soul and spirit go down to Paradise like always, God's process never changes. The Old Testament Saints went to rest in Paradise, the New Testament Saints go to rest in Paradise, and the Millennial Saints will go to rest in Paradise where all saints await their appointed time to be reunited with their new body for all eternity.

---

96 Dan.12:13

While we may be able to understand man is three-in-one enclosed within a living body, our ability to picture how God can exist as three-in-one is often limited. If the earth is God's footstool, how does He fit into the Ark of the Covenant or the Holy of Holies, yet be everywhere else in the universe at the exact same time? I understand it by seeing God's all-knowing Soul is God the Father, God the Spirit is the Holy Spirit, and God the Body is Jesus. As a human being, who sees only partially, it is difficult to package it all together. The fact that it is difficult for me to understand does not make it untrue. It just means my finite mind cannot understand everything on this side of eternity.

Perhaps I can make it simpler and share a big failure on my part in the process. I was witnessing to an open-minded Rabbi in training. I was sure God wanted us to talk about how God was three-in-one just as we were. I brought up that we were created in God's image. He quickly cut me off and said the Tanakh says God was addressing all His beings when He said, "let us create man in our image." His position means man was in the combined image of God, His angels, and living beings. This allowed man to have a soul, body, and spirit, but not God. I was dumbfounded and had no response. Afterward, I asked God what went wrong. Did I not hear Him correctly? God's immediate response was that I asked Him what to talk about, but did not ask Him how to go about it. I decided by myself how to go about it. After that episode, I then asked Him how He wanted me to do it should there ever be a next time.

The response He gave me started with proving man has a soul, body, and spirit. Most Jews will agree with this point, but for those who do not, point out the Scriptural support from the Tanakh. Then use support for God, having all three can be examined.

God's soul is revealed through references like Leviticus 26:11 *"I will set My tabernacle among you, and My soul shall not abhor you,"* Leviticus 26:30 *"I will destroy your high places, cut down your incense altars, and cast your carcasses on the lifeless forms of your idols; and My soul shall not abhor you,"* and Isaiah 42:1 *"Behold! My Servant whom I uphold, My Elect One in whom My soul delights! I have put My Spirit upon Him,"* which covers two things as it establishes God has both a Soul and a Spirit.

God reveals He has a spirit also through other Tanakh verses. Genesis 6:3 *"And the Lord said, "My Spirit shall not strive with man forever, for he is indeed flesh,"* and Isaiah 44:3 *"... I will pour My Spirit on your descendants, And My blessing on your offspring."*

Those Scriptures reveal two of the three. Perhaps God's Body is harder to describe and understand, with our small inadequate minds. I believe that has more to do with us trying to put God's body in some sort of container in the way we think about things, and we really should not be limiting God in that way. If we start with the understanding that God's Body has a physical nature to it, which is also supernatural, then the following verses should make sense and prove God has a Body.

His body is not exactly like our body, but it functions similar to ours in that God can walk and talk with Adam and Eve in the garden, and has hands He used to create coverings of skin for them and yet flashes of rays can come out of them.[97] Isaiah 66:1 says Heaven is where He sits on His throne, and the earth is His footstool. Trying to make God the Father fit into a form with actual hands, feet, face, and voice, as we understand, is like putting something supernatural into a natural, manmade box, and expecting the box to keep the supernatural

---

97 Gen. 3:21, Hab. 3:4

contained in it until reopening the box. Scripture says God has hands, feet, and voice, but it also says they do not exist as ours do.

The concept of God being three-in-one shouldn't be a hard one for us who live in today's world. A cell phone is a physical item (its body). Yet, like a human's soul, it has different internal electronics that define it and give it life. Otherwise, it is an empty vessel. Each cell phone has its own unique features making them all different from each other like phone numbers, memories with pictures, etc. In addition to its soul and body, it has a wireless feature that functions as the spirit within man. God had the original wireless capability, and it is called the Holy Spirit. Our wireless human spirit, when we let it, communicates with God's wireless Holy Spirit. Our cell phone's wireless feature, when we direct it, communicates with the more extensive wireless system that connects all of us who have them. All believers are connected with each other and God through God's extensive Holy Spirit network. I understand how people hundreds of years ago might have struggled with God as a three-in-one concept, but we have many examples of that concept today.

Supernatural God has dimensions we do not have. Habakkuk 3:4–6, describes God as having a fever following His feet and hands that somehow had rays flashing out of them. God is three in one; we just do not have a way to understand that completely.

His brightness was like the light; He had rays flashing from His hand, And there His power was hidden. Before Him went pestilence, And fever followed at His feet. He stood and measured the earth; He looked and startled the nations.

In Genesis 3:8–9, it says God was walking in Eden and spoke to Adam. Many verses tell us God can walk, talk, and see because He has hands, feet, and a voice. *And they heard the sound of the Lord God walking in the garden in the cool of the day, and Adam and his wife hid themselves from the presence of the Lord God among the trees of the garden. Then the Lord God [spoke] called to Adam and said to him, "Where are you?"*

A pivotal Scripture to prove God has a Soul (Father), Body (Jesus), and Spirit (Holy Spirit), and they are all God in one package is Psalm 110:1. God is quoted as saying, *"The Lord said to my Lord."* The Gospels record Jesus repeated this many times, so we could not mistake the fact that Jesus was God, and God co-exists as Father, Son, and Holy Spirit. How else can the Lord say to my Lord?

Considering when the Rapture happens and where our soul and spirit go when our body dies, directs our attention to 1 Thessalonians 4:13–17. *But I would not have you to be ignorant, brethren, concerning them which are asleep, that ye sorrow not, even as others which have no hope For if we believe that Jesus died and rose again, even so them also which sleep in Jesus will God bring with him. For this we say unto you by the word of the Lord, that we which are alive and remain unto the coming of the Lord shall not prevent them which are asleep. For the Lord himself shall descend from heaven with a shout, with the voice of the archangel, and with the trump of God: and the dead in Christ shall rise first: Then we which are alive and remain shall be caught up together with them in the clouds, to meet the Lord in the air: and so shall we ever be with the Lord.* As Apostle Paul answers this question to the Thessalonian, the keywords are "asleep," "died," "are now asleep," they are not up in the third heaven worshipping, and other activities. Apostle Paul is answering one of the questions the Thessalonians had about their brethren that had died. He told them not to worry, for they that are asleep will be raised up first. That place of asleep-sleep-rest, as we have learned, is the Paradise side of Hell. Between verses 13 through 17, Paul states that they are asleep or sleep three times. This is very consistent with what the Old Testament teaches and indeed what many of the early Christians, such as Polycarp, taught. Then in verse 16, we see Jesus descends from His place, in His Father's heaven, and the dead are raised first. They are raised from their slumber. So, either they are asleep in the Father's heaven, or they are asleep on the good side of Hell. Paul says the same thing in 1 Corinthians 15. Verse 6 says some believers have fallen asleep already, verse eighteen talks about those who have fallen asleep in Christ, and verse twenty says Jesus was the first raised from them that slept. Clearly, Jesus went down to the place where our souls go to sleep. It is your eternity, so it is your homework to do. As for me, I believe if I die before Jesus comes for me in the Rapture, I will go down to rest in Paradise, where all the church saints are. Not because of what I have done, but because of what Jesus did for me.

Older versions like KJV and ASV, and also, the newer NKJV, refer to the Bride in the third heaven as the "wife." You cannot be the wife up there if you are not married. I find it quite awkward if Jesus somehow married up there to souls without bodies. Nor is it plausible they all came down to the clouds, got their new bodies, met those who were still alive on the earth, immediately got married in the clouds between the Father's heaven and Earth. Then as fast as we get married in the clouds, while Satan and all his angels are creating chaos right behind us, we are then on Earth in the midst of the Armageddon battle. I cannot speak for anyone else, but to me, there are too many contradictions with this and other scripture to accept a Post-Tribulation Rapture. Then again, your opinion may vary; it's your eternity to investigate.

Revelation 19 says that all the "wives" of Christ are in the third heaven before the Father's Throne and coming down as part of the army with Jesus. That army includes those of us who were raised up last because we were still alive on the earth. *Let us be glad and rejoice and give Him glory, for the marriage of the Lamb has come, and His wife has made herself ready." Let us be glad and rejoice, and give honour to him: for the marriage of the Lamb is come, and his wife hath made herself ready. And to her was granted that she should be arrayed in fine linen, clean and white: for the fine linen is the righteousness of saints. And he saith unto me, Write, Blessed are they which are called unto the marriage supper of the Lamb. And he saith unto me, These are the true sayings of God.*

The Post-Tribulation teachings that everything somehow happens "in the clouds" above Earth, and virtually at the end of the Seven-year Tribulation period, makes no sense no matter how hard you try and make it work with Revelation 19. The meaning of wife in Revelation 19 is a short topic, appropriately in another chapter, as it causes us to determine the root of the Greek word "gamos" and the implication of God's usage of the Greek word Kai in the Book of Revelation. Some Bible versions like the NIV and NAS avoid the controversy by neutering Scripture and calling her the Bride as in not married yet. Still, in reality, the Bride can't be there "ready" for the marriage if she doesn't have her "new" Raptured body to wear her white linen and ride down from the Father's heaven on white horses. Revelation 19:7 and 9 say the Bride is coming to Earth for the wedding supper. How can they come to Earth for the Wedding Supper if they have not yet been married in the third heaven before the Father? Besides, getting Raptured to the clouds and married there means the marriage is actually in the Earth's atmosphere, not God the Father's heavenly house. God's word is very specific, and you cannot change it to agree with what you were taught or were thinking.

When talking about end times prophecy, it is fundamentally important for people to understand that in death, our soul and spirit go down to the good side of Hell. If a person can understand that, then end times prophecy is simpler to understand, and false teachings are more readily recognized. A person can understand prophecy in the Scriptures, but they will have to work much harder at it if they think they go straight to the third heaven upon death. In my opinion, it is a key that helps unlock the proper handling of the Rapture and end-time prophecy.

Truly our God is beyond all we can conceptualize and thoroughly comprehend. It is reassuring that He has planned the end of time well before the beginning of time. He has designed all of mankind and will be with everyone through to their appointed time. His Word has been set down for all who want to know more about Him and His ways with an open invitation to come to Him, ask your questions, and receive His answers, and perhaps even a few visions from Him. Believing in your heart that He is Lord guarantees rest in Paradise until your appointed time, a new Raptured body, a celebration like no other, and a choice place to spend eternity. What is in your eternity?

For Further Study

To invite you to understand what is in your eternity, The One True God is saying to you:

> *"Call to Me, and I will answer you, and show you great and mighty things, which you do not know."*

> —JEREMIAH 33:3

- Matthew 12:40; Ephesians 4:9–10

- Psalm 110:1 quoted by Jesus Matthew 22:44, Mark 12:36, Luke 20:42, and Acts 2:34

- Luke 16, Luke 23:43, Ephesians 4:8–10, and 1 Samuel 28:13–15.

- Job 3:11–19; Isaiah 57:1–2, Daniel 12:13

- John 20:17; Acts 1:9–11.

- Psalm 2:9; Revelation 2:27, 12:5, 19:15, 20:7–9; Zechariah 14:16–19

- Zechariah 14:7; Jude 1:14; Revelation 19:7–14

- Jeremiah 30

- Luke 21:11; Matthew 24:6–8

- John 14:1–3, Matthew 25:1–12, Luke 13:23–28, and Luke 21:36.

- 1 Thessalonians 1:10, 5:4 & 9; 2 Thessalonians 3:3; Revelation 3:10

- John 16:33, Acts 14:22; 2 Timothy 3:12

- Isaiah 26 and 27

CHAPTER SIXTEEN

BOOK OF DANIEL
MADE SIMPLE

God gave mankind His written word to guide our daily lives and to reveal His nature and character. Occasionally while studying the Bible, His message is simple at first but then becomes more complicated. The Book of Daniel can be that way for some of us. Taking a simple approach and focusing on the main point provides a way to find what God is revealing through the prophet Daniel.

The main message in Daniel is centered on the four kingdoms that rule over Israel, starting with the Babylonians and ending with the Romans. God gives Daniel three different dreams describing those four kingdoms. Each covers additional detail about the four empires. God provides those details, but we must not allow them to distract us and cause us to lose sight of what God is trying to tell us. These are the only four kingdoms that matter, and the fourth kingdom ends when Jesus rules from Jerusalem for one thousand years. God says there are only four, and He says multiple times that He will destroy the fourth ruling empire.

The three different visions and explanations given to Daniel are:

1. The first is found in Daniel, chapter two. It is Nebuchadnezzar's dream, which God revealed to Daniel with the exact contents of the dream and the meaning of the four kingdoms represented by the statue of gold, silver, bronze, and iron.

2.   The second vision is described in Daniel, chapter seven. It consists of four beasts, a lion, a bear, a leopard, and the fourth beast with iron teeth. This vision came in the first year of King Belshazzar, who had replaced King Nebuchadnezzar.

3.   The third vision is detailed in Daniel 8 and comes in the third year of Belshazzar's reign.

The three different visions given to Daniel are about four empires that will rule over Israel. Daniel explains the first three are the Babylonians, the Medes–Persians, and the Grecian Empires. The fourth was evidenced during Jesus' days on Earth as the Roman Empire. No empire conquered the Roman Empire, nor has there been one since the Romans.

It is essential to understand these four kingdoms ruled over and in Israel, when Israel as a land existed. Even Nebuchadnezzar established rule and reigned for a short time in Israel, appointing Gedaliah as the governor of Judah.[98] When the second kingdom, the Medes and Persians governed, they allowed the Israelites to return to their land and rebuild Jerusalem and their Temple. The occupation of Israel by foreign rule continued through the Grecian and Roman Empires. The fourth occupation in the land of Israel ends with the destruction of Jerusalem and the Temple in AD 70. Israel ceased to be a country, and so there has not been another since the fourth. Israel did become a nation again about nineteen hundred years later in 1948. Since then, no other country has ruled over them. God said there were only four kingdoms until He rules from Jerusalem, so, what happened to that fourth kingdom? Well, it is crucial to understand that when Jesus re-

---

98 2 Kings 25:22

turns to reign for the millennium, He will destroy the fourth kingdom. The fourth kingdom has yet to be defeated and exists today, perhaps in a weakened condition, but it will regain strength and rule over and in the land of Israel.

Several Scriptures point to the final Antichrist ruler declaring himself to be God in the rebuilt Temple. I believe current self-governed Israel will sign over their sovereignty to another power for seven years of protection and peace. Standing in the rebuilt Temple, the leader of this agreement will declare he is God as proof he is the king of the twelve tribes of Israel. However, Daniel has told us how this ends, as the stone cut without hands will destroy that fourth kingdom, and Jesus shall rule from Jerusalem.

There is some evidence of a reformed Roman Empire that will sign the seven-year peace treaty with Israel. We must investigate to see if there is more information. Daniel 9:26, says the "antichrist of all antichrists" is to come from the people who destroyed Jerusalem and the Second Temple. The Roman General Titus gave the orders to destroy the Second Temple during the days of the Apostles. He further instructed the forces to bring all the booty from their destruction to Rome. Many historical documents record this event. General Titus sent Josephus, a Jewish historian, to Jerusalem to negotiate with Israel. That effort failed, so the general gave orders to destroy the Temple and Jerusalem. Josephus documented the events of this encounter. There may still be Temple booty hidden somewhere in Rome today. The fourth empire of *iron* weakened with clay is the last part of the fourth kingdom, the Roman Empire. Clay is not a metal and is a contaminant reducing the strength of the iron, so, the end days of this fourth empire is not as strong as they were. Christ comes and destroys this fourth empire upon His return to reign from Jerusalem.

Chapter one relates that Nebuchadnezzar conquers Judah and makes off with the prized articles of the Temple, but most Israelites are left alive. A few of them were chosen to serve in the King's palace. Of those, Daniel, Hananiah, Mishael, and Azariah were singled out by God. He chose them because they did not defile themselves with the king's delicacies and wine. When facing certain death in the fiery furnace Hananiah, Mishael, and Azariah answered the king by stating matter-of-factly that their God was able to save them from death. They continue by saying that even if He decided not to, it would not change anything. To them, that would signify it was their time to meet God because their purpose on Earth was completed.[99] God saved them from the fiery furnace, and later, He saved Daniel in the lions' den.

In the book of Daniel, God established His power, which easily overcomes any man-made situation. He also set in stone the proper character of believers, highlighting the need for them to fear Him only, rather than fearing man.[100] God continues to promote Daniel, Hananiah, Mishael, and Azariah in the eyes of their captors and blesses them with knowledge and skill in literature and wisdom. God gifts Daniel with the ability to understand visions and dreams, which reveal the primary purpose of the Book of Daniel. God established why He liked these four Israelites and entrusted prophecy that affects all mankind to Daniel because of his strong character. Those prophecies include the first and second coming of Jesus to reign on the earth. Daniel reveals the first time He was rejected but makes it clear rejection will not be an option the second time.[101]

Daniel's visions, involving the four kingdoms, span across

---

99 Dan. 3:17–18
100 Isa. 11:2; Matt. 10:28
101 Dan. 9:26, Dan. 2:44

time. They stretch from the days of Nebuchadnezzar to the day when Jesus defeats the Antichrist at the start of the Millennium. Daniel's first dream interpretation is for Nebuchadnezzar. God gave Nebuchadnezzar a dream where he sees four kingdoms that start with him and end with the coming of the Messiah to reign and rule on Earth. He didn't understand the dream but was desperate to have it interpreted. He threatened to kill all his magicians, astrologers and sorcerers if they were unable to explain it to him. God gave the key to understanding the dream to Daniel. This message is so important to God that he brings these four kingdoms up three different times to Daniel. The first time in Chapter Two, verse forty, makes it clear there are only four kingdoms, and the fourth ends at the hands of the God of Heaven. In this chapter, God establishes that there will only be four important kingdoms that rule in and over Israel until He (Jesus) puts an end to that and sets up His kingdom without end. To date, that is about twenty-six hundred years and counting, as Jesus has yet to come and rule.

Because of the importance of these four kingdoms and how it all comes to an end, God gave Nebuchadnezzar the dream and Daniel the ability to interpret it. But God wants to show us more details about these four kingdoms so we can be sure there are only four that matter, and they take us into the thousand-year reign of Jesus from Jerusalem. It is imperative to keep that in mind and never get creative and add or subtract from God's Word. So, God shows Daniel the four different kingdoms that matter, three different ways and with increasing detail. The more detail God gives us, the more likely it is to create confusion. So, when in doubt, refer back to Nebuchadnezzar's dream in Daniel 2. It is clear and will help keep us from getting derailed.

Daniel, chapter seven, details the second vision of the four kingdoms. It is in the first year of King Belshazzar who followed in Nebuchadnezzar's footsteps. In this version, Daniel sees the kingdoms as four beasts, instead of four metals. He sees a lion, a bear, a leopard, and a fourth beast that was different than anything Daniel had ever seen. The interpretation of the vision depicts the four beasts as the four kings of four kingdoms. It foretells that the fourth beast would be overcome by a realm that is an everlasting kingdom of the Most High. Once again, we see God defeats the fourth kingdom and replaced it with His eternal kingdom.

Daniel 8 describes the third version stating it was in the third year of King Belshazzar. This time Scripture identifies two of the beasts with more detail. The second beast is called a ram with two horns. I am not sure why God chose to describe the second kingdom after Nebuchadnezzar in three different ways. We find it illustrated as a kingdom of silver in its chest and arms, then a bear, and finally, a ram with two horns. The ram with two horns represents the Medes and Persians who join forces and defeat King Belshazzar. An interesting fact here is that Daniel knew who was eventually going to conquer King Belshazzar before "Mene, Mene, Tekel, Upharsin" mysteriously appeared on a wall at Belshazzar's party.

In Daniel 8, Greece, the third kingdom, is represented by a goat. So, the third kingdom described through the three visions has a belly and thighs of bronze, is a leopard, and then is a goat. Alexander the Great conquered the Persians and Medes, which is the ram with two horns, but when he died suddenly, the kingdom was split between four of his generals. The four generals are described in Daniel 7:6 by the dominion given to the four heads, and in Daniel 8:8 as the four notables. It sounds like a movie title, "The Four Notables."

The most confusing kingdom is the fourth. It is easy to see Jesus, the stone formed without hands, will conquer it when He returns, but where is this fourth kingdom today? Daniel is given the names of the first three kingdoms, but not this one. What or who took over the empire that belonged to Alexander the Great? Before exploring this, we must define the land area being discussed.

It all starts with Nebuchadnezzar, who conquered and controlled a large landmass consisting of at least parts of current-day Iran, Iraq, Afghanistan, Turkey, Syria, Saudi Arabia, Jordan, Israel, Lebanon, Egypt, parts of Central Asia, Pakistan, and Macedonia-Greece. The key in all of this is Israel, of course. So, what empires ruled over the stated land areas and inside of Israel? We know that, in chronological order, the Babylonians, Medes and Persians, Greek Hellenistic, and Romans all ruled over that landmass, which included Israel. However, in AD 70, Jerusalem and the Second Temple were destroyed, and the Israelites endured Diaspora. A unique point here is that only two kingdoms have ever destroyed Jerusalem and the Temple, and removed Israelites from the land. They are the Babylonian and Roman Kingdoms. There is more significance to this than some give. The vision never names the fourth kingdom, and in many respects, it is a mystery kingdom, especially since it does not seem to exist today. There was no Israel to rule over from the time the Temple was destroyed in AD 70 until 1948 when they became a nation again. Because there are only four kingdoms to rule over Israel, one of those four must be reborn just as Israel was. Then Israel must submit sovereignty to this empire's rule, and that sounds exactly like what we know today as the One World Order. The books of Daniel and Revelation affirm this will happen through a seven-year treaty. That agreement will allow them to build the Third Temple. That fourth kingdom must also contain iron. It seems this means Israel will submit to a reformed Roman Empire (iron with clay) for seven years for protection and peace.

Daniel 9 contains a prophecy concerning seventy weeks. God punished Israel with a seventy-year exile in Babylon because, in their disobedience, they did not allow the ground to rest every seventh year. When you compute seven times seventy years, it yields four hundred and ninety years of missed rest for the land. The seventy weeks of years talked about in Daniel 9 is also seventy weeks times seven or four hundred and ninety years, as well. The first thing to keep in mind is that these seventy weeks are not consecutive years. I believe misunderstanding this point has confused people trying to account for four hundred and ninety successive years. Otherwise, we could add the seven weeks of years to the sixty-two weeks of years and arrive at the death of Jesus on the cross. Following that logic, by adding the last seven years, then we would know when Jesus was going to return and reign from Jerusalem. That would mean that when Jesus died, AD 30, plus the last seven years takes us to AD 37. The destruction of the Temple came much later, revealing the seventy weeks of years cannot be consecutive. That is why they were broken down into three groups in Daniel. The seven weeks, sixty-two weeks, and one week are three separate events, each having separate start and stop times. As a way to explore this topic, I will work in reverse beginning with the last week of years.[102] The seven-year covenant with the coming Antichrist starts this seventieth, or last week of years. That prince has not yet come, but he will soon. Until this happens, there will be no Third Temple that allows for the restart of the Israeli sacrifices during that last week of years. The Antichrist, whose abominations make the Temple desolate, will bring an end to those sacrifices. It has been about two thousand

---

102 Dan. 9:26–27

years since the death of Christ, and there is still no seven-year covenant allowing Israel to build the Third Temple and restart their sacrifices. While it seems imminent, there are a few things that must fall into place first.

A quick summary of the start and stop events for the three different periods in Daniel 9:

1. First seven weeks of years: This is a total of forty-nine years of decreeing to rebuild Jerusalem and the Temple. The decrees did not contain the same information making it difficult to know where these forty-nine years fit. This time period has ended, and the total effort didn't go smoothly evidenced by at least three, if not four, decrees. One was by Cyrus around 537 BC, a second by Darius 520 BC, a third by Artaxerxes 457 BC. There was possibly a fourth by Artaxerxes in 445 BC. Some say that the fourth was simply a duplicate that confirmed Artaxerxes' original decree. While there is not a way to pinpoint this, there is enough information to estimate its timing.

2. The second timeframe of sixty-two weeks of years: This is a total of four hundred and thirty-four years ending with the death of Jesus. If Jesus died in AD 30, this would indicate this period started around 404 BC. This is only an example because we don't know when God considered the rebuilding of the Second Temple and Jerusalem completed. Since there were so many different decrees, we know Israel had difficulty getting this done. What we do know for certain is that the destruction of the Second Temple did not complete the seventy weeks of Daniel. The pertinent facts are that there was no peace treaty

or covenant signed with Roman forces, and nobody stood in the Temple and declared he was God. Additionally, the last week is only seven years long, and the Second Temple was not destroyed until AD 70 or about 40 years after Christ died on the cross. The end marker for these 62 weeks is very clear as it ended with Christ's death in AD 30.

3.   The third timeframe of 1 week of years or the seventieth week: This is a total of seven years starting with the seven-year covenant between Israel and the Antichrist of all antichrists. The Antichrist kills the two witnesses revealed in Revelation 11, defiles the Temple at the half-way point, and demands all people must worship him as if he is God.[103] All of these elements are clear indications that this last week has not yet started.

The last week brings us to the end of the four Kingdoms described by Daniel through three different visions over the reign of two Babylonian Kings, Nebuchadnezzar and Belshazzar.

---

103 Rev. 13

For Further Study

To invite you to understand what is in your eternity, The One True God is saying to you:

> *"Call to Me, and I will answer you, and show you*
> *great and mighty things, which you do not know."*
>
> —JEREMIAH 33:3

- The Book of Daniel

- Daniel 2:34–35, 44–45

- Daniel 2:44, Zechariah 9:9–10, Zechariah 14:9–11, Revelation 20:6

- Daniel 9:27, Matthew 24:15, and 2 Thessalonians

CHAPTER SEVENTEEN

GREEK WORD GAMOS

I will cover two Greek words as defined via the Strong's and Thayer's reference materials that I use. Revelation 19:7, in the KJV, NKJV, DARBY, GNV, WYC, YLT, and other literal translations translate "gamos" to wife. Literal translations are those which translate word for word, as opposed to easier to read translations that use thought for thought equivalents. All are good, and it is the Holy Spirit that leads and guides us into all Truth. Some of them, like the Common English Version, say, "the wedding day of the Lamb is here, and His Bride is ready." No matter how it is worded, there should be no mistake that the "Bride" means the believers in Christ's free gift of Grace. They are in Heaven getting married, and then they come down to Earth for the Wedding Supper, which always comes after the wedding. No wedding, no wedding supper. Not only that but in order to be the ready Bride, we have to have our Raptured incorruptible bodies. No Rapture, then no Bride present and ready for marriage. This occasionally seems complicated, so, the next section is to provide you with more facts.

Strong's Concordance: Hebrew #1060 gameo (gam-eh'-o); #1062; to wed; used of either sex
KJV-- marry (to lead in marriage; take to wife).

Thayer's Greek Lexicon: #1060 gameo-

1.   to lead in marriage, take to wife

    a. to get married, to marry

    b. to give oneself in marriage

    c. to give a daughter in marriage

The usage of the Greek word "gameo" above (#1060) is the word used when the Bridegroom comes to take his Bride. It is a derivative of the more general word "gamos" (#1062) listed below.

> 1062 gamos (gam'-os); of uncertain affinity; nuptials: KJV—marriage, wedding. (Strong's)
> 1062 gamos-

> 1. a wedding or marriage festival, a wedding banquet, a wedding feast

> 2. marriage, matrimony (Thayer's)

The Greek word gamos is not the proper word concerning a man coming for his Bride, but rather it is used to generically refer to a wedding, or a wedding banquet, as can be evidenced in the definitions above. For example, we see the generic use of "gamos" (#1062) when Jesus attends the marriage at Cana and makes wine. As implied, at Cana, "marriage" (#1062) means Jesus made wine for the wedding supper happening right then, as opposed to being a future date:

- *And both Jesus was called, and his disciples, to the marriage. And when they wanted wine, the mother of Jesus saith unto him, They have no wine. John 2:2–3 KJV*

Another place that #1062 (gamos) is used is in Revelation 19:

- *And he saith unto me, Write, Blessed are they which are called unto the marriage supper of the Lamb. And he saith unto me, These are the true sayings of God. Revelation 19:9 KJV*

The important point is that in Revelation 19, the Bridegroom and Bride were married in Heaven, and are coming down for the

"Wedding Supper." Note that the King James Version and many others call it the "supper." You don't have the marriage supper before the marriage. They are married, and this "wife" is up in the third heaven. The Seven-year Tribulation period is over. Now Jesus, the Groom, and the Church, His Wife, are coming out of the place Jesus prepared in His Father's house. Then they go to the Wedding Supper on Earth.

• *Let us be glad and rejoice and give Him glory, for the marriage of the Lamb has come, and His wife has made herself ready. Rev. 19:7 NKJ*

Here it is translated "wife" (gamos #1062), but many newer versions of the Bible blur this, perhaps not wanting to offend anyone concerning the location of the Rapture. Regardless, the Greek word is "gune," and it refers to "wife." In doing a search in the New Testament for "gune," which is #1135, it is either translated as wife or married woman. One example is *Wives, submit to your own husbands, as is fitting in the Lord. Husbands, love your wives and do not be bitter toward them. Colossians 3:18–19NKJ*

Strong's Concordance: Greek #1135 gune (goo-nay'); probably from the base of 1096; a woman; especially, a wife: KJV-- wife, woman.

Thayer's Greek Lexicon: #1135 gune-

1. a woman of any age, whether a virgin, or married, or a widow

2. a wife; used of a betrothed woman

For Further Study

To invite you to understand what is in your eternity, The One True God is saying to you:

> *"Call to Me, and I will answer you, and show you*
> *great and mighty things, which you do not know."*
>
> — JEREMIAH 33:3

- Revelation 19

- Colossians 3

CHAPTER EIGHTEEN

LETTER TO SON JAKE

Hi Jake,

Because you asked about Thessalonians, in general, I thought that I should provide some background that many have not considered. Then it is up to you and God. I really like the fact that you are not taking somebody's word for it, but rather digging into scripture like the Bereans did to see if "these things were true." I know that referring to the Bereans is a bit too common, as some are memorizing and repeating another man's writings about scripture, rather than sticking to what the Bible is saying about digging in yourself, and taking what is written straight up within the context around it. I am not saying there is anything wrong with memorizing scripture, just pointing out that knowing what is there without personal understanding is a big problem, from my perspective. This is why the seven aspects of the Holy Spirit (Isaiah 11) include both "knowledge" and "understanding." At first, that seems redundant, but they are two separate things. That and you really need the OT & NT together to be properly balanced and grounded in scripture. An important piece, always, is to ask God to reveal His Truth and to cause the nonsense to crumble and blow away like fine dust in the wind. Be patient and wait, as He will connect the dots in His time. God may rarely be early, but He is never late. Yes, I am a bit of a stickler concerning all of this, but it is "My Eternity," and I am not trusting that to anyone but Jesus. We should all be accepting responsibility for our own Eternity. Piece by piece, year by year, God has been working on me as I let Him. Some years have been better than others. I am as human as anybody and do not always let Him do that. I'll never be perfect, and it takes time to grow through all the stages from an infant to an elder in our maturity. It is one of those continuous improvement processes that, with a willing heart and mind, really does improve with time and effort. Not all grow up to be elders in their walk with God, but that is their choice. We all have our own "free will" to choose. Regardless, God knows how to use us all. He will use some to plant, others to do some watering, but only God causes the growth (1 Corinthians 3:5–8). So, we should be doing what God has given us to do, and then get out of the way so that God can do what He does.

Do not confuse God's grace with works. They are two completely different things. Grace being God's unmerited free gift if we accept it and has nothing to do with storing treasures up in heaven through good works with the abilities God has placed in us. We do not all have the exact same capabilities, but we all have the ability to deliver on the capabilities that God has given to us. Some it is through sports, others music or in business, there are skilled teachers and intercessors. Many, many different natural capabilities that allow the least of us to be difference makers as we allow God to come through us in those areas. Many times it may seem a small thing to us, but it is not to God. Do not grow weary, but rather do good to all, as you have the opportunity, especially to those who are brothers and sisters walking with God (Galatians 6:7–10).

By the way, I am not saying to ignore what others say and do concerning scripture, but I am saying that all is in God's hands, do your best to hear what He is saying and search scripture to see if those things are true. It is your eternity, not anyone else's, and discerning the difference matters or the works we do becomes about us and not God. The works being subtle and not in your face, being effective, not destructive. We all have to be able to support what we believe with the (entire) Bible in mind. It is not a book written by man, and we need God's help to understand Him and His scripture. Reasoning and rationalizing with our own small (finite) minds does not provide good fruit, which is why the Bereans were commended for digging into the written Word as opposed to the Thessalonians. Either what is said is consistent with all scripture, or it is not. No gray area there. In sticking with colors, man likes to create the gray area, but God is very black & white. The catch is that you really have to know "and" understand all the scripture to be in balance (OT & NT). Jesus gave each of us a brain and His Holy Spirit to do that, and we just need to press into Him and wait for Him to provide clarity in His timing. Let us not be accused of having itchy ears when we meet our Maker (2 Timothy 4:3–4). Heresy comes from itchy ears, and the apostles were fighting that back in their day, and it still continues. The enemy never rests and is very good at what he does. We can see it throughout the Church today. There are more different versions to end times prophecy than I have the desire to count. The many different arguments and support by men may be powerful, but only one can be right. That alone should really bother people and get them digging to discern the Truth. God holds each of us, individually, accountable for what we have done in the flesh, so, playing the blame game serves absolutely no useful purpose. It is your eternity, so, press in for Truth. God will give you what you need when you need it.

Moving onto Apostle Paul, what he did, concerning end times prophecy, was to write at least two letters to the Thessalonians. They are core to what we are investigating here. Yes, there are basic things that Paul does in all of his letters like "Hi, from Paul & Silvanus & Timothy," the church name he is writing to, peace and a word of praise and thanksgiving or blessing. In the end, Paul then finishes up with some practical matters, some personal greetings, a personal remark, and a prayer. In the midst of all that is the meat or main reason, he is writing. Sometimes there are multiple reasons as to why he is writing, but both the letters to the Thessalonians surround the same end-times topic. The key is to understand the main reason or reasons as to "why" Paul is writing.

To set the stage, we see in 1 Thessalonians 2 that Paul is telling them that what he had told them previously about the rapture, in person, was, in fact, the Truth and nothing but the Truth. 1 Thessalonians 2:2–3 Paul acknowledges that he and others had "indeed" suffered in Philippi and came to them in many conflicts, but their words and teachings were not affected by that in any way, shape, or form. That they delivered 100% Truth, there was zero uncleanliness or deceit in what they spoke, and they were not changing anything. That put the church at Thessalonica in a bind because they had been hearing other teachings that conflicted with Apostle Paul's, and they thought both sides were credible. So, they were hoping that Paul was wrong and trying to give him an easy out for some understandably bad teachings. Apostle Paul would have none of that, and we can see in Paul's second letter to them, 2 Thessalonians 2:5 that Paul is quite upset at the Thessalonians as not only did he tell them the truth about the rapture (once) in person (as stated in 2 Thessalonians 2:5), he had (also) sent Timothy on a second visit "before" he wrote 1 Thessalonians as stated in 1 Thessalonians 3 (1 Thessalonians 3:1–6). So, on four different occasions, two in person and two by letter, Paul tried to set the record straight. It is unclear if the Thessalonians ever got it straight. The order of events was:

1. Paul and his group were there in person, instructing the Thessalonians on the rapture, amongst other things.

2. Paul heard reports while in Athens that seriously disturbed him, so, he sent Timothy back to them (1 Thessalonians 3:1–3) to set things straight.

3. Upon Timothy's return to Paul, Paul then wrote 1 Thessalonians to hammer the main points home concerning the fact that they are not appointed to wrath (1 Thessalonians 1:10 & 1 Thessalonians 5:3–5) and exactly how the rapture event works and where it is relative to other end-time events (1 Thessalonians 4:all).

4. Somehow, after the two different visits and then the 1 Thessalonians letter, Paul had to write 2 Thessalonians. 2 Thessalonians 1 is all about God (finally) repaying those who have persecuted the Church. In chapter 2, Apostle Paul lays out, once again, the sequence of end-times events, and it seems that he is pulling out even more hair, if he has any left, as seen in 2 Thessalonians 2:5 when he says "Do you not remember that when I was with you, I told you these things?". Apostle Paul sounds quite frustrated over the fact that they still do not get it. I am sure he would be equally frustrated with the Church today and the mess we have made with end times prophecy.

The answer as to why the Thessalonians were having trouble discerning who was telling them the Truth will be answered, using scripture, but onto the letters Paul wrote to the Thessalonians to identify better the problem Apostle Paul was dealing with, first.

Starting with 1 Thessalonians, we need to understand the main reason why Paul wrote 1 Thessalonians. It was to clear up misconceptions about the rapture/gathering up of the Bride of Christ (Church) for the wedding. As part of that, Paul sets the context for when this capturing up of the Bride happens. Whether or not it is before or around the very end of the seven-year Tribulation time period identified by Daniel 9:27 & 12:11, Revelation 11:2 (first half of the seven years) & Revelation 13:5 (last half of the seven years). I get that some will argue against God's one or two verse support, but there is overwhelming support in many locations throughout the Bible that will be shown in this note to you.

You have already picked up on something in 1 Thessalonians chapter 1, where God says in verse 10 that "Jesus who delivers us from the "wrath" to come" (NKJV). It is His Bride-Church that He is delivering from His wrath of 7 Seal Judgments, which is still (yet) to come. Who else would Jesus be delivering from His wrath? There are some in high places within the Body-Church that are stuck in their very bad "late Tribulation" teachings or worse and have to play games with the rest of God's Word as to when God's wrath starts. To avoid this problem, they teach that God's wrath doesn't really begin with the opening of the first Seal, but rather much later. Intelligent people can build a compelling argument, but the simple fact is that it is Jesus opening all of these 7 Seals of wrath (Revelation 5:4–10); they are not Satan's seven seals. Satan does not have any seals to open. None mentioned in any of the Bible versions I read. It is God-Jesus' wrath being unleashed, starting with Seal 1. Either the Bride of Christ is here on earth being miraculously protected through those 7 Seal Judgments, or we have already been raptured, as stated in Isaiah 26:19–21. If the Bride really is here on earth and protected, then who exactly is Satan persecuting in Revelation 12:17? Who is the Antichrist killing for rejecting to wear the mark of the beast, not worshiping his image in Revelation 20:4? Either the Bride is raptured up to the Father's heaven to become the wife of Christ, or we are being killed as martyrs for rejecting to worship the beast or his image. So, which is it? Well, I contend that the Bride of Christ is protected from the 7 Seal judgments of God, but are there more locations that say that besides 1 Thessalonians 1:10 and Isaiah 26:20–21 through 27:1? A quick list of all that I remember, including the two, just mentioned:

- Revelation 3:10, *"I will also keep you from the hour of trial which shall come upon the whole world."* There is only one trial that comes upon the "whole" world, post-Noah's flood, and this one is both longer and greater in magnitude (Jeremiah 30:7–9; Luke 17:26–30; 2 Peter 2:4–9). 2 Peter 2:9 clearly says that God knows how to deliver the godly when He punishes the unjust in His day of judgment.

- Zephaniah 2:2–3 *Before the decree is issued, Or the day passes like chaff, Before the Lord's fierce anger comes upon you, Before the day of the Lord's anger comes upon you! 3 Seek the Lord, all you meek of the earth, Who have upheld His justice. Seek righteousness, seek humility. It may be that <u>you will be hidden</u> In the day of the Lord's anger* (NKJV). Like Isaiah 26:20, God says here that His chosen group is "hidden" in the day of His anger (7 Seal judgments). In fact, in just these two verses, we see the day of the Lord's anger (7 Seal judgments) mentioned three times. There should be no question as to the fact that (a) those seeking God are hidden, and (b) this happens in the day of the Lord's wrath/anger (7 Seals) being poured out upon all the earth. If someone wants to argue differently, they can. It is their Eternity, not mine. As for me, I do not see God as being tricky or that He writes things that only those of very high intellect can understand. To me, God means what He said. He wrote things that we all can understand, and I have no intention of changing the meaning of what He said. If it makes plain sense as is, do not look for any other sense, lest we turn it into nonsense. God means it as He said it, or else He would have said it differently. God certainly did not leave it up to man to fill in the blanks or interpret what He was saying. I think that we all understand what a convoluted mess that would be.

- Mathew 25:6–10 *"And at midnight a cry was heard: 'Behold, the bridegroom [a]is coming; go out to meet him!' 7 Then all those virgins arose and trimmed their lamps. 8 And the foolish said to the wise, 'Give us some of your oil, for our lamps, are going out.' 9 But the wise answered, saying, 'No, lest there should not be enough for us and you; but go rather to those who sell, and buy for yourselves.' 10 And while they went to buy, the bridegroom came, and those who were ready went in with him to the wedding, and the door was shut* (NKJV). This uniquely parallels the already mentioned Isaiah 26:20–21, as there are a group of people that are properly prepared when Jesus comes to receive His people, and Matthew 25:10 ends with the door being shut behind them. That is the exact same thing that

God says in Isaiah 26:20, and I'll now add Luke 13:23–25 to this "shut door" action.

- Luke 13:23–25 *Then one said to Him, "Lord, are there few who are saved?" And He said to them, 24 "Strive to enter through the narrow gate, for many, I say to you, will seek to enter and will not be able. 25 When once the Master of the house has risen up and shut the door, and you begin to stand outside and knock at the door, saying, 'Lord, Lord, open for us,' and He will answer and say to you, 'I do not know you* (NKJV)

- Luke 21:36 *"Watch therefore, and pray always that you may be counted worthy to escape all these things that will come to pass, and to stand before the Son of Man."* (NKJV)

- John 14:1–4 *"Let not your heart be troubled; you believe in God, believe also in Me. 2 In My Father's house are many [a] mansions; if it were not so, [b], I would have told you. I go to prepare a place for you. 3 And if I go and prepare a place for you, I will come again and receive you to Myself; that where I am, there you may be also. 4 And where I go, you know, and the way you know."* (NKJV) There is so much here and I have covered it elsewhere, so, I will just say that many change what is written here. If there is no pre-Tribulation rapture, then the Church is raised up into the clouds at or very near the end of the 7 Seals, including those that were still alive on the earth, and they all come straight back down to the earth for the 1000 year reign of Jesus from Jerusalem. If that were true, then there is no point in Jesus going to the Father's house to build mansions (there) for His Bride-Church. At least for those who were alive on the earth at His Rapture-Catching up event, as we would never go up to see the Father's House. All we would do is to meet Jesus in the air/clouds and then come straight to earth. Some may try to paint this as referring to the New Jerusalem (Revelation 21), so be careful. The New Jerusalem is part of the new heaven and new earth, as verse 1 says that the first heaven and first earth (that we live on now) had passed away. So, the New Jerusalem is well after the 1000 year reign of Jesus on earth, and it is (also) after God's final judgment (White Throne Judgment).

- 1 Thessalonians 5:8–10 "*⁸ But let us who are of the day be sober, putting on the breastplate of faith and love, and as a helmet the hope of salvation. ⁹ For God did not appoint us to wrath, but to obtain salvation through our Lord Jesus Christ, ¹⁰ who died for us, that whether we wake or sleep, we should live together with Him.*" (NKJV)

- 1 Thessalonians 1:10 "*and to wait for His Son from heaven, whom He raised from the dead, even Jesus who delivers us from the wrath to come.*" (NKJV)

- Isaiah 26:20–21 Come, my people, enter your chambers, And shut your doors behind you;
  Hide yourself, as it were, for a little moment, Until the indignation is past. *²¹ For behold, the Lord comes out of His place to punish the inhabitants of the earth for their iniquity* (NKJV); So, we see God telling His people (Church) to enter their chambers and shut the doors behind them for a "little" moment, which is not a long time and certainly nothing close to forever. I included this, plus scripture from Zephaniah, as some claim that the Rapture event is "not" in

the OT. They mock others for their belief in the "hidden-secret" rapture. In this verse and (also) in Zephaniah, God uses the word (Hide – Hidden), these are God's words, not mine or others who read it the same way. Be careful. You may be mocking God with your words and actions. The timing of this is (also) quite clear as it is when the Lord punishes the entire earth, finally punishes Leviathan/Satan, and slays the reptile that is in the sea (see Isaiah 27:1).

In summarizing the scriptures (above), they should show that the Bride-Church is saved-hidden-protected from God's seven seals of judgment, and that is stated in both the OT & NT. I do not know how post-Tribulation or other disbelievers in the pre-Tribulation Rapture of the Bride of Christ can argue around all of these proofs and feel good about doing that, but glad that I am not one of them. There was a point in time where I tried, and I just could not get there based on the evidence presented here and other Biblical locations.

1 Thessalonians 1:10 is an odd way to end the first chapter, and it's not just this chapter that ends with reference to the rapture event that saves believers from God's wrath. It does make sense if you determine for yourself that the "main" reason why Paul wrote this letter educating the Thessalonians was about the rapture event. Please keep in mind that I started off early in this letter stating that somehow Paul had to communicate with the Thessalonians 4 times. Starting with Paul and the gang being there, then he sent Timothy because he didn't like what he had heard. So, that makes 1 Thessalonians Paul's third attempt to set them straight on this topic, with 2 Thessalonians the fourth. While you will have to take some time to sort this out for yourself, it is Your Eternity. As the head of your household, you must ask God for the Truth and lead them accordingly. As for me, I believe that both these

letters were written to correct errors concerning the rapture-gathering up that existed even back in Paul's day. If it was a problem back then, it should be no surprise that it is (also) a problem today.

God knew this would happen and wrote scripture in a way that His teachings would stand, for those searching, even today. That we could see that the Bride-Church was going to be delivered from God's wrath poured out in the seven-year Tribulation period. That we were not to be discouraged and to be ready with plenty of oil in our lamps. However, because the enemy is relentless and we are not perfect, Satan has been successfully chipping away at this and all things God for thousands of years. Satan was very successful even amid Paul's teachings to the Thessalonians. We all need to understand the depth and breadth of the depravity of mankind. God gave us all free will. He was never interested in a bunch of mindless robots following Him around. Unfortunately, man's free will has led mankind in a grotesque downward spiral that exists today. I am not talking just about the depravity that has led to the "Me Too" movement and sex trafficking. There are many more examples. Man's free will is such a problem that it is even an issue in Jesus' future 1000 year reign of True peace on earth. This is the reason that Jesus has to rule with a rod of iron (Revelation 12:5) throughout His 1000 year reign. After those peaceful 1000 years, Satan is let loose for a time, and men using their freewill, flock after him. Too many to be counted (Revelation 20:7–8). As hard as that may seem to be to believe, it is written, and it shall happen.

Moving onto 2 Thessalonians, chapter one is all about God (finally) repaying those who have been persecuting the Bride of Christ - Church. While Paul seems to be doing his best at being encouraging, he is clearly distressed with the fact that after all he has done, in person and in writing a letter (1 Thessalonians), he now has to write a second letter (see 2 Thessalonians 2:5). You may be wondering what has the Thessalonians rattled yet again. Turn to 2 Thessalonians 2:1–3, and you will see that it involves the gathering-rapture up of the Bride-Church to Jesus when He comes for them. They at least understood that the rapture was a physical raising up and transformation of their flesh bodies to a new incorruptible one like what Jesus now has. However, it seems that someone had convinced them, someone that they had much respect for as "if from" Paul himself (see verse 2), that they had not been worthy enough and missed the gathering-rapture up to Jesus. So, Paul has to talk them away from the edge of the cliff and convince them as to why they had not missed it. It is not like they had cell phones, so, word got around pretty slowly back then. Paul, in 2 Thessalonians 3:6 straight out, tells them to withdraw from every brother who does not teach according to the traditions they have received from Paul. Those are pretty tough words but had to be spoken, and we will see later on that Paul is not done addressing this problem, that a certain group had created.

When we finish 2 Thessalonians we are all left to wonder who the people were that got the Thessalonians all worked up, and what exactly did they teach. Believe it or not, God does not leave us guessing. We just have to pay attention and look for it. The answer is covered in the two letters Paul wrote to encourage brother Timothy who was going to carry the mantle for Paul, so to speak, because Apostle Paul was about to become a martyr in Rome. The letters to Timothy were two of the last three letters that Paul wrote (Titus was the other). In 1 Timothy, Paul is really hot under the collar concerning Hymenaeus and Alexander. So much so, that he says that he has delivered them to Satan (1 Timothy 19–20) because they shipwrecked the faith of some. The letters have more of a personal tone to them as they were written to just Timothy, and they had been through a lot of tough travels together. Paul was probably unaware that the two letters would survive to this day, but God knew that they had to be a part of the future New Testament to answer a big open-ended question concerning 2 Thessalonians 2:1–3. Who were those people that got the Thessalonians all shook-up, and what did they teach? I am sure that Timothy knew what Paul was saying in 1 Timothy 1:19–20, so, Paul did not have to elaborate, but that does not do us much good today. However, Paul answers what the issue was in 2 Timothy. In 2 Timothy 2:16–18, Paul adds Philetus to the group (Hymenaeus and Alexander), who have strayed from the Truth and teaching that the "resurrection is already past." Paul says that message has spread like cancer/gangrene. Well, gangrene is, in fact, both fast and deadly, and this was difficult for the Thessalonians to shake. With the Roman army gathering around Jerusalem, it would be easy for them to think that it was the end, and they had not been good enough to be raptured up. The news did not travel quickly back then, and if Paul or Timothy had been there with them, they would have known they had not missed anything. With this in mind, it is time to take another look at 2 Thessalonians 2:1–3. There were too many Thessalonians that thought that they were not good enough and did, in fact, miss the gathering up to Jesus, and they had to stick it out through the seven-year Tribulation period. Apostle Paul got word of this and wrote 2 Thessalonians. He had to tell them it was total nonsense, that they had missed nothing and made it quite clear why in chapter 2. If what they were experiencing was not what Paul described in verses 4–12, then they had not missed the gathering-rapture up to Jesus. I get that some want to teach that the resurrection is a spiritual thing or the rapture event is right at or near the end of the seven years, but then there is no reason to fear missing the event. It is what it is, and they do have to go through all the events Paul his stated in 2 Thessalonians 2. In addition, Paul says in 2 Timothy 2:16–18 that this has "overthrown" the faith of some. No reason to have your faith overthrown if you are supposed to "cowboy" up and ride it out to the very end. As a matter of fact, all Apostle Paul has to do is say there is no such thing as a pre-Tribulation or pre-Wrath rapture, we have to be here to the very end. Yes, be scared and be prepared, but that was not the message was it. The message was that they (a) did not miss the rapture, so, no need to be all shook-up about anything, and (b) he gave them the proof as to why they had not missed the rapture. Interestingly, the proof that Paul gave also serves as instruction for those who do miss the rapture event as to what they will see as conclusive, beyond a shadow of a doubt evidence, that they are in that period when the 7 Seals are being opened (2 Thessalonians 2:3–4). Make no mistake, there shall be a man that sits in the (rebuilt) Israeli Temple and require all to worship him as God.

It was well known, back then, that Christians were going through all sorts of brutal deaths in Rome, and Paul would, too. Nothing new about being a Christian and being martyred in some fashion. What would throw me and others off would be if we were told that we would escape the wrath to come (1 Thessalonians 1:10; 1 Thessalonians 5:3–5 and others already mentioned), only to hear from someone like Hymenaeus, Alexander, or Philetus that I or we were "not good enough" and missed the gathering up to Jesus in the rapture. If I was doing everything in my power to do what I was taught, and that had not been good enough to make the rapture, then why keep trying? I can see how that would overthrow the faith of some, back then and even today. Thankfully, that is not what happens, according to Paul, who goes to great lengths in 2 Thessalonians 2 to set the record straight and that they have not missed the rapture unto Jesus. While they did not understand everything surrounding the rapture event, at least they (finally) understood that the rapture was yet to come and not be discouraged. Apostle Paul's frustration with the whole thing enters into both letters to Timothy. Despite their best efforts to educate the Thessalonians and shoot down the teachings of Hymenaeus and the others, it had spread like cancer or gangrene. So, Paul sees the need to encourage his good friend Timothy and brother in Christ, to shake it off and stand fast to what he had been taught. To endure the hardship "as a good soldier of Jesus Christ" (2 Timothy 2:1–3). One last comment of 1 Thessalonians 2 that I believe ties into this, is that Apostle Paul makes it a point to restore his credibility and that of his team. It seems unthinkable to us that he would have to do that in one letter, but he actually has to do that in both Thessalonian letters. Those teaching heresy at the Thessalonian church were wolves in sheep's clothing and quite good at it. Despite what Apostle Paul had taught at his first visit; he had to triple down after that to extinguish the flames of heresy in Thessalonica.

In case anyone seems to think that Apostle Paul's main motive for writing 1 Thessalonians was something other than the gathering or rapture to Jesus, Paul goes into a deep dive on the rapture event in chapter 4. It should be noted that in all of Apostle Paul's writings, as well as whenever the Bible talks about the gathering-rapture to Jesus in the OT or NT, it never says anything along the lines of being prepared by acquiring some sort of land-compound, storing away rations and whatever else would be required to survive the 7 Seals of judgment. I know that everyone who has spent at least a little time at church knows this, but it is worth repeating because the Great Commission is to be fishers of men, which tends to be a very dangerous job. Which is why I asked your wife to be if she was prepared to die for what she believed in. God never asks us to remove ourselves from accomplishing the Great Commission, but rather says that we should not fear the man who can destroy the body, but rather God who can destroy the soul (Matt 10:27–28). Nowhere in the commission to be fishers of men does it say to build a "safe-haven."

1 Thessalonians 4:17 says that we who are alive when Jesus comes for his Bride-Church, that we will be gathered-raptured up to meet them in the clouds. That is why it is called a gathering up and not a resurrection. You have to be dead to have your body resurrected from the earth, and these people are still alive. I realize that some will try to twist this and somehow wrap it into the first Resurrection (Revelation 20:4–6). What they fail to understand is that God wrote it exactly as He did so that no man could somehow combine the rapture with the first Resurrection. There are no live people accounted for in Revelation 20:4–6. God says that there is a price to pay for changing what He wrote, and teachers pay an even larger price (James 3:1; Matthew 5:17–19; Revelation 22:18–19). If anyone is alive at the rapture, then they cannot be resurrected from death as they are, in fact, alive. Changed in the twinkling of an eye with their new body, yes, but they were not dead when that happened. The rapture is all about the Groom coming for His Bride-Church (those dead & alive). While some teach that the perfect wedding means that we meet in the clouds and then come straight down for the battle and all the gore of Armageddon, I believe that the Bible teaches us much differently. I think that the Lord knows how to throw a beautiful wedding above and beyond what any man and woman can imagine. I believe that the example that Jesus spoke of in John 2, the way the Jewish wedding was back in Jesus' day, is the perfect example of how it works and why that

event ended up in the Bible. It was a seven-day event. By the way, a day in Daniel 9 and 12 is defined to be a year in the Tribulation period. So, those seven days represent seven years, and we see that throughout Revelation 11, 12, and 13.

Concerning God knowing how to throw a Wedding, in John 2, not only did Jesus turn water into wine, it was the finest wine served at the wedding. In addition, Jesus made 120 to 160 gallons of it (John 2:6–10). That was quite the party. Not only did they drink all of what they originally thought was enough, but Jesus also had to make another 120 to 160 gallons to cover the event. It is a bit hard to imagine how much that is and why Jesus made so much, especially when the people throwing the party thought that they had enough wine for the event. There are 16 eight-ounce cups in a gallon. In using the lower number of 120 gallons, that means there were at least 1,920 glasses of wine that Jesus made to cover for the rest of the party. If you count a standard glass of wine to be 4 ounces, then the number of glasses Jesus made is close to 4,000. I doubt that Jesus made all that wine to allow a bunch of rowdies to continue to drink themselves into oblivion, so why did he do that? Apparently, they did not have trouble feeding everyone because Jesus did not provide extra food. It is because a wedding in Jesus' day lasted seven days, and they ran out of wine before the seven days were up. Today's weddings are a shortened version. I will briefly cover the order of events in Jesus' day, below. It is important to see the similarities in this to what Jesus says about His wedding to His bride (Church).

- The young man would approach the young woman and her father with a marriage contract

- The most important piece being the price he was willing to pay

  - Jesus bought us by paying the price for our sin, through His death

- If the terms were suitable, the bride and groom would drink a glass of wine together to complete the agreement

- Upon agreement, the groom would include in his speech "I go to my father's house to prepare a place for you" (John 14:1–3)

- At his father's house, the bridegroom prepared a bridal chamber, a little mansion, in which they would spend their first seven days together, before emerging to join in on the wedding feast (John 14:1–3)

- A key feature of this was that the groom could not go for his bride until the father said he was fully prepared and could go

  - Jesus said this very thing to His disciples (Matthew 24:36; Mark 13:32)

- While the bride is waiting, she has things to do, and one of them is to ensure she has an oil lamp ready that is full of oil, in case the bridegroom came in the night, and that should sound just like Matthew 25:1–12

- Traditionally, the groom would come with his groomsmen to claim his bride in the middle of the night, and someone in the party would shout enough in advance to wake the bride who would light her lamp and grab her things

- When getting to the father's house, the bridegroom and bride would enter into the place that he had prepared and "shut the door behind them" (Isaiah 26:20; Matthew 25:10, Luke 13:23–25, Revelation 12:8)

- The friend of the bridegroom would stand near the door waiting for the bridegroom to announce that the marriage had been consummated, and then would go to the wedding guests stating the good news and the wedding celebration would continue for the entire seven days

- At the end of the week, the married couple would open the door and emerge from the bridal chamber that had been prepared in the father's house, for the first time, and join in on a joyous meal (wedding feast) that concluded the matrimonial week

- After the wedding feast, the married couple permanently depart the father's house, as will the Bride of Christ when they return to earth for the 1000 year reign of Jesus as defined in Revelation 20

I get that some may think that the rapture, wedding, and return to earth for the 1000 year reign of Jesus all happens in an instant in the clouds, with an almost immediate return to the earth at Armageddon (post-Tribulation ideology). However, that provides no allowance for those that were alive on the earth to enter into God the Father's house to their mansions that Jesus went to prepare for us. I do hope that those who believe this way are beginning to understand that this wedding that God has planned is a big-BIG event that we can scarcely imagine the glorious time we will have. War and a bunch of death all over the place at Armageddon just doesn't cut the mustard compared to any wedding ceremony I know of. It is hard enough to imagine all the devastation that is going to take place on earth through the opening of the 7 Seals of judgment, as written in Revelation. But that should also help us to understand how tremendous and peaceful the Wedding of the Bride of Christ will be up in the Father's house, during that timeframe. God the Father will hold nothing back for His Son's Wedding. The way the Bible reads to me, along with a vision providing details, there is no such thing as God doing a negative Wedding. Weddings are supposed to be a joyous event. If God is calling the shots, and He is, I cannot help but believe that the event will be more joyous than I or any human could imagine. So, I do not get why some would believe in the Bride of Christ being raised up in the clouds only to then return immediately back to earth for war at the very end of seven miserable years. Not only that, but post-Tribulation types say that upon death, their partial existence of soul and spirit (only) go up straight to God the Father's house to their mansions. If true, I call foul play on God, because then I and others like me that are alive would never get to see our mansions in the Father's house (third heaven), if the rapture happened as I type. Of course, as previously covered in a different chapter, Saint Polycarp (AD 69–156) appointed to be a lead pastor by Apostle John to the Church of Smyrna (Turkey), taught against the heresy that we go straight to the Father's house upon death, because we do not. That we actually follow in the same footsteps of Jesus and the OT saints. That our soul and spirit go down to Paradise to await our resurrection at our appointed time (the rapture event). At that point, we would all go together, dead and those alive, to the Father's house to the mansions that Jesus has prepared for us (John 14:1–3), and we would be up there the entire time (7 years). If you understand that Jesus has full control over both the good (Paradise) and bad sides of Hell-Hades-Sheol, then this should all feather together nicely. If not, I hope that something does not pass the sniff test. Ask God and wait for His answers. After all, it is YOUR eternity. Do your homework. People who say that the pre-Tribulation rapture is a new teaching in the past 200 years have not done their homework, and that has caused a big problem concerning end-times teaching. I have done my homework, concerning the earliest of church fathers, and it is worth repeating concerning Polycarp & Irenaeus, two early Church fathers.

We need to remember that the good (Paradise-Abraham's Bosom) and bad sides of Hell are below the earth (see 1 Samuel 28:13–15, Luke 16:19–end), not up above where the Lake of Fire is. They taught that when we die, we DO NOT go straight to the Father's heaven as an incomplete person (i.e., with no body). Rather, we go to and are at complete rest-peace in Paradise, of which Jesus has complete control over. So, when we are there, we are at peace in the presence of Jesus. Satan has no power there or anywhere in Hell, even the bad side where the rich man went (Luke 16:19–27). It is important to note that in these verses, this is a real conversation that took place between the rich man and Lazarus, so they are not asleep as we know it when going to bed at night. Jesus has these keys, not Satan, and that was true in the OT, as pointed out already in 1 Samuel 28. Polycarp, a martyr of the early church, who was appointed by Apostle John to be head of the church at Smyrna, taught this very point. I know what Apostle Paul taught, and it is the same as Polycarp. Satan has no power over Paradise (good side) or the other (bad) side where the rich man's soul and spirit "still are." It all belongs to Jesus (Luke 16), who has the keys to Hell (I prefer to call it Hell instead of Hades or some other name) and death (Revelation 1:18). If this were not true, then evil would rule and contaminate both sides. There would be no rest anywhere. Below is a short clip on what Polycarp and Irenaeus taught and can be found by anyone on the internet:

> *If, then, the Lord observed the law of the dead, that He might become the first-begotten from the dead, and tarried until the third day "in the lower parts of the earth;" then afterwards rising in the flesh, so that He even showed the print of the nails to His disciples, He thus ascended to the Father; - [if all these things occurred, I say], how must these men not be put to confusion, who allege that "the lower parts" refer to this world of ours, but that their inner man, leaving the body here, ascends into the super-celestial place? For as the Lord "went away in the midst of the shadow of death," where the souls of the dead were, yet afterward arose in the body, and after the resurrection was taken up [into heaven], it is manifest that the souls of His disciples also, upon whose account the Lord underwent these things, shall go away into the invisible place allotted to them by God, and there remain until the resurrection that event; then receiving their bodies, and rising in their entirety, that is bodily, just as, awaiting the Lord arose, they shall (only then) come thus into the presence of God. "For no disciple is above the Master, but every one that is perfect shall be as his Master." As our Master, therefore, did not at once depart, taking flight [to heaven], but awaited the time of His resurrection prescribed by the Father, which had also been shown forth through Jonas, and rising again after three days was taken up [to heaven]; so ought we also to await the time of our resurrection prescribed by God and foretold by the prophets, and so, rising, be taken up, as many as the Lord shall account worthy of this [privilege].*

Like you, Jake, I am a little surprised at how many get all hung up about the last Trump mentioned in 1 Corinthians 15:52. This is the only time that there is a reference to the "last" trumpet. God does not call the (rapture) trumpet in 1 Thessalonians the "last" trumpet. Nor does God call the 7th Trumpet in Revelation the "last" trumpet. Nor does God call the "great" trumpet the last trumpet in either Isaiah 27:13 or Matthew 24:31. God is very precise and does not make mistakes. So, either the translation to English is wrong in all of these cases, or there is only one "last" trumpet listed in the Bible, and that is in 1 Corinthians 15:52. I do not think that I need to remind you that "great" and "last" are not the same word in Greek or Hebrew, they are different words with different meanings, and God would have ensured that Apostle Paul would have called the trumpet in 1 Thessalonians 4:16 the "last" trumpet if it was. However, it was not the last trumpet, so Paul did not equate it to the last trumpet. This means that we have to take a deeper look at the context around what Apostle Paul said in 1 Corinthians 15:52. Paul coined it the last trumpet, but why in just this one spot? Obviously, it is the last trumpet of something, but there are many possibilities. Is it the last trumpet of the Feast of Trumpets or some other feast? Is it the last trump of the Church Age? Is it the last trumpet of all time (i.e., when God makes a new heaven and earth (Revelation 21), in which there is no more time after that? Does this mean that God will stop blowing trumpets forever and ever? If yes to that, it is worth noting that there will be plenty of trumpet blowing during Jesus' (unchallenged) 1000 year reign from Jerusalem in cele-bration of the different feasts (see Zech 14), so, that would mean the last trumpet would have to happen well after the 1000 year reign of Christ (Revelation 20) and has no impact on the rapture up of the Bride of Christ. The biggest problem the Church, in general, has today, is the lack of understanding of what God is telling us about future end times in Revelation 20.

Just saying that we all need to be careful, relative to Scripture and the context that comes with it. We should not be putting the word "last," where "great" is. They are two different Greek words (New Testament was written in Greek, not Hebrew), and we certainly should not be adding the word "last" in front of the trumpet stated in 1 Thessalonians 4, when God did not put it there. Fortunately, the context of the last trumpet is given in 1 Corinthians 15. Context matters, so be careful and always look for context before taking a stand. Going back to 15:24–28, it says the "end" comes, and Jesus delivers the kingdom up to His Father. Verse 25 says that cannot happen until Jesus puts all enemies underneath His feet, and Jesus has to reign until then, with verse 26 (of 1 Corinthians 15) saying that the last enemy to be destroyed is death. Remember that in Revelation 20:7–10, God says that Satan will lead one last uprising, and that is well after the "rapture" event. That is well after Jesus returns to earth to rule from Jerusalem for 1000 years. Not only that but Revelation 20:11–15 clearly shows that there is another resurrection, which we know happens in the twinkling of an eye for the Great White Throne judgment. However, this time it is for all of the dead, good and bad that had not gotten their new bodies. This would include those believers living in Jesus's 1000 year reign from Jerusalem. Revelation 20:14 says that this event is when All of Death and Hell (Hades) is (finally) cast into the Lake of Fire. This is when Jesus completes all things. It is when all His flocks come together as one (John 10:16), and Jesus delivers everything up to God the Father, and God becomes all in all (1 Corinthians 15:28). As a side note and previously discussed, we know that the Lake of Fire and Hell are not the same place, because you cannot cast Hell into the

Lake of Fire if they are the same thing. You can't cast something into itself.

Getting back to 1 Corinthians 15:24–28, the end of "ALL" death cannot happen until Revelation 20 is complete. 1 Corinthians 15:54–55 feathers perfectly into the Great White Throne (final) theme set in 15:24–28, where death is finally/completely swallowed up in victory, and there will no longer be any such thing as death because Jesus has truly finished all things as written including overcoming (all) death and then, only then, hands it all up to God the Father (1 Corinthians 15:24). Only then is death, which came from sin, completely dealt with. The main point in all of this is that despite Apostle Paul's coining the phrase "last trump" in 1 Corinthians, he makes no reference in either 1 Thessalonians or 2 Thessalonians to the "rapture" trump being the "last" trump. Nor does he make any reference, in either of the Thessalonian letters, to the rapture being the final event where death is completely overcome when there is no more death, and Jesus then delivers the kingdom up to God the Father. To close the door on this, God refers to a "Great" Trumpet, not the same as "Last" Trumpet, twice in His scripture. When looking, you will find that the trumpet in 1 Thessalonians 4:16 is "not" called Great, nor is it referred to as the Last. One of the Great Trumpet references is in Isaiah 27:13 and the other in Matthew 24:31 (NKJV). If you read those in context of the scripture around them, both occur before the 1000 year reign of Jesus from Jerusalem. In addition, the Greek word for "great" in Matthew 24:31 is "megas" meaning big, great, loud, or mighty. Keep in mind that the NT is written in Greek and the OT in Hebrew, so I am not trying to play games here to make a point. God knows and would hold me accountable for doing that. The Hebrew word for "great" in Isaiah 27:13 is "gaw-dole," meaning great, high, loud, mighty, more, or much. So, whether we are talking Greek or Hebrew, the meaning of Great doesn't change, and there are zero references to "last" in the definitions of "great" in either language. However, the Greek word "last" in 1 Corinthians is "eschatos" meaning last, final, or end of. To me, the correct translation to English should be something along the lines of "end of all things trumpet," not last trumpet.

There is only one mention of a "Last" Trumpet in the Bible (1Corinthians 15:52), and it is connected to when "death is swallowed up in victory" a couple of verses later (verse 54). We know that all of death is (completely) swallowed up in victory, with death being the "last enemy" (1Corinthians 15:26), and well after Jesus's 1000 year reign at the Great White Throne judgment (Revelation 20). Maybe it now makes sense as to why it would have been better if the translation had been the "end of" all things trumpet instead of "last" trumpet. It isn't about the trumpet. It is about the message announced by the trumpet within the context of scripture surrounding it. We all need to remember that God is the one who is saying to not add or subtract to or from His scripture, and I am just attempting to repeat where God put "the last trumpet" within the context around it and pointing out that none of the other trumpets called out in the Bible are called "last." Only this one in 1 Corinthians 15:52. Be careful. Do not attempt to force the rapture-catching up trumpet listed in 1 Thessalonians 4:16 to being the "last" trumpet. Also be careful when trying to equate the "last" trumpet to Jesus' return to earth to reign for 1000 years, as there is a second resurrection well after that, where "all" of the dead are raised up in the twinkling of an eye at the Great White Throne judgment (Revelation 20:11). We would be well served by giving Saint Irenaeus the last word on this, as he taught: *It is He who is Himself able to extend both healing and life to His handiwork, that His words concerning its [future] resurrection may also be believed; so also at the end, when the Lord utters His voice "by the last trumpet," the dead shall be raised, as He Himself declares: "The hour shall come, in which all the dead which are in the tombs shall hear the voice of the Son of man, and shall come forth; those that have done good to the resurrection of life, and those that have done evil to the resurrection of judgment."* We can see that Saint Irenaeus is referring directly to the second resurrection at the Great White Throne Judgment where the last of both good and evil are raised up. It is the only time the evil are raised up with new bodies. That is the "last trumpet" spoken of by Apostle Paul in 1 Corinthians 15:52, and it marks the end of all evil, forever. Do not take my word for it. It is up to you to do your homework on all these matters. It is Your eternity, weigh the cost in the balance. No one can serve two masters. They will be loyal to only one of the two (Luke 16:13).

Returning to 1 Thessalonians 5, God draws a serious distinction between those that are raptured-gathered up before the "Day of the Lord" or "day of wrath" happens, and those that are left behind in 5:1–10. In 1 Thessalonians 5:2–4, 9, we see two references, along with 1 Thessalonians 1:10, that says the Bride-Church is delivered from the "wrath to come." The context is that we are delivered from "God's wrath to come," from God's opening of His 7 Seals. Yes, we will have tribulations from Satan while alive on earth, most certainly, but we, the Bride of Christ, will not be around for God's wrath. I believe that Luke 19:11–15 ties in nicely with the pre-Tribulation rapture and safe from God's wrath. Jesus told this parable to them as they thought Jesus was going to bring in the kingdom of God immediately, but Jesus knew that he was going to the cross in death that very week. So, in this parable, Jesus tells them that what they thought is not true through a parable. In this parable, which is a true account representing what would happen, Jesus says He will be going into a faraway country to receive a kingdom (gentiles) first, before returning. As the parable goes on, the Nobleman (Jesus) gave His servants, in the home land, money to do His business till He returned, but the local citizens hated him, and they said that they would not have this man reign over them. Which we know was true as they asked for Barabbas to be set free instead of Jesus (John 18:39–40). Then in Luke 19:15, it says that when the Nobleman (Jesus) returned, having already received His kingdom (Bride-Church), He returns to Israel. Which is what Paul (also) states in Romans 11:25, when he writes "for blindness in part has happened to Israel until the fullness of the gentiles has been completed." Jesus is telling His followers that His kingdom is not yet and that He will not return to Israel and set up His kingdom until He has received a "far away kingdom" (rapture of His Bride-Church). As I type this, Jesus has not yet received His Bride-Church, but this will happen, and when it does, God's full attention will be back on Israel. Going back to Luke 19:14, His (local) Israeli citizens hated Him and would not allow Jesus to reign over them. But we know that Jesus will return after He receives His faraway kingdom (Bride), and what is left of Israel will "then" be saved (Romans 11:26–27). Luke 19:27 ends the parable with Jesus having His enemies slain upon His return at Armageddon. Pretty hard stuff to swallow, but there is nothing pretty about Noah's flood in Genesis 7, or blood up to the horses' bridles for one thousand six hundred furlongs (Revelation 14:20). A furlong is 660 feet or one-eighth of a mile. That would be blood for 200 miles, and it is unclear to me if that is an area number, but we know that the valley of Megiddo (Armageddon) is 36 miles long and 15 miles wide, so, the area of that valley is 540 square miles and 200 square miles of blood would easily fit into that valley. That is a staggering number, but an army of 200 million (Revelation 9:16) is (also) a staggering number, and it will take a lot of land to provide for that large of an army. Not as staggering number of men today, with a world population over 7 billion, but back when Revelation was written, there were only 200–300 million people on the earth. The earth didn't have a population of 1 billion until the 1800s.

Jake, hopefully, you can see why I have been making such a big deal about knowing what the "day of the Lord" actually means, and why it is different from "the Lord's Day" and (also) "latter days." The Lord's Day is Sunday. It is the day Jesus rose from the dead, and why many of us go to church on Sunday (see Revelation 1:10). The "Day of the Lord" is when Jesus starts to reign with a rod of iron in what I call the Age of Judgment, as the Age of Grace or Church Age that we currently live in is over. Jesus's reign of Judgment starts with the opening of His 7 Seals as described in Revelation. It is when He starts pouring His wrath/Judgment out against those not hidden/raptured/caught-up (Bride-Church). This is the beginning of the seven-year Tribulation, as we are not appointed to God's wrath Luke 21:36, 1 Thess. 1:10, 1 Thess. 5:9, Isaiah 26:19–21, Zephaniah 2:2–3, Revelation 3:10, to name a handful. I mean, how many times does God have to say this for men to believe it? Sorry, but I get fired up because people against the Pre-Tribulation rapture have no response for stuff like this. Work hard to understand the context. 1 Thessalonians 5:1–11 establishes that the rapture event just described in 1 Thessalonians 4 has nothing to do with being in the "day of the Lord." Verse 1 says that the Church has nothing to worry about concerning the "times and seasons" because we will have protection from God as Apostle Paul states in verses 2–11. Yes, we will miss God's wrath as we will be gone via the pre-Tribulation rapture.

For those that speak against the pre-Tribulation rapture of the Church, they have us still here on earth, somehow being protected through the opening of the 7 Seal disasters. In addition, that is despite God saying that most believers will be killed for refusing to worship the Antichrist, refusing the mark of the beast (Revelation 20:4). I fail to see how that is God's divine protection of His Church if we are dying at the hands of the Antichrist. Jesus says that when He returns to earth to reign, will He find faith on earth (Luke 18:8)? Those that go through that period of wrath are, I believe, the lukewarmers (not enough oil in their lamps), that are left behind, but finally catch on fire for Jesus. God does call them "virgins" (too) in Matthew 25. Why? I believe that is because they are, but procrastination got the best of them, and they figure it out, but when they do, they have missed the rapture and not part of the Bride of Christ. Many in the church today can discern, by actions, that there are plenty of lukewarmers in the Body (Revelation 3:14–16). That has nothing to do with judging, and it has everything to do with discerning, as we have been instructed to do, by Jesus and that topic is covered elsewhere in this book. Either people have enough oil in their lamps to go up as the Bride at the wedding, or they do not. Half full of oil does not cut it. Those are not my words; they come straight from Jesus in Matthew 25. We are supposed to discern in order to avoid all sorts of trouble, and let Jesus "judge" the actual motivation of people's hearts (Luke 16:15). We are to discern their actions to be of "proper" help when and where we can, but not to be reeled into thinking and/or doing things unless God is telling us to. Yes, I understand how difficult that can be, as it is human nature to be way ahead or way behind what God is doing. Sort of the old saying that "timing is everything." Just saying that in 1 Thessalonians 5 and 2 Thessalonians 2:1–5, Paul cannot say that the church had "no reason" to worry unless there was "no reason" to worry. The only way there is no reason to worry, even today, is because the rapture-catching up of the Bride-Church event, covered in 1 Thessalonian 4, whenever it happens in time, that it does come first before God's 7 Seal Judgments start to be opened by Jesus (Revelation 5). Just saying that if the rapture-gathering up happened any other time, somewhere in the midst of the 7 Seal Judgments, there is plenty for the Bride of Christ to worry about. Nothing good happens starting with Seal 1, and it only gets worse from there. All seven are God's Seals, and all are opened by Jesus. This should not be complicated unless man makes it that way, and we are all guilty of that along the way. What matters is admitting it and moving on in the Lord.

Thankfully the Bible gives us lots of support, starting with 1 Thessalonians 5:2, which clearly states that Paul is talking about "the day of the Lord," "the day of His wrath-anger," or "in that day." They all point to the same time period, and it is so critical to understand what period of time scripture says this actually is. "The day of His wrath or that day" is not the same time period as the "Latter Days or Last Days." All references to "that day" are either that actual day or a direct reference to the Day of God's wrath (starting with the opening of the 7 Seals). Because of scripture, we know that a day to God can be a 24 hour day as described in Genesis 1, or a thousand years (2 Peter 3:8; Psalm 90:3–5), or a day is a year as described in Daniel 9:20–27. The day of the Lord or "that day" is when God starts His "reset" and starts dealing directly with sin through His 7 Seals. God is no longer watching and taking notes. It is when God, the Father directs His Son (Jesus) to step out and start His rule with a rod of iron. God does not do His reset until after the "latter days," which we live in today. We know that God starts His reset by ruling over rebellious mankind with His "rod of iron" (Psalm 2:9, 149:8; Isaiah 10:34, 26:21; Revelation 2:27; 12:5; 19:15). This should be compelling evidence that the rapture event happens before Jesus starts His reign of judgment by opening the first of 7 Seals. Yes, some do claim that the 7 Seals are open already, somehow, and we have been in the midst of the seven seals for quite a while. Others believe that we are somehow past all of that, and we already live in Jesus' Millennial (1000 year) reign. However, we should be able to see that Jesus has yet to start His reign, as things are as they have always been, and (absolutely) none of His Judgments have been poured out yet, at least not exactly as described in Revelation. Again, some may claim otherwise, but study their words closely and research scripture for context. Just because an extremely intelligent person can talk a good story, does not mean that what they said properly fits God's context around the scripture being discussed. When reading 1 Thessalonians 5:2 & 3 together, that scripture clearly states that the "day of the Lord" (day of the Lord's Wrath) comes like a thief in the night. That it comes with "sudden destruction," and "they shall not escape." Look closely at the grammar in 5:3, as it says they and them. Those terms do not apply to the Church (i.e., us, we, you, and me). Looking even more closely, in 5:4, Paul transitions from them to you (us) and says that we the Bride-Church are not in darkness and because we are not in darkness "that Day or Day of the Lord" will not overtake us as a thief in the night. The rapture-gathering up that Paul is talking about will catch others that are not prepared by surprise, but not the believers that are ready and have their lamps full of oil. After all, that is who Paul wrote the Thessalonian letters to. It was written to believers in Jesus. Yes, what is said there still applies, because the day of the Lord's wrath has yet to come. None of the seven seals has been opened. Neither the Thessalonians, back then, nor us (today) have reason to worry as to the times or seasons (1 Thessalonians 5:1), just make sure your lamp is full of oil (Matthew 25:1–13). Pretty simple.

Looking even closer into 1 Thessalonians 5, Apostle Paul never tells us, not even once, that we should be doing anything differently than what the church has always done. In verses 6–8, he's saying not to sleep as the others sleep but to watch and be sober, to put on the breastplate of faith and love, to put on the helmet of salvation. That is what the Bride-Church has been trying to do for the past ~2000 years, nothing has changed, and that is how you make sure your lamp is full of oil. Then in verse 9, Paul says that "God did not appoint us to wrath." If we just stick to what scripture says, at least to me, this should be very clear as to how it works. God tells us multiple times in 1 Thessalonians and other locations, that the Church is not appointed to God's wrath (1 Thessalonians 1:10, 5:4, & 5:9; Revelation 3:10; Isaiah 26:20; Zephaniah 2:3). So, do your homework and ask God. Do not be guilty of just repeating what you have heard from someone you like, even me.

Finishing up 1 Thessalonians 5, Paul states where we will be during the time of God's wrath (day of the Lord) in verses 9–10. We will be living together with Him. There is only one way for those awake (alive) and sleeping (in death) can live together with Him, and that is in our new bodies. The only way that can happen is through the Rapture event, as covered in both 1 & 2 Thessalonians. If we are "living" with Him, because we (Church) are not appointed to wrath, we are no longer on the earth, which means we are not here for His 7 Seal Judgments. Critical thinking, with the Lord's help, is a top priority. We all need to ask ourselves if we are doing what God is asking of us, or are we spending our time and money acquiring land and assets to survive God's wrath? His 7 Seal judgments, or are we plowing all our efforts into being "fishers of men" (Matt 4:19; Mark 1:17)? One of those two actions results in the fulfillment of the Great Commission, and the other does not. In the end, everything I try to do is all about investing in the Great Commission with the ability God has given me, to be fishers of men. Am I really good at it? Well, I'd like to think that I am better at it than 20–30 years ago. Scripture says to discern and use good judgment by listening to Him, but it does not say to run, hide, and be prepared to fight to the bitter end. Be encouraged, despite appearances, because, in the end, Jesus has a much better plan. If we need manna, He will provide it, or come for us as it is our time.

As shown here, both 1 & 2 Thessalonians have everything to do with the rapture event. The Thessalonians had a hard time believing what Apostle Paul was teaching on it, and Paul being Paul was determined to set the record straight with everything he had. That is why God ensured that these two letters were included in the Bible. The Apostles fought all types of heresy in the early Church, and this was one of them. Actually, there was more than one type of heresy concerning the rapture that Paul had to straighten out, but this one had staying power that really hit Apostle Paul hard, as already covered in his last couple of letters which went to Timothy, concerning Hymenaeus in particular. Paul had to directly intervene with the Thessalonians at least four times that we know of, so, Hymenaeus must have been a very persuasive person to cause someone like Apostle Paul so much trouble.

The rapture battle still continues, in even more variants, today. The enemy is good at throwing garbage around, and none of us are bulletproof. We like to think that we are bulletproof, but we are not. There are large ministries that would probably crumble if they confessed that they were wrong about their version of the end times. At least that is what the enemy has them believing, so they are backed into a corner and working double time to defend their view. Of course, it's better for them if they did confess and then let scripture interpret scripture, rather than to continue what they are doing, which involves rewriting parts of the Bible to be what they need it to be to match their manmade teachings. I am not saying that they are not saved because God's Grace covers all sin. Yes, (intentionally) misrepresenting scripture is sin (see Matthew 5:17–19; Revelation 22:18–19; Matthew 7:15–23). In the case of false teaching, not all who teach and do falsely in Jesus's name will have their name written in the book of life (Matthew 7:21–23). Regardless, it is Jesus' call as to whose name is written in the Book of Life, not mine or anybody else's. Only God knows the intent of the heart. However, we are warned to be aware and discern false teachings, to beware of those that come in sheep's clothing, but are ravenous wolves (Matthew 7:15–23). Discerning is much different than judging, but many stumble over that.

The Thessalonians were every bit as intelligent as anyone in the Church today, and even better informed as they had the likes of Paul and Timothy teaching them. So, the real question is what had them so bent out of shape that Paul had to directly address the rapture topic on at least four different occasions that we know of, to them? The first time being in person, but they did not believe him, and they even gave Paul an out (1 Thessalonians 2:1–3). I do believe that God has provided plenty of answers through visions, dreams, and scripture to many over the years to refute others who do not believe in a Pre-Tribulation Rapture. The visions, dreams, and words I have received were most likely necessary to provide me with the confidence I needed to speak out. They could have only come from one of two sources. They are either from God or the devil. There is no in-between, and that should point out how important it is for everyone to do their homework and search the scriptures like the Bereans. Memorizing and being able to spit out scripture is nice, but if you cannot do that within the context of (all) scripture, then there is a lack of understanding that can lead to false beliefs. Thankfully, there is much more to God than any man can comprehend, and He knows the intent in our hearts. As Apostle Paul says in 1 Corinthians 13, we see in part, even Paul and the other Apostles, and we do not all have the same gifting. I firmly believe that if I had been born a thousand years ago, God would not have given me this "part" needed for the end times, because that was too far away and not as important. But then that is everyone's job to search the scripture, pray, and wait on God to determine if what is stated is Truth revealed from Him or manmade nonsense.

Love ya, Dad

About the Author

Craig D. Beltrand is a graduate of the United States Air Force Academy with a degree in business and the University of Colorado, Colorado Springs, with a degree in electrical engineering. He served in the United States Air Force as an ICBM launch officer and later as a design engineer for defense products. In his late twenties he decided to seek out the truth and was surprised by supernatural encounters with the One True God. This book goes into depth concerning those encounters and how they corroborate scripture, as written in the Christian Bible. However, writing a book about God and our eternity was about as far away as the east is from the west for him. Schooling prepared him for work in the military as an officer and later as an engineer, but God had other ideas. Craig learned that God does exist, does speak to us, and has spoken directly with many people over thousands of years, as documented in the Bible. God has never changed, so ask and be surprised yourself!

Made in the USA
Las Vegas, NV
03 September 2021